I0009827

Learning Android Google Maps

Integrate Google Maps with your Android application to offer feature-rich and interactive maps

Raj Amal W.

[PACKT] open source*
PUBLISHING   community experience distilled

BIRMINGHAM - MUMBAI

Learning Android Google Maps

Copyright © 2015 Packt Publishing

All rights reserved. No part of this book may be reproduced, stored in a retrieval system, or transmitted in any form or by any means, without the prior written permission of the publisher, except in the case of brief quotations embedded in critical articles or reviews.

Every effort has been made in the preparation of this book to ensure the accuracy of the information presented. However, the information contained in this book is sold without warranty, either express or implied. Neither the author, nor Packt Publishing, and its dealers and distributors will be held liable for any damages caused or alleged to be caused directly or indirectly by this book.

Packt Publishing has endeavored to provide trademark information about all of the companies and products mentioned in this book by the appropriate use of capitals. However, Packt Publishing cannot guarantee the accuracy of this information.

First published: September 2015

Production reference: 1240915

Published by Packt Publishing Ltd.
Livery Place
35 Livery Street
Birmingham B3 2PB, UK.

ISBN 978-1-84969-886-3

www.packtpub.com

Credits

Author
Raj Amal W.

Reviewers
Dmytro Danylyk

Janos Gyerik

Commissioning Editor
Usha Iyer

Acquisition Editors
Vivek Anantharaman

Usha Iyer

Divya Poojari

Content Development Editor
Siddhesh Salvi

Technical Editor
Rahul C. Shah

Copy Editors
Sonia Cheema

Akshata Lobo

Project Coordinator
Kranti Berde

Proofreader
Safis Editing

Indexer
Monica Ajmera Mehta

Production Coordinator
Arvindkumar Gupta

Cover Work
Arvindkumar Gupta

About the Author

Raj Amal W. has almost three years of real-time working experience with Android technology and has helped many developers complete their projects on time with high-quality standards as an Android developer for a private company. Raj is an open source evangelist and encourages others to use open source software. He writes about Android and Linux at http://www.learn2crack.com.

About the Reviewer

Dmytro Danylyk was a finalist at Google Apps Developer Challenge 2012 and he was also nominated to apply for the Google Developer Expert program.

Dmytro loves the freedom and flexibility that open source projects offer as these qualities blend well with his personality. He is also the author of open source libraries for Android, which have received 5,000+ stars.

He likes all things about Stack Overflow: from answering questions and earning reputation to unlocking badges for special achievements and improving posts by editing or commenting on them.

When Dmytro has some free time, he writes technical articles. He is a keen speaker and tries to share his knowledge and experience at different events whenever he can.

He is also a big fan of technologies, such as Android, flat design, Stack Overflow, Git, and IntelliJ IDEA. You can reach him by visiting his website at `http://dmytrodanylyk.com`.

www.PacktPub.com

Support files, eBooks, discount offers, and more

For support files and downloads related to your book, please visit www.PacktPub.com.

Did you know that Packt offers eBook versions of every book published, with PDF and ePub files available? You can upgrade to the eBook version at www.PacktPub.com and as a print book customer, you are entitled to a discount on the eBook copy. Get in touch with us at service@packtpub.com for more details.

At www.PacktPub.com, you can also read a collection of free technical articles, sign up for a range of free newsletters and receive exclusive discounts and offers on Packt books and eBooks.

https://www2.packtpub.com/books/subscription/packtlib

Do you need instant solutions to your IT questions? PacktLib is Packt's online digital book library. Here, you can search, access, and read Packt's entire library of books.

Why subscribe?

- Fully searchable across every book published by Packt
- Copy and paste, print, and bookmark content
- On demand and accessible via a web browser

Free access for Packt account holders

If you have an account with Packt at www.PacktPub.com, you can use this to access PacktLib today and view 9 entirely free books. Simply use your login credentials for immediate access.

Table of Contents

Preface

This book completely covers the Android Google Maps API, which helps users to integrate the Google Map functionalities with their Android applications. This book also has real-time examples, which makes the learning process simpler and smoother.

What this book covers

Chapter 1, *Setting Up the Development Environment*, shows you how to install Android Studio and Eclipse IDE; configure Android SDK; create an Android virtual device in Windows, Mac, and Linux; and download the Google Play services.

Chapter 2, *Configuring an API Key and Creating Our First Map Application*, explains you how to obtain an API key from Google Cloud Console. It also helps you create your first Map application.

Chapter 3, *Working with Different Map Types*, helps you learn about the different map types, such as hybrid, terrain, and indoor as well as the lite mode.

Chapter 4, *Adding Information to Maps*, helps you understand how to add markers, overlays, and information windows to the map.

Chapter 5, *Interacting with a Map*, explains how to add custom controls, toolbars, gestures, and events to the map.

Chapter 6, *Working with Custom Views*, helps you change different camera views and animate the camera. It also helps you with map padding.

Chapter 7, *Working with Location Data*, helps you learn how to work with real-time location data (GPS data) and integrate it with an Android application.

Chapter 8, *Knowing about the Street View*, explains you how to add Street View to the map and use custom location in it.

Chapter 9, Google Maps Intents, explains you how to complete certain tasks using the native Google Maps application and Google Maps Intents.

Chapter 10, Creating a Custom Map Application, helps you create a real-time full fledged Android application using the map concepts learned in the previous chapters.

Appendix, Answers to Self-test Questions, covers the answers to all the self-test questions that appear at the end of every chapter.

What you need for this book

To practice the code you need a perfectly working PC or Mac with the OS of your choice. The important software required is Android Studio or Eclipse with ADT plugin. It is recommended to use Android Studio over Eclipse as the support for Eclipse may end anytime in future. It is also recommended to have a physical Android device for testing apps as it is faster than the virtual device.

Who this book is for

If you are an Android developer and want to integrate maps into your application, then this book is definitely for you. This book is intended for novice Android application developers who would like to get up and running with map-rich applications using Google Maps. Some basic development experience would be helpful, but it's not essential.

Conventions

In this book, you will find a number of text styles that distinguish between different kinds of information. Here are some examples of these styles and an explanation of their meaning.

Code words in text, database table names, folder names, filenames, file extensions, pathnames, dummy URLs, user input, and Twitter handles are shown as follows: "Now, extract the downloaded ZIP package and run the `eclipse.exe` executable."

A block of code is set as follows:

```
dependencies {
    compile 'com.google.android.gms:play-services:7.5.0'
    compile 'com.android.support:appcompat-v7:21.0.3'
}
```

When we wish to draw your attention to a particular part of a code block, the relevant lines or items are set in bold:

```
if(db.getMarkerCount() > 0){
        List<Marker> markerList = db.getAllMarkers();
        for (int i = 0; i < db.getMarkerCount(); i++) {
            Marker mkr = markerList.get(i);
```

Any command-line input or output is written as follows:

```
sudo dpkg --add-architecture i386
sudo apt-get update
```

New terms and **important words** are shown in bold. Words that you see on the screen, for example, in menus or dialog boxes, appear in the text like this: "Now, check the **Developer Tools** box and select **Next**."

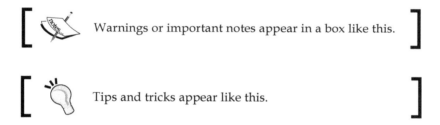

> Warnings or important notes appear in a box like this.

> Tips and tricks appear like this.

Reader feedback

Feedback from our readers is always welcome. Let us know what you think about this book—what you liked or disliked. Reader feedback is important for us as it helps us develop titles that you will really get the most out of.

To send us general feedback, simply e-mail feedback@packtpub.com, and mention the book's title in the subject of your message.

If there is a topic that you have expertise in and you are interested in either writing or contributing to a book, see our author guide at www.packtpub.com/authors.

Customer support

Now that you are the proud owner of a Packt book, we have a number of things to help you to get the most from your purchase.

Downloading the example code

You can download the example code files from your account at http://www.
packtpub.com for all the Packt Publishing books you have purchased. If you
purchased this book elsewhere, you can visit http://www.packtpub.com/support
and register to have the files e-mailed directly to you.

Downloading the color images of this book

We also provide you with a PDF file that has color images of the screenshots/diagrams
used in this book. The color images will help you better understand the changes in
the output. You can download this file from https://www.packtpub.com/sites/
default/files/downloads/Learning_Android_Google_Maps_ColorImages.pdf.

Errata

Although we have taken every care to ensure the accuracy of our content, mistakes
do happen. If you find a mistake in one of our books—maybe a mistake in the text or
the code—we would be grateful if you could report this to us. By doing so, you can
save other readers from frustration and help us improve subsequent versions of this
book. If you find any errata, please report them by visiting http://www.packtpub.
com/submit-errata, selecting your book, clicking on the **Errata Submission Form**
link, and entering the details of your errata. Once your errata are verified, your
submission will be accepted and the errata will be uploaded to our website or added
to any list of existing errata under the Errata section of that title.

To view the previously submitted errata, go to https://www.packtpub.com/books/
content/support and enter the name of the book in the search field. The required
information will appear under the **Errata** section.

Piracy

Piracy of copyrighted material on the Internet is an ongoing problem across all
media. At Packt, we take the protection of our copyright and licenses very seriously.
If you come across any illegal copies of our works in any form on the Internet, please
provide us with the location address or website name immediately so that we can
pursue a remedy.

Please contact us at copyright@packtpub.com with a link to the suspected pirated material.

We appreciate your help in protecting our authors and our ability to bring you valuable content.

Questions

If you have a problem with any aspect of this book, you can contact us at questions@packtpub.com, and we will do our best to address the problem.

Setting Up the Development Environment

Android is the most popular mobile operating system and it has a market share of more than 80 percent. Over 1 million Android devices are shipped each day. Android can run on low-end hardware with 512 MB RAM as well as high-end hardware with 4 GB RAM. It is based on the open source Linux kernel. Due to its open source nature, OEMs prefer Android over other operating systems. The Google Play store now has over a million applications. This makes Android the favorite operating system for users and developers. Some of the unique features that differentiate Android from the others are:

- You can develop Android apps on any platform, whether it is Mac, Linux, or Windows

- Android has top-notch documentation, which makes it the most developer-friendly platform

- Android apps can be easily published in Google Play compared to the lengthy review process in the iOS app store

Development environment setup is the first and most important step in the software development process. Improper setup will lead to build errors.

In this chapter, we will cover the following topics:

- The importance of Android Google Maps
- **Integrated Development Environment** (**IDE**) to develop Android applications
- Setting up Android Studio
- Setting up Eclipse with the ADT plugin
- Setting up an **Android Virtual Device** (**AVD**) for testing
- Exploring Android Studio
- Additional helpful stuff

The importance of Android Google Maps

In this section, you will learn the importance of Android Google Maps. It helps to seamlessly integrate Maps with your Android application. It provides location data in a graphical form that enhances the user experience while helping you to create real-time, map-based applications similar to Waze and Uber. Google Maps is superior in comparison to all the other maps. You can display a label or marker over the map. You can provide turn-by-turn navigation and get directions between two locations. These are the some of the points that make Android Google Maps special.

An example of a map application

One of the great examples of a map-based application is Waze. It is a GPS-based, social map application and was developed by two Israeli software engineers. It was bought by Google in 2013 for an amazing 1.2 billion USD. Waze now has more than 50 million active users. Users who want to try Waze can download it from the following link:

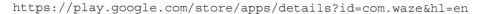

```
https://play.google.com/store/apps/details?id=com.waze&hl=en
```

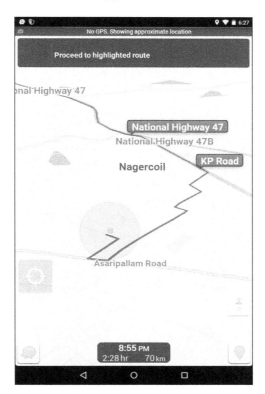

IDEs for developing Android applications

Integrated Development Environment (IDE) makes coding easier by providing a built-in compiler, debugger, syntax highlighting, autocompletion, project layout generation, project structure overviews, unit testing, and an app launcher. The two IDEs used for Android application development are:

- Android Studio IDE
- Eclipse IDE

Each IDE has its own advantages. Let's learn about both the IDEs a bit more in detail.

Android Studio

Android Studio is Google's official IDE to develop Android applications. It was introduced by Google in 2013 at their annual developer conference Google I/O. After over a year and a half of active development, Android Studio hit its official stable release 1.0 in December 2014. It was based on IntelliJ IDEA software. Let's see how it differs from Eclipse:

- It provides a live layout editor with real-time rendering (WYSIWYG)
- It uses the Gradle build system against the traditional Apache ant build system
- It provides advanced code completion
- It has inbuilt template-based wizards for common Android designs
- It offers built-in support for Google Cloud Platform, which helps integrate **Google Cloud Messaging** (**GCM**) and the App Engine seamlessly
- It provides support for Android Wear

The following screenshot displays the typical Android Studio interface with the Dracula theme:

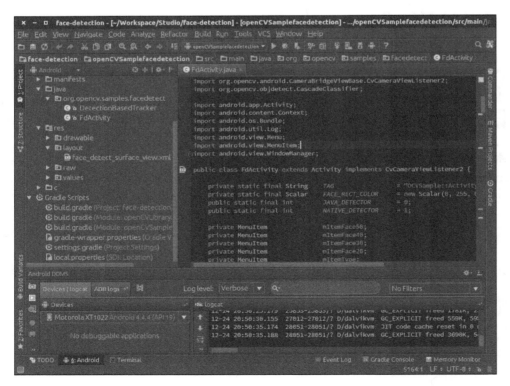

System requirements for Android Studio

The system requirements for Android Studio for various operating systems are listed in the following table:

Windows	OS X	Linux
Microsoft Windows 8/7/ Vista/2003 (32 or 64 bit)	Mac OS X 10.8.5 or higher, up to 10.9 (Mavericks)	GNOME or KDE or Unity desktop
2 GB RAM minimum, 4 GB RAM recommended	2 GB RAM minimum, 4 GB RAM recommended	2 GB RAM minimum, 4 GB RAM recommended
400 MB hard disk space plus at least 1 GB for Android SDK, emulator system images, and caches	400 MB hard disk space plus at least 1 GB for Android SDK, emulator system images, and caches	400 MB hard disk space plus at least 1 GB for Android SDK, emulator system images, and caches
Java Development Kit (JDK) 7	Java Runtime Environment (JRE) 6 Java Development Kit (JDK) 7	Oracle Java Development Kit (JDK) 7
Optional for accelerated emulator: Intel processor with support for Intel VT-x, Intel EM64T (Intel 64), and Execute Disable (XD) Bit functionality	Optional for accelerated emulator: Intel processor with support for Intel VT-x, Intel EM64T (Intel 64), and Execute Disable (XD) Bit functionality	GNU C Library (glibc) 2.11 or later

Eclipse

Eclipse has been one of the most popular IDEs among Android developers since its inception. Eclipse was the first officially supported IDE and it is still thriving today. Eclipse is a general purpose IDE; with standalone Eclipse, it's hard to develop anything. It has specialized plugins for almost everything and it has an awesome bundle for Android called the **Android Developer Tools** (**ADT**) plugin, which enables Eclipse for Android application development. The following screenshot shows the Eclipse interface:

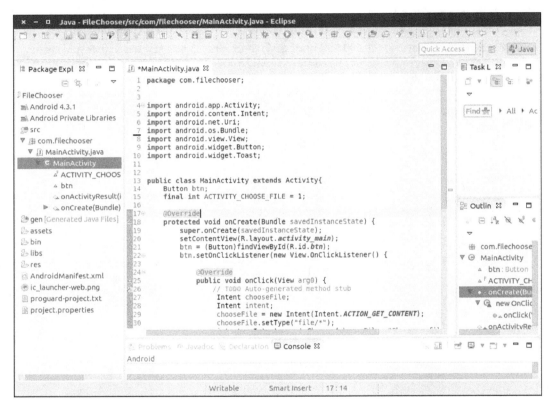

Choosing one IDE over another

Android Studio IDE needs more RAM, while Eclipse is lightweight. Android Studio provides more features than Eclipse, and it is very easy to add dependencies such as the Google Play services library in Android Studio. While the choice depends on you, and my personal favorite is Android Studio, Eclipse can work well with 2 GB of RAM. The rest of the system requirements are the same as Android Studio.

Google recommends us to use the official Android Studio IDE and switch from Eclipse to Android Studio, since it will receive the latest updates.

Setting up Android Studio

In this section, you will learn how to set up the official Android Studio IDE on different desktop platforms.

Windows

Java Development Kit (JDK) is essential for the functioning of Android Studio.

1. Download and install the latest version of JDK from `http://www.oracle.com/technetwork/java/javase/downloads/index.html`. Download the correct architecture, x86 for the 32-bit OS, as shown in the following screenshot:

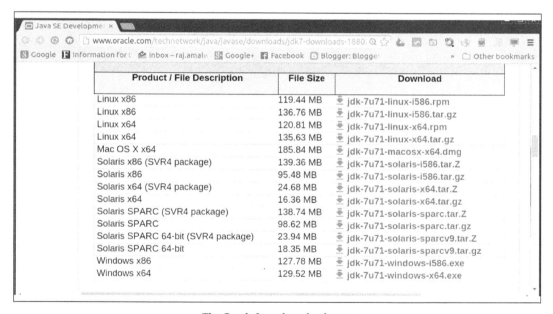

The Oracle Java download page

2. Next, install and configure Android Studio on your PC. Download the Android Studio bundle from `http://developer.android.com/sdk/index.html`.

3. Run the downloaded executable and follow the onscreen instructions, as shown in the following screenshot:

4. Next, we will see the following screen:

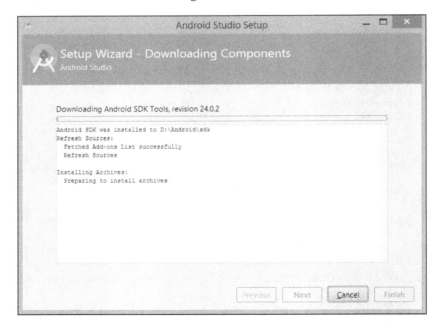

It may take some time for it to install. It may download some of the required components. Now, you have successfully installed Android Studio with SDK.

Mac OS X

We need JDK for Android Studio to work.

1. Download JDK 7 for OS X from `http://www.oracle.com/technetwork/java/javase/downloads/index.html`.

2. Open the downloaded `.dmg` file. A window will appear with a `.pkg` file. Double-click to launch the installer and follow the onscreen instructions:

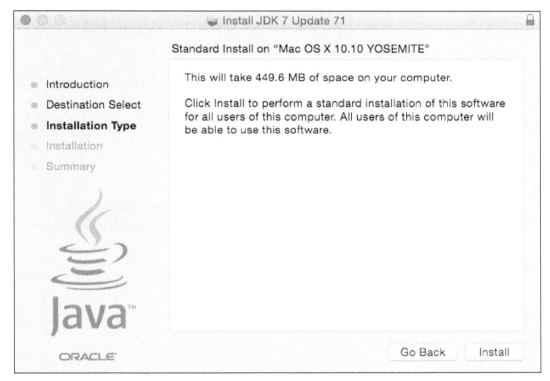

JDK 7 installation on Mac OS X

Google recommends us to use JRE 6 for optimized font rendering. Similarly, download and install JRE 6.

3. Next, download and install Android Studio.

4. Download Android Studio for OS X from `http://developer.android.com/sdk/index.html`.

5. Open the downloaded `.dmg` file. Drag and drop Android Studio in the `Applications` folder:

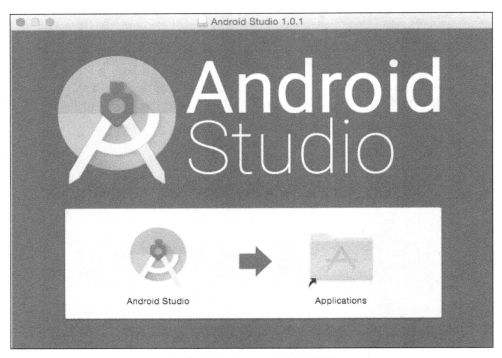

Android Studio setup in Mac OS X

6. Then, open Android Studio and continue with the setup process. Now, you have set up Android Studio on OS X.

Linux

Ubuntu is one of the most popular Linux distributions, which is based on Debian. Here, I am giving instructions to set up Android Studio in the Ubuntu distribution. The Ubuntu version I am using is version 14.10.

The first major requirement is the installation of Oracle Java. It is not available in the official Ubuntu PPA repository. So, we are going to download and install it from a third-party PPA repository.

1. Open the Terminal or use the shortcut key *Ctrl* + *Alt* + *T*. Install Oracle Java 7 using the following commands. Enter it one by one:

   ```
   sudo add-apt-repository ppa:webupd8team/java
   sudo apt-get update
   sudo apt-get install oracle-java7-installer
   ```

2. You can install Oracle Java 8 by replacing the last command with the following:

   ```
   sudo apt-get install oracle-java8-installer
   ```

3. Now, let's check whether we have setup Android Studio correctly. Enter the following command in the Terminal:

   ```
   java -version
   ```

   It should return an output similar to the following:

   ```
   java version "1.8.0_25"
   Java(TM) SE Runtime Environment (build 1.8.0_25-b17)
   Java HotSpot(TM) 64-Bit Server VM (build 25.25-b02, mixed mode)
   ```

   If you are using the 64-bit distribution of Ubuntu, you need to install some packages to get the 32-bit applications supported. If you are using version 13.10 or above, use these commands in the Terminal:

   ```
   sudo dpkg --add-architecture i386
   sudo apt-get update
   sudo apt-get install libncurses5:i386 libstdc++6:i386 zlib1g:i386
   ```

   For the earlier versions of Ubuntu, use the following command:

   ```
   sudo apt-get install ia32-libs
   ```

4. Now, our initial setup is done. Download Android Studio for Linux from http://developer.android.com/sdk/index.html.

5. Extract the downloaded ZIP package. Navigate to the android-studio/bin directory and execute the studio.sh shell script. Android Studio will start. Follow the onscreen instructions.

Now, you have set up Android Studio on Linux.

Setting up Eclipse with the ADT plugin

In this section, you will learn how to set up the Eclipse IDE with ADT on different desktop platforms.

Windows

The Oracle Java JDK is required for the functioning of Eclipse.

1. Follow the same instructions given in the *Setting up Android Studio* section for installing Java. After installing Java, let's proceed to the next step.

2. Next, we need to download the Eclipse IDE. Visit the following link and download the Eclipse IDE for Java developers: `https://eclipse.org/downloads/index.php`.

3. Now, extract the downloaded ZIP package and run the `eclipse.exe` executable. Eclipse will be running. We need to set up SDK and download the Android SDK standalone installer from `http://developer.android.com/sdk/index.html`.

4. Run the downloaded executable and follow the onscreen instructions.

5. Set up the ADT plugin in Eclipse. Open Eclipse and select **Help | Install New Software**.

6. A dialog box will appear. Enter the following URL and hit *Enter*: `https://dl-ssl.google.com/android/eclipse/`. Wait until it fetches information.

7. Now, check the **Developer Tools** box and select **Next**. Accept the agreements and the ADT plugin will be downloaded and installed. Then, Eclipse will restart and ADT will be integrated with Eclipse successfully. Select **Window | Preferences**.

8. Set the SDK location in the **Android** section. Hit **Apply**. Success! You have done it.

Mac OS X

Follow the same instructions given in the *Setting up Android Studio* section for Installing Java. After you have installed Java, proceed to the next step:

1. Visit `https://eclipse.org/downloads/index.php` and download the OS X version of the Eclipse IDE for Java developers.

2. Open the downloaded archive. Drag the `eclipse` folder to the `Applications` directory. To open Eclipse, open the Eclipse executable from the `eclipse` folder in the `Applications` directory. Next, we need to set up SDK. Download the Android SDK Tools standalone package for OS X from `http://developer.android.com/sdk/index.html`.

3. Extract the downloaded SDK package. The ADT plugin setup is same as the setup on Windows. Now, you have set up Eclipse ADT with SDK on OS X.

Linux

Follow the same instructions given in the *Setting up Android Studio* section for Installing Java. After you have installed Java, proceed to the next step:

1. Now, we need to download the Eclipse IDE. Visit `https://eclipse.org/downloads/index.php` and download the Linux version of the Eclipse IDE for Java developers.

2. Extract the downloaded ZIP package and run the Eclipse executable. Eclipse will be running. Next, we need to set up SDK. Download the Android SDK Tools standalone package for Linux from `http://developer.android.com/sdk/index.html`.

3. Extract the downloaded SDK package. The ADT plugin setup is same as the setup on Windows. Now, you have set up Eclipse ADT with SDK on Linux.

Downloading and setting up Google Play services

The Google Play services SDK is required to work with Google Maps. Google Play services can be only installed from the SDK Manager.

1. Open the SDK Manager via Android Studio by selecting **Tools** | **Android** | **SDK Manager**.

2. You can open the SDK Manager via Eclipse by selecting **Window** | **SDK Manager**.

The following screenshot shows the Android SDK Manager:

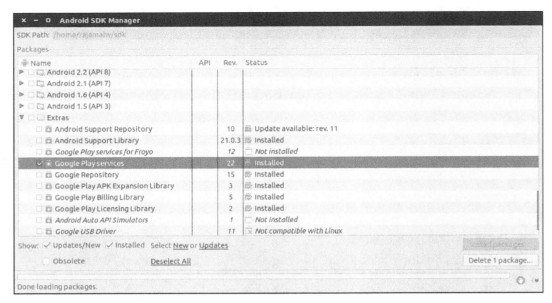

Android SDK Manager

3. Scroll down to the bottom. Under the **Extras** section, check **Google Play services** and select **Install packages**. The Google Play services package will then be downloaded and installed. If it is successfully installed, it will show the status as **Installed**.

Downloading the Google APIs System Image

We need the Google APIs System Image to test the Google Maps application on our PC. These system images have Google Play services preinstalled, which helps us test our Maps application. Open SDK Manager. Under each Android API section, you will find a Google APIs system image. You can use the ARM image or x86 image as per your own requirements. Now, select and install the system image.

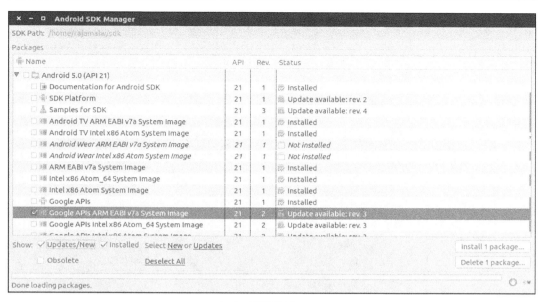

Android SDK Manager

Setting up AVD for testing

AVDs are used to virtually test the app on your PC. You may not have different versions of Android with different screen resolutions. To overcome this issue, AVDs are used to virtually create a number of devices and test whether the app runs perfectly on a particular version of Android. One thing to note is that AVDs are much slower compared to physical devices. Now, let's create an AVD to test our Google Maps Android application. The AVD Manager looks a bit different in Android Studio than in the traditional one. There are two different targets of an AVD, they are:

- Pure AOSP target, which does not contain any additional apps
- Google API target, which has Google Play services preinstalled

The different architectures available are x86 and ARM.

Setting up AVD from Android Studio

In this section, we will set up AVD from the Android Studio IDE by performing these steps:

1. Open AVD Manager in Android Studio by navigating to **Tools | Android | AVD Manager**. The following window will appear:

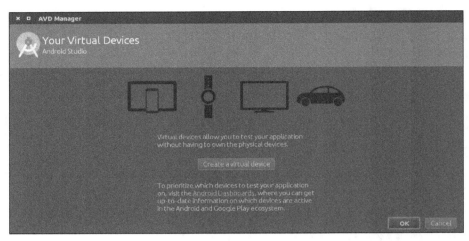

AVD Manager

2. The following screenshot shows how to select the virtual device:

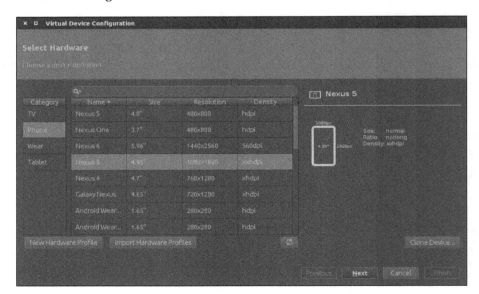

Selecting the virtual device

3. The next step is to select a system image. The following window will appear. Select a system image with the Google APIs target. The x86 system images have better emulation speed than an ARM system image. Then, select **Next**.

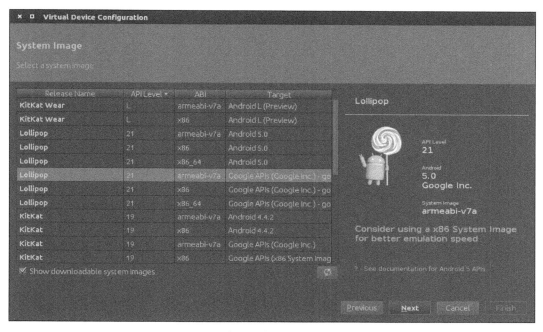

Selecting the API target

4. In the next screen, you can change some advanced settings. They are:
   ° You can change the amount of RAM of your virtual device
   ° You can change the internal and SD storage size
   ° You can use your PC's webcam to support the Android camera
   ° Enabling host GPU helps for better emulation speed as it uses your PC's graphics processor to render

The following screenshot shows these additional options:

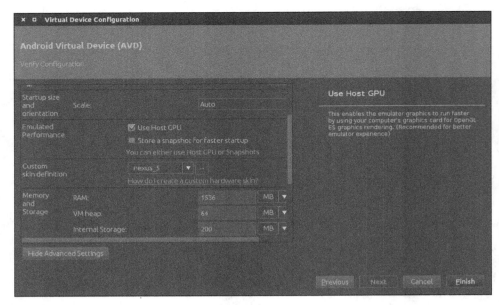

Additional options

5. After changing the settings, finally select **Finish**. You will see a screen with a list of virtual devices created. To start a virtual device, press the green button under the **Actions** section.

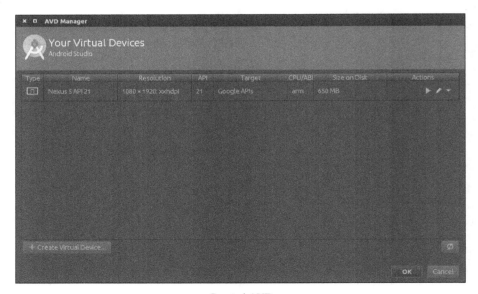

Created AVD

It may take some time for the emulator to start according to the speed of your PC.

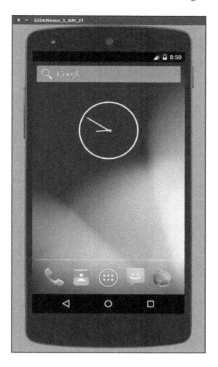

The preceding screenshot shows an emulator running Android Lollipop 5.0 with the Google API.

Setting up AVD from Eclipse

In this section, we will set up AVD from the Eclipse IDE by performing these steps:

1. Let's see how to create an AVD from the Eclipse IDE. Open the AVD manager in Eclipse by navigating to **Window | Android Virtual Device Manager**.

2. In the **Android Virtual Device (AVD) Manager** window, you will see the list of virtual devices created with the predefined device definitions.

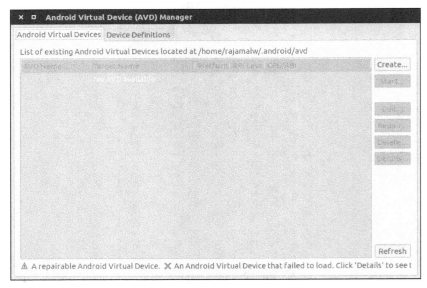

AVD Manager

The following screenshot shows the AVD Manager with the device definitions:

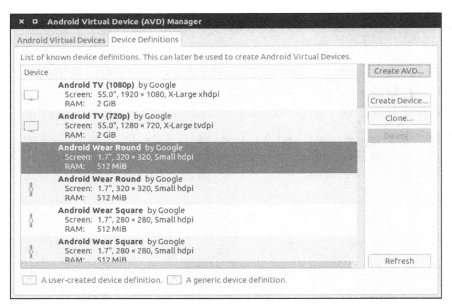

AVD Manager with device definitions

3. To create a new virtual device, select a device configuration and click on the **Create AVD** button. The following window will appear. You can change the advanced configurations, amount of RAM, and so on.

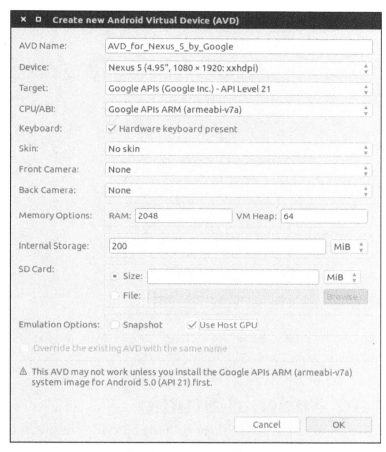

Creating a new virtual device

4. Then, press **OK**. Your virtual device will be created. The following window will appear with the list of virtual devices created:

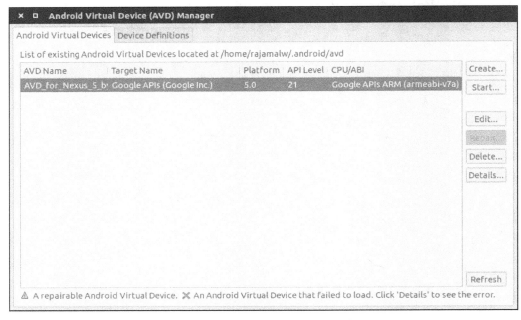

Created virtual devices that are listed

5. To start the virtual device, select a virtual device from the list and press the **Start...** button. The emulator will be running.

Exploring Android Studio

Let's see how we can do some basic things with the official Android Studio IDE. You can change the appearance of Android Studio as you wish. It has some inbuilt themes like:

- The IntelliJ theme, which is the default theme
- The Dracula theme, which is a dark cool theme

You can change the theme by navigating to **File** | **Settings** | **Appearance**.

Creating a sample application

Let's create our first sample Android application using Android Studio.

1. To create a new project, select **File | New Project**. The following window will appear:

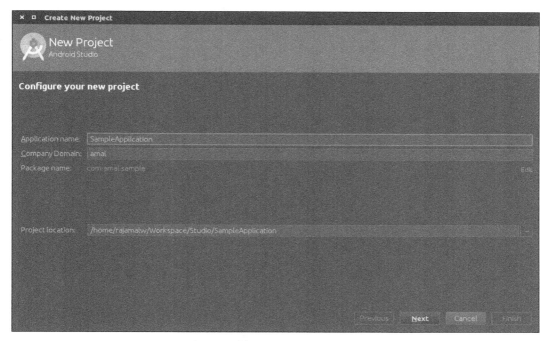

The wizard for creating a new project

2. Enter the values in **Application name:**, **Company Domain:**, and **Package name:**. Then, select the project location.

3. In the next screen, you need to select the minimum SDK version that your application supports. Targeting your application for a lower SDK version ensures that your application runs on a maximum number of devices. As of now, KitKat has a market share of 34 percent.

4. In the next screen, you need to select an activity template. This template helps you to simplify the task. For our sample application, select **Blank Activity**.

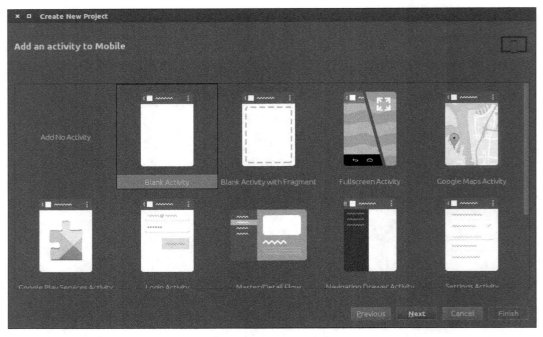

Selecting an activity template

5. In the next screen, you should enter the name of your main activity and the name for your main layout. **Menu Resource Name** is for the action bar menu layout file.

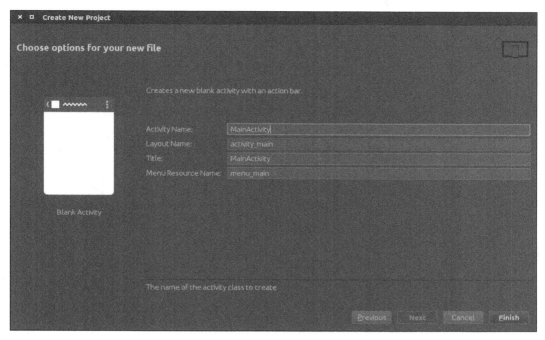

Defining the name for the activity and layout

6. Then, click on **Finish**. Wait for some time until Gradle builds your project information.

   Your sample app template is now created. Let's now explore Android Studio.

   The section on the left-hand side is the project explorer and the section on the right-hand side is the code editor. You will see three folders: manifests, java, and res inside your app. The manifests folder contains our application's AndroidManifest.xml file. The java folder contains our Java classes, which make our Activities, Fragments, and other functions. The res folder contains all our layout files and styles.

7. Now, run your application on the Android emulator or on your own physical device. To run the application, you can click on the green Run app icon in the toolbar or you can select **Run | Run app**.

You will see the text **Hello World** in TextView. Physical devices are a lot faster than the Android emulator, which runs on your PC.

Exporting the Android application as APK

Your Android app should be exported as APK and signed to be able to publish it in the Google Play store and install it on your device. In order to sign an APK, you need to create a key store. Let's see how to export in Android Studio.

1. Select **Build | Generate Signed APK**.

2. The **Generate Signed APK Wizard** window will appear. You need to create a new key store by selecting the **Create new** button. Enter the required details. One of the fields in the **Certificate** section needs to be nonempty. You can leave the rest of the fields empty. The minimum validity should be 25 years.

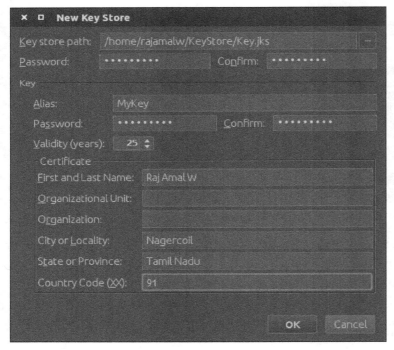

Creating a new key store

3. Then, select **OK**. Your new key store will be created. If you have already created a key store, you can use it. It is recommended to sign different apps you create with the same key store. Key store is used to authenticate you. So, keep your key store safe. Note that, if you lose your key store, you can't update your app published in Play store.

The following screenshot shows the Generate Signed APK Wizard window:

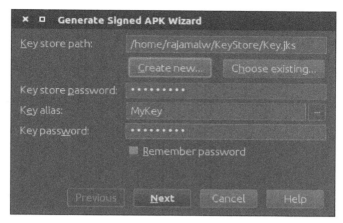

Generate Signed APK Wizard

4. Then, select **Next**. In the next window, you should select the destination folder of your APK. Then, select the build type, whether it is **Release** or **Debug**. While running our app on the virtual device, it will run in the **Debug** mode. You cannot distribute a **Debug** build in Play store. The **Release** build is the final build that can be uploaded to the Play store in which the app must be signed with your own certificate. Finally, select **Finish**. Your APK will be generated.

Additional helpful stuff

Let's see some things that will help in app development such as ADB, configuring the Java environment variable, and API levels.

Using Android Debug Bridge

Android Debug Bridge (**ADB**) is an inbuilt command-line tool, which helps us communicate with our virtual device or physical device.

The ADB tool can be found within our SDK directory. It is available at **sdk | platform-tools**.

Ubuntu users can easily install ADB by using the following command and directly accessing ADB from the command line:

```
sudo apt-get install android-tools-adb
```

To access ADB from any directory, if you are using older versions, you need to export the path of the `adb` directory. It can be done by using the following command:

```
export PATH=${PATH}:/home/rajamalw/sdk/platform-tools/
```

Here, I have given the path of my `adb` directory. To validate it for all the terminal sessions, you can add this line in the `.bashrc` file located in your home directory.

For detailed information on ADB, refer to the official documentation at `http://developer.android.com/tools/help/adb.html`.

Let's see some of the `adb` commands we mostly use:

```
adb devices
```

This command displays all the devices that are attached to your PC. It would return an output similar to the following:

```
List of devices attached
ZX1B325BRZ        device
```

To work with your own physical device, you must enable the **USB Debugging** option in the **Developer** options.

To install an APK on my device via ADB, I used the following command. Replace `myappname` with the name of the APK:

```
adb install myappname.apk
```

The following `adb` command can be used to copy the `image.png` file from the SD card to your PC:

```
adb pull /sdcard/image.png
```

The following command can be used to copy the `image.png` file from your PC to the root of your SD card:

```
adb push image.png /sdcard/
```

The following is the most important command for Android developers, which helps them to debug the app, and to know why and when it is crashing. This displays the logs from the device. The IDE shows the logcat messages too, both in Android Studio and Eclipse with the ADT plugin:

```
adb logcat
```

The following command lands you in the shell using which you can execute some common Linux commands on your device:

```
adb shell
```

Configuring JAVA environment variables

While starting Android Studio, you may get a **JAVA_HOME is not set** error. Let me show you how to fix this error.

1. Open **Control Panel** and select **System**.

2. Then, go to **System protection** | **Advanced** | **Environment Variables...** | **System variables**.

3. Then, create a new variable and provide a variable name as JAVA_HOME and a variable value as a path to your Java installation.

Android API levels

This is just for reference and to give you an idea about API levels. Each API level corresponds to each framework revision of Android, starting from API level 1 to API level 22. Android Lollipop 5.1, which is the latest API level, corresponds to API level 22. KitKat 4.4 corresponds to API level 19, while Gingerbread corresponds to API level 8 and 9.

Self-test questions

Q1. What is Google's official IDE for Android app development?

1. Android Studio
2. Eclipse

Q2. Android Studio uses the Apache ant build system.

1. True
2. False

Q3. Name an Android app that uses Map.

1. Waze
2. Duolingo
3. Evernote

Q4. ADB can be used to debug your Android application.

1. True
2. False

Q5. What are the architectures that AVD supports?

1. ARM
2. x86
3. MIPS
4. Both 1 and 2

Summary

In this chapter, we have seen some basic things that are required to kick start our app development. This will help us to avoid errors that may be due to some misconfigurations.

You have learned how to set up Android Studio and Eclipse on various platforms. Then, you have learned about the advantages of each IDE over the other, and how to create an AVD. You created a sample application. Finally, you learned about some additional stuff such as ADB and setting Java environment variables.

In the next chapter, we will see how to obtain the API key, SHA1 fingerprint and develop our first Maps application.

2
Configuring an API Key and Creating Our First Map Application

In the first chapter, we learned how to set up a development environment to kick-start an app development process. In order to install our Google maps application, we need to register our maps application in the Google Developer Console with our SHA1 fingerprint. This can be obtained by using the Java keytool and it is used in an authentication process. Let's learn about it in detail in this chapter.

In this chapter, we will cover the following topics:

- Generating the SHA1 fingerprint on Windows, Linux, and Mac OS X
- Registering our application in the Google Developer Console
- Configuring Google Play services with our application
- Adding permissions and defining the API key
- Creating our first map application
- Common problems and solutions

Generating the SHA1 fingerprint

Let's learn how to generate the SHA1 fingerprint on different platforms one by one.

Windows

The keytool usually comes with the JDK package. We use the keytool to generate the SHA1 fingerprint. Navigate to the `bin` directory in your default JDK installation location, which is what you've configured in the `JAVA_HOME` variable, for example, `C:\Program Files\Java\jdk 1.7.0_71`. Then select, **File | Open command prompt**.

Now, the command prompt window will open. Enter the following command, and then hit the *Enter* key:

```
keytool -list -v -keystore "%USERPROFILE%\.android\debug.keystore" -alias
androiddebugkey -storepass android -keypass android
```

You will see an output similar to this:

```
. . . . . . . . . . . .
Valid from: Sun Nov 02 16:49:26 IST 2014 until: Tue Oct 25 16:49:26 IST
2044
Certificate fingerprints:
    MD5:   55:66:D0:61:60:4D:66:B3:69:39:23:DB:84:15:AE:17
    SHA1:  C9:44:2E:76:C4:C2:B7:64:79:78:46:FD:9A:83:B7:90:6D:75:94:33
. . . . . . . . . . . .
```

Next, note down the SHA1 value, which is required to register our application with the Google Developer Console:

Chapter 2

The preceding screenshot is the typical output screen that is shown when the command is executed.

Linux

We are going to obtain the SHA1 fingerprint from the debug.keystore file, which is present in the .android folder in your home directory. If you want to install Java directly from PPA as given in *Chapter 1*, *Setting Up the Development Environment*, open the Terminal and enter the following command:

```
keytool -list -v -keystore ~/.android/debug.keystore -alias
androiddebugkey
-storepass android -keypass android
```

This returns an output similar to what we obtained in Windows as shown previously. Note down the SHA1 fingerprint that we will use later.

If you've installed Java manually, you need to run the keytool from the keytool location. You can export the Java JDK path as follows:

```
export JAVA_HOME={PATH to JDK}
```

After exporting it, you can run the keytool as follows:

```
$JAVA_HOME/bin/keytool -list -v -keystore ~/.android/debug.keystore
-alias
androiddebugkey -storepass android -keypass android
```

This command produces the following output:

```
×  –  □   rajamalw@AMAL-WORKSTATION: ~
rajamalw@AMAL-WORKSTATION:~$ keytool -list -v -keystore ~/.android/debug.keystor
e -alias androiddebugkey -storepass android -keypass android
Alias name: androiddebugkey
Creation date: 2 Nov, 2014
Entry type: PrivateKeyEntry
Certificate chain length: 1
Certificate[1]:
Owner: CN=Android Debug, O=Android, C=US
Issuer: CN=Android Debug, O=Android, C=US
Serial number: 2fadd356
Valid from: Sun Nov 02 16:49:26 IST 2014 until: Tue Oct 25 16:49:26 IST 2044
Certificate fingerprints:
        MD5:  55:66:D0:61:60:4D:66:B3:69:39:23:DB:84:15:AE:17
        SHA1: C9:44:2E:76:C4:C2:B7:64:79:78:46:FD:9A:83:B7:90:6D:75:94:33
        SHA256: 1C:31:76:CE:DD:D1:CE:63:A7:FF:8E:69:3B:26:38:28:AF:B0:4D:7E:A6:
92:8D:FF:DF:85:FA:77:16:2B:B2:A7
        Signature algorithm name: SHA256withRSA
        Version: 3

Extensions:

#1: ObjectId: 2.5.29.14 Criticality=false
SubjectKeyIdentifier [
KeyIdentifier [
```

[33]

Mac OS X

Generating the SHA1 fingerprint on Mac OS X is similar to Linux. Open the Terminal and enter the following command. It will show an output similar to what we've obtained in Linux. Note down the SHA1 fingerprint that we will use later:

```
keytool -list -v -keystore ~/.android/debug.keystore -alias
androiddebugkey -storepass android -keypass android
```

Registering in the Google Developer Console

Registration is one of the most important steps in our process. Our application will not function without obtaining an API key from the Google Developer Console. Follow these steps to obtain the API key:

1. Open the Google Developer Console from `https://console.developers.google.com`. Click on the **Create Project** button.

2. A new dialog box will appear. Give your project a name and a unique project ID. Then, select **Create**:

3. As soon as your project is created, you will be redirected to the project dashboard. On the left-hand side, under the **APIs & auth** section, select **APIs**.

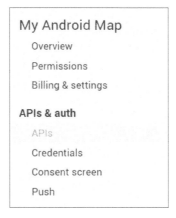

4. Then, scroll down and enable **Google Maps Android API v2**:

5. Next, under the same **APIs & auth** section, select **Credentials**. Now, select **Create new key** under **Public API access**, and then select **Android key** as shown in the following dialog:

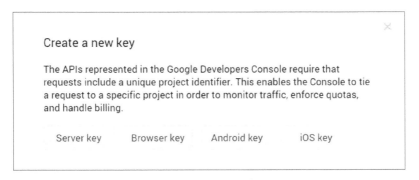

6. In the next window, enter the SHA1 fingerprint we noted in our previous section followed by a semicolon and the package name of the Android application we wish to register. For example, my SHA1 fingerprint value is `C9:44:2E:76:C4:C2:B7:64:79:78:46:FD:9A:83:B7:90:6D:75:94:33`, and package name of the app I wish to create is `com.raj.map`. I will then enter it as this: `C9:44:2E:76:C4:C2:B7:64:79:78:46:FD:9A:83:B7:90:6D:75:94:33;com.raj.map`.

7. You should enter the value as shown in the following screenshot:

Create an Android key and configure allowed Android applications

This key can be deployed in your Android application.

API requests are sent directly to Google from your client Android device. Google verifies that each request originates from an Android application that matches one of the certificate SHA1 fingerprints and package names listed below. You can discover the SHA1 fingerprint of your developer certificate using the following command:

```
keytool -list -v -keystore mystore.keystore
```

Learn more

ACCEPT REQUESTS FROM AN ANDROID APPLICATION WITH ONE OF THE CERTIFICATE FINGERPRINTS AND PACKAGE NAMES LISTED BELOW
One SHA1 certificate fingerprint and package name (separated by a semicolon) per line. Example:
45:B5:E4:6F:36:AD:0A:98:94:B4:02:66:2B:12:17:F2:56:26:A0:E0;com.example

C9:44:2E:76:C4:C2:B7:64:79:78:46:FD:9A:83:B7:90:6D:75:94:33;com.raj.map

Create   Cancel

---

8. Finally, select **Create**. Now our Android application will be registered with the Google Developer Console, and it will display a screen similar to what is shown here:

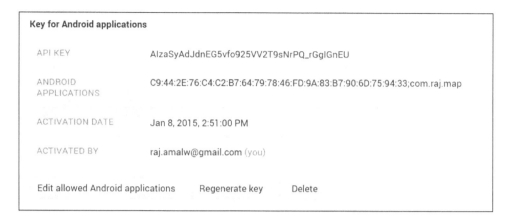

9. Note down the API Key from the screen. It will be similar to this: `AIzaSyAdJdnEG5vfo925VV2T9sNrPQ_rGgIGnEU`.

Configuring Google Play services

Google Play services include the classes required for our map application. So, it is required to set it up properly. It differs for Eclipse with the ADT plugin and Gradle-based Android Studio. Let's take a look at both separately. It will be simple.

Android Studio

Configuring Google Play services with Android Studio is very simple. You need to add a line of code to your `build.gradle` file, which contains the Gradle `build` script required to build our project. There are two `build.gradle` files. You must add the code to the inner `app` folder's `build.gradle` file. The following screenshot shows the structure of the project:

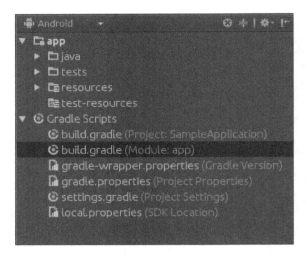

The code should be added to the second Gradle build file that contains our app module's configuration. Add the following code to the dependencies in the Gradle build file:

```
compile 'com.google.android.gms:play-services:7.5.0
```

The structure will be similar to the following code:

```
dependencies {
    compile 'com.google.android.gms:play-services:7.5.0'
    compile 'com.android.support:appcompat-v7:21.0.3'
}
```

The `7.5.0` in the code is the version number of Google Play services. Change the version number according to your current version. The current version can be found from the `values.xml` file present in the `res/values` directory of the Google Play services library project.

The newest version of Google Play services can be referred to from `https://developers.google.com/android/guides/setup`.

That's it. Now resync your project. You can sync it like this: **Tools** | **Android** | **Sync Project with Gradle files**.

Now, Google Play services will be integrated with your project.

Eclipse

Let's take a look at how to configure Google Play services in Eclipse with the ADT plugin. First, we need to import Google Play services into the workspace. Then, select **File** | **Import**.

The following window will appear:

In this window, select **Android** | **Existing Android Code Into Workspace**.

Then, select **Next**. In the next window, browse the `sdk/extras/google/google_` `play_services/libproject/google-play-services_lib` directory. It is given in the following image:

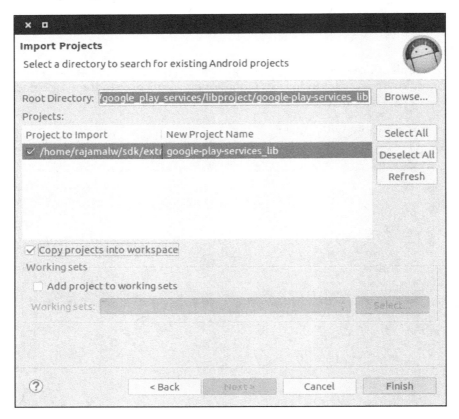

Finally, select **Finish**. Now `google-play-services_lib` will be added to your workspace. Now, let's take a look at how to configure Google Play services with our application project. First, select your project. Then, right click on | **Properties**.

In the **Library** section, select the following: **Add** | **google-play-services_lib**.

Next, select **OK**; `google-play-services_lib` will be added as a library to our application project. The following screenshot shows this:

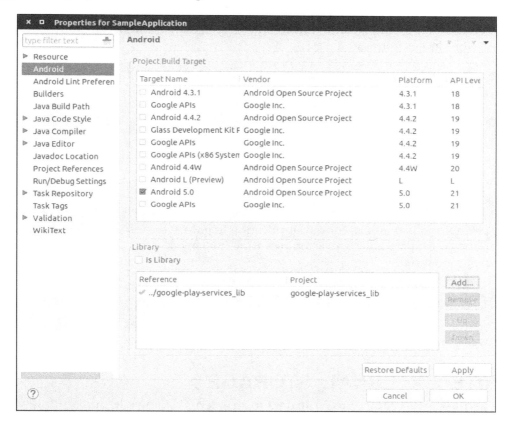

In the next section, we will take a look at how to configure an API key and add permissions that will help us to deploy our application.

Adding permissions and defining the API key

The permissions and API key must be defined in the `AndroidManifest.xml` file, which provides essential information about applications to an operating system. The OpenGL ES version must be specified in manifest, which is then required to render the map and also different versions of Google Play services.

Adding permissions

Three permissions are required for our map application to work properly.

The permissions should be added inside the <manifest> element. The four permissions are as follows:

- **INTERNET**
- **ACCESS_NETWORK_STATE**
- **WRITE_EXTERNAL_STORAGE**
- **READ_GSERVICES**

Let's now take a look at what these permissions are for.

INTERNET

This permission is required for our application to gain access to the Internet. Since Google Maps mainly works on real-time Internet access, access to the Internet is essential.

ACCESS_NETWORK_STATE

This permission gives information about networks and whether we are connected to a network or not.

WRITE_EXTERNAL_STORAGE

This permission is required to write data to an external storage. In our application, it is required to cache map data to an external storage.

READ_GSERVICES

This gives permission to read Google services.

The permissions are added to AndroidManifest.xml as follows:

```
<uses-permission android:name="android.permission.INTERNET"/>
<uses-permission android:name="android.permission.ACCESS_NETWORK_
STATE"/>
<uses-permission android:name="android.permission.WRITE_EXTERNAL_
STORAGE"/>
<uses-permission android:name="com.google.android.providers.gsf.
permission.READ_GSERVICES"
/>
```

There are some more permissions that are currently not required. We will learn about these in later chapters.

Specifying the Google Play services version

The Google Play services version must be specified in manifest for the functioning of maps. It must be within the `<application>` element.

Add the following code to `AndroidManifest.xml`:

```
<meta-data android:name="com.google.android.gms.version"
        android:value="@integer/google_play_services_version" />
```

Specifying the version 2 of OpenGL ES

Android Google maps uses OpenGL to render the map. Google maps will not work on devices that do not support version 2 of OpenGL. Hence, it is necessary to specify this in the manifest.

It must be added within the `<manifest>` element similar to permissions. Add the following code to `AndroidManifest.xml`:

```
<uses-feature
        android:glEsVersion="0x00020000"
        android:required="true"/>
```

The preceding code specifies that version 2 of OpenGL is required for the functioning of our application.

Defining the API key

The Google maps API key is required to provide authorization to the Google maps service. It must be specified within the `<application>` element.

Add the following code to `AndroidManifest.xml`:

```
<meta-data
    android:name="com.google.android.maps.v2.API_KEY"
    android:value="API_KEY"/>
```

The `API_KEY` value must be replaced with the API key we noted earlier in the Google Developer Console.

The complete `AndroidManifest` structure after adding permissions, specifying OpenGL, the Google Play services version, and defining the API key, is given as follows:

```xml
<?xml version="1.0" encoding="utf-8"?>
<manifest xmlns:android="http://schemas.android.com/apk/res/android"
    package="com.raj.sampleapplication"
    android:versionCode="1"
    android:versionName="1.0" >



    <uses-feature
            android:glEsVersion="0x00020000"
          android:required="true"/>



    <uses-permission android:name="android.permission.INTERNET"/>
    <uses-permission android:name="android.permission.ACCESS_NETWORK_
STATE"/>
    <uses-permission android:name="android.permission.WRITE_EXTERNAL_
STORAGE"/>
    <uses-permission     android:name="com.google.android.providers.
gsf.permission.READ_GSERVICES" />



    <application>



    <meta-data android:name="com.google.android.gms.version"
            android:value="@integer/google_play_services_version" />
    <meta-data
              android:name="com.google.android.maps.v2.API_KEY"
                android:value="AIzaSyBVMWTLk4uKcXSHBJTzrxsrPNSjfL18
lk0"/>



    </application>
</manifest>
```

Creating our first map application

Creating our map application with Android Studio is very simple. Android Studio has inbuilt templates that help us to create our map application easily through some simple steps. The first method to do this is by editing the layout from the Android studio inbuilt template. Select **File | New Project**.

In the next screen, select the target Android SDK version and minimum Android SDK version that your application supports.

In the following screen, select activity as **Google Maps Activity** and select **Next**, as shown in the following image:

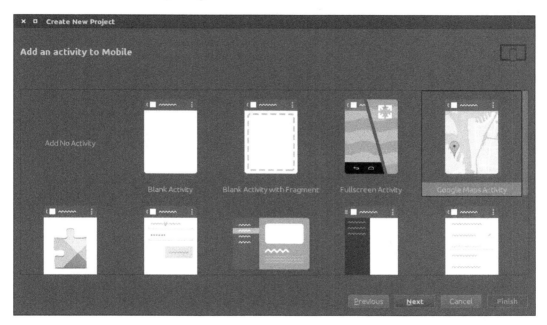

In the following screenshot, enter a name for activity and layout:

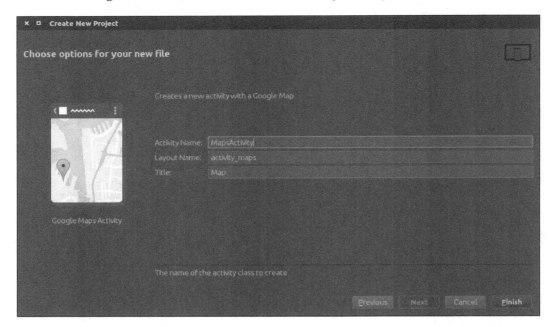

Finally, select **Finish**. Our map project will be created and all the permissions of the other components are added by default. Our job is to paste the API key to the google_maps_api.xml file, which is present in the folder res/values.

However, if you create an application in Eclipse, you need to add the permissions and other components manually and also configure Google Play services to get everything working. After configuring everything, let's proceed to the coding part, which is amazing.

Working with a layout

Add the following code to your main activity's layout file. The file is typically activity_main.xml, but in my case, it is activity_maps.xml:

```xml
<?xml version="1.0" encoding="utf-8"?>
<fragment xmlns:android="http://schemas.android.com/apk/res/android"
        android:id="@+id/map"
        android:layout_width="match_parent"
        android:layout_height="match_parent"
        android:name="com.google.android.gms.maps.MapFragment"/>
```

activity_maps.xml

This is the simplest way to load the map. The `android:name` attribute in the preceding fragment specifies the `MapFragment` class to instantiate the layout. The `android:id` attribute defines a unique ID for our fragment.

Optional (for old APIs)

This code only works for API 12 or greater (that is, Honeycomb or later; it can also be called a modern API). To support lower versions of Android, such as Gingerbread, you need to use `SupportMapFragment`.

To use `SupportMapFragment`, replace the last line in the preceding fragment code with the following code:

```
android:name="com.google.android.gms.maps.SupportMapFragment"
```

Working with the Activity class

Now, let's proceed to the `Activity` class. To get a basic map application running, we don't need anything special. Just link the activity to our main layout, which contains `MapFragment` or `SupportMapFragment`.

Use the following code in your main activity. For me, it is `MapsActivity.java`:

```
package com.raj.map;

import android.app.Activity;
import android.os.Bundle;

public class MapsActivity extends Activity {

    @Override
    protected void onCreate(Bundle savedInstanceState) {
        super.onCreate(savedInstanceState);
        setContentView(R.layout.activity_maps);

    }}
```

MapsActivity.java

The first line of our code defines the package name of our project. Replace this with the package name you've created.

The next two lines import the `Activity` and `Bundle` classes, which are required essentially to run a basic Android application.

`MapsActivity` is the name of our class, which is a subclass of the `Activity` super class.

When our `MapsActivity` is launched, the `onCreate()` method is called first, which loads the layout defined in `activity_maps.xml`.

Optional (for old APIs)

If you've used `SupportMapFragment` instead of `MapFragement` to support lower version devices, your `MapsActivity` should extend to the `FragmentActivity` class, which contains the support library to support lower versions of Android. You can download the support library from SDK Manager. If you are using Android Studio, you need to download the support repository.

Now, run your application in an Android emulator or a physical device. The basic application will work. For faster performance, it is better to use a physical device. You will get output similar to what is shown in the following screenshot:

Adding MapFragment programatically

In the last section, we added `MapFragment` in our layout file directly. In this section, we are going to create `MapFragment` dynamically in our activity. Open your main layout and enter the following code:

```
<LinearLayout xmlns:android="http://schemas.android.com/apk/res/
android"
    android:layout_width="match_parent"
    android:layout_height="match_parent"
    android:orientation="horizontal">
    <FrameLayout
        android:id="@+id/content_frame"
        android:layout_width="match_parent"
        android:layout_height="match_parent" />
</LinearLayout>
```

activity_maps.xml – code 3

In the preceding code, we use `FrameLayout`, which is used to display a single child view. Here, `FrameLayout` is the child of `LinearLayout`.

Next, we've defined `content_frame` as the unique ID for the `FrameLayout`.

Then, in our activity code, we will replace the contents of `FrameLayout` with `MapFragment`.

Use the following code in your main activity:

```
package com.raj.map;

import android.app.Activity;
import android.app.Fragment;
import android.app.FragmentTransaction;
import android.os.Bundle;

import com.google.android.gms.maps.MapFragment;

public class MapsActivity extends Activity {
    Fragment mapFragment;

    @Override
    protected void onCreate(Bundle savedInstanceState) {
        super.onCreate(savedInstanceState);
```

```
setContentView(R.layout.activity_maps);

mapFragment = MapFragment.newInstance();
FragmentTransaction fragmentTransaction =
        getFragmentManager().beginTransaction();
fragmentTransaction.add(R.id.content_frame, mapFragment);
fragmentTransaction.commit();

}}
```

`MapsActivity.java`

In the preceding code, `mapFragment` is the object of the `Fragment` class. The `FragmentTransaction` class provides APIs to add, remove, and replace a fragment.

We create `fragmentTransaction` as an object for the `FragmentTransaction` class. Then, we use the `add()` method to insert `MapFragment` in `FrameLayout`.

Finally, the `commit()` method is called to apply the changes.

Optional – for older APIs

To support devices with API 11 or lower, we need to use the support library to provide compatibility.

Use the following code in your main activity:

```
package com.raj.map;

import android.os.Bundle;
import android.support.v4.app.Fragment;
import android.support.v4.app.FragmentActivity;
import android.support.v4.app.FragmentTransaction;
import com.google.android.gms.maps.SupportMapFragment;

public class MapsActivity extends FragmentActivity {
    Fragment mapFragment;

    @Override
    protected void onCreate(Bundle savedInstanceState) {
        super.onCreate(savedInstanceState);
        setContentView(R.layout.activity_maps);

        mapFragment = SupportMapFragment.newInstance();
```

```
        FragmentTransaction fragmentTransaction =
                getSupportFragmentManager().beginTransaction();
        fragmentTransaction.add(R.id.content_frame, mapFragment);
        fragmentTransaction.commit();

    }}
```

MapsActivity.java

The preceding code provides the same functionality as the previous code. This code uses the SupportMapFragment class instead of the MapFragment class to support lower API devices.

When you notice the import statement in the preceding code, you will see that the classes are imported from android.support.v4.app.

The android.support.v4.app package provides classes to support backward compatibility. Now you need not worry about backward compatibility problems that arise.

Next, run the code in the emulator or physical device; you will then see your app running.

In the next section, we are going to take a look at the GoogleMap object.

Using the callback method

A callback function is a function you provide to another code, allowing it to be called by this code. The GoogleMap object can be obtained from MapFragment. You can get the GoogleMap object directly, but it may return null sometimes, which makes the application likely to crash. So, a callback will handle this scenario seamlessly. To enable a callback on our MapFragment, call the getMapAsync() method on MapFragment. Our activity must implement the OnMapReadyCallback interface.

We must use the onMapReady() method to handle the callback. Both getMapAsync() and the callback will be called on the main thread. It has the GoogleMap object as a parameter. Let's implement this in our activity. Take a look at the following code:

```
    package com.raj.map;

    import android.app.Activity;
    import android.os.Bundle;
    import android.widget.Toast;

    import com.google.android.gms.maps.GoogleMap;
```

```java
import com.google.android.gms.maps.MapFragment;
import com.google.android.gms.maps.OnMapReadyCallback;

public class MapsActivity extends Activity implements
OnMapReadyCallback {


    @Override
    protected void onCreate(Bundle savedInstanceState) {
        super.onCreate(savedInstanceState);
        setContentView(R.layout.activity_maps);
        MapFragment mapFragment = (MapFragment) getFragmentManager()
                .findFragmentById(R.id.map);
        mapFragment.getMapAsync(this);

    }
    @Override
    public void onMapReady(GoogleMap map) {

        Toast.makeText(getApplicationContext(),"Map Ready",Toast.
LENGTH_LONG).show();
        map.setMyLocationEnabled(true);

    }

}
```

`MapsActivity.java`

In the preceding code, `MapsActivity` implements the `OnMapReadyCallback` interface.

The `getMapAsync()` method is used to enable the callback on the main thread. The callback method is defined in `onMapReady()`, which has the `GoogleMap` object as the parameter.

Here, we show a toast message in the callback method. For those of you who do not know what a toast is, it is a pop up used to display messages.

The `setMyLocationEnabled()` method is used to enable the `location` button on `MapFragment`, and you can use this button to set your current location in maps using GPS.

Now, run the project. You will see the toast message and **location** button.

Use SupportMapFragment in order to support lower API devices.

The GoogleMap object

The `GoogleMap` object helps us to use the Google maps API effectively and to implement many features in our application.

Some of the features are as follows:

- It can be used to add markers, overlays, and so on
- It can be used to add controls, such as pan and zoom

The `GoogleMap` object can be initialized as follows:

```
GoogleMap map = ((MapFragment)
getFragmentManager().findFragmentById(R.id.map)).getMap()
```

Similarly, use `SupportMapFragment` and `SupportFragmentManager` to support lower API devices.

After initializing the `GoogleMap` object, you can use methods on the `GoogleMap` object. For example, consider this code:

```
map.setMyLocationEnabled(true)
```

The preceding code enables the **location** button on the map fragment.

In the next section, let's take a look at some of the commonly faced problems while executing or running a program.

Common problems and solutions

Common problems and their solutions are as follows:

- `java.lang.RuntimeException`: The API key is not found – Logcat.

  Your application will crash before opening. This is caused because the API key is not found in manifest.

  To fix this, add the API key to `AndroidManifest.xml`

- `Authorization failure` – Logcat: Your application will display an empty map on opening. This is caused because you have entered an invalid API key. You may have missed some strings in the key.

  To fix this, enter the API key without missing anything

- This application will not run unless you update Google Play services: This error is caused because you are using a lower version of Google play services than the version you used in your application.

  If you are using a physical device, you can fix this error by updating the Google Play services version. If you are using an emulator with the Google API, the only way to update is from the SDK Manager.

Self-test questions

Q1. What tool can we use to generate the SHA1 fingerprint?

   1. Gradle
   2. Keytool

Q2. In which Gradle build script file can we add dependencies for Google Play services?

   1. `build.gradle`
   2. `settings.gradle`

Q3. What permission can we use to get network information?

   1. **INTERNET**
   2. **ACCESS_NETWORK_STATE**

Q4. Which object is used to access the Google Maps API?

   1. `Fragment`
   2. `MapFragment`
   3. `GoogleMap`

Q5. Which fragment can we use to access Google Maps in lower API devices?

   1. `MapFragment`
   2. `SupportMapFragment`

Q6. Which function is used to handle the callback in our Google Maps application?

   1. `onMapReady()`
   2. `onMapReadyCallback`

Summary

In this chapter, we learned some more basic stuff that is required to create a basic map application.

We covered how to generate the SHA1 fingerprint on different platforms, registering our application in the Google Developer Console and generating an API key. We also configured Google Play services in Android Studio and Eclipse, and added permissions and other data in manifest, which is essential. Then, we created our first working Map application and tested it in an emulator. We also solved the compatibility issue by using support libraries. Finally, we learned about the callback method and the `GoogleMap` object.

In the next chapter, we will learn the implementation of different map types. Enjoy learning!

3
Working with Different Map Types

In our previous chapters, we learned how to set up a development environment to kick-start an app development process, registered our application in the Google Developer Console and obtained an API key, explored the permissions required, and lastly, we also learned about the `GoogleMap` object. In this chapter, we are going to learn about working with different types of maps.

We will cover the following topics:

- The need for different types of maps
- The different types of maps and the differences
- Implementing different types of maps
- Working with indoor maps
- Using the Lite mode

The need for different types of maps

Each map has its own advantages and disadvantages. For example, a normal map is good for navigation, whereas, a satellite map is not. A satellite map does not display labels, while other maps do. So, it is necessary to use different types of maps for different types of applications.

Delving into different types of maps and their differences

Currently, Google maps offers four different types of maps to integrate with applications. These are as follows:

- Normal
- Hybrid
- Satellite
- Terrain

Let's take a look at the differences between different types of maps.

Normal map

A normal map has the following characteristics:

- This is a normal, typical map
- This includes man-made features, natural features, rivers, and so on
- Labels are shown.

Here is a screenshot of a normal Google map running on a device:

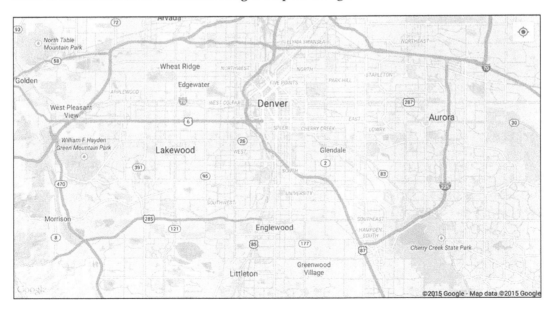

Satellite map

A satellite map has the following characteristics:

- This map displays images that are captured using a satellite
- No roads are shown on this kind of a map
- No labels are shown

This is a screenshot of a satellite map running on a device:

Hybrid map

A hybrid map has the following characteristics:

- This map is the combination of a normal and satellite map, respectively
- This kind of a map displays roads and labels

This is a screenshot of a hybrid map running on a device:

Terrain map

A terrain map has the following characteristics:

- This kind of a map displays topographic data
- It displays roads and labels
- It displays 3D elevation for mountains and other geographical data

Here is a screenshot of a terrain map running on a device:

Implementing different types of maps

Make sure you have registered your application in the Google Developer Console and obtained the API key for it. Then, set up Google Play services and define the API Key in manifest. Now, let's see how to implement different types of maps in our application.

Create a new Android application in Eclipse or Android Studio. Let's see the code needed for a layout file. The easiest way to load a map is using a MapFragment class. The code for the layout is the same as the one we used in the previous chapter:

```xml
<?xml version="1.0" encoding="utf-8"?>
<fragment xmlns:android="http://schemas.android.com/apk/res/android"
        android:id="@+id/map"
        android:layout_width="match_parent"
        android:layout_height="match_parent"
        android:name="com.google.android.gms.maps.MapFragment"/>
```

activity_maps.xml

Using a normal map

The first step is to initialize a `GoogleMap` object. Then, we should call the `setMapType()` method on the `GoogleMap` object, which takes the same type of the map as an argument. Now, let's see the code for our activity:

```java
package com.raj.map;

import android.app.Activity;
import android.os.Bundle;

import com.google.android.gms.maps.GoogleMap;
import com.google.android.gms.maps.MapFragment;
import com.google.android.gms.maps.OnMapReadyCallback;

public class MapsActivity extends Activity implements
OnMapReadyCallback {

    MapFragment mapFragment;

    @Override
    protected void onCreate(Bundle savedInstanceState) {
        super.onCreate(savedInstanceState);
        setContentView(R.layout.activity_maps);
        mapFragment = ((MapFragment)   getFragmentManager().
findFragmentById(R.id.map));
        mapFragment.getMapAsync(this);

    }

    @Override
    public void onMapReady(GoogleMap map) {
        map.setMapType(GoogleMap.MAP_TYPE_NORMAL);
    }
}
```

MapsActivity.java

The `MAP_TYPE_NORMAL` constant loads the normal map. Now, if you execute the application, you will see a normal Google map rendered in it:

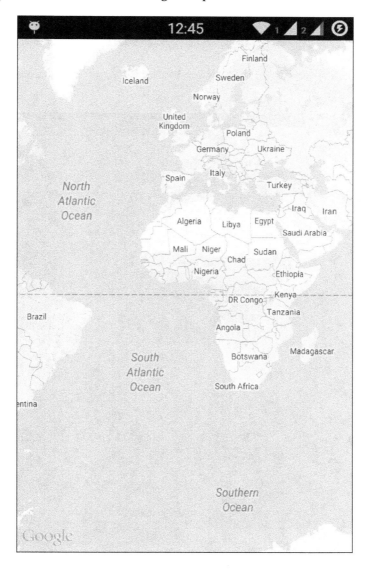

Using a satellite map

It is very simple to implement a satellite map. To do this, just use the constant
`MAP_TYPE_SATELLITE` in the `setMapType()` method:

```
map.setMapType(GoogleMap.MAP_TYPE_SATELLITE);
```

Now, execute the application. You will see the satellite map rendered in
your application:

Using a hybrid map

Similarly, use the constant MAP_TYPE_HYBRID in the setMapType() method:

```
map.setMapType(GoogleMap.MAP_TYPE_HYBRID);
```

Now, you will see a hybrid map rendered in your application:

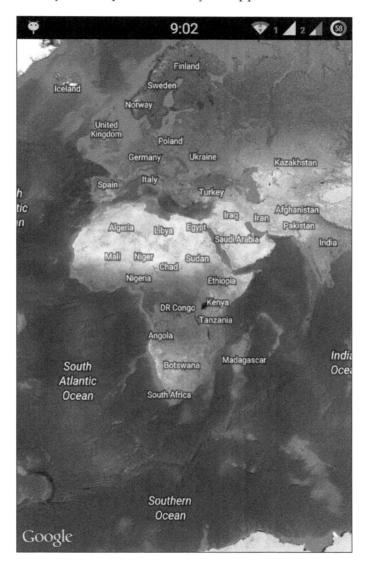

Using a terrain map

Similarly, use the constant `MAP_TYPE_TERRAIN` in the `setMapType()` method:

```
map.setMapType(GoogleMap.MAP_TYPE_TERRAIN);
```

Now, you will see a terrain map rendered in your application:

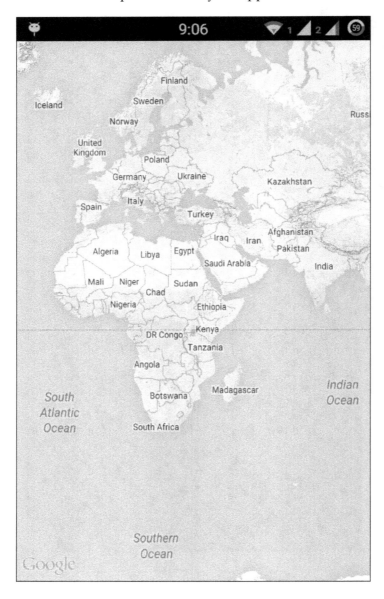

What if I don't need anything?

I have decided to display nothing. What shall I do? There is a way. Using the constant `MAP_TYPE_NONE` will render an empty grid for us, thus creating a custom application.

Until now, we have seen how to use different types of maps. Now, let us create a custom application that displays the different types of maps according to user selection.

We have already seen how to create a sample map application. Next, use the following code for an XML layout:

```xml
<LinearLayout xmlns:android="http://schemas.android.com/apk/res/
android"
    xmlns:tools="http://schemas.android.com/tools"
    android:layout_width="match_parent"
    android:layout_height="match_parent"
    android:orientation="vertical"
    tools:context=".MapsActivity">
    <fragment
        android:id="@+id/map"
        android:layout_width="match_parent"
        android:layout_height="400sp"
        android:name="com.google.android.gms.maps.MapFragment"/>
    <Button
        android:id="@+id/button"
        android:layout_width="match_parent"
        android:layout_height="wrap_content"
        android:text="None" />
</LinearLayout>
```

`activity_maps.xml`

The preceding code has `MapFragment` and a button as a parent of `LinearLayout`. In our previous examples, `MapFragment` is scaled to the full height of the screen. This is done to limit the height of `MapFragment` in order to display the button. This button is used to select a map according to user needs.

Next, create an XML file named `popup.xml` in the `res` | `menu` folder, such that its structure should be as follows: `res` | `menu` | `popup.xml`.

Here is the code for popup.xml:

```xml
<menu xmlns:android="http://schemas.android.com/apk/res/android">

    <item
        android:id="@+id/action_normal"
        android:title="Normal"/>
    <item
        android:id="@+id/action_satellite"
        android:title="Satellite"/>
    <item
        android:id="@+id/action_hydrid"
        android:title="Hybrid"/>
    <item
        android:id="@+id/action_terrain"
        android:title="Terrain"/>

</menu>
```

popup.xml

This is used to display a pop-up menu that contains all the four types of maps.

The next step is to code the activity. The following code performs all the functions for this activity:

```java
package com.raj.map;

import android.app.Activity;
import android.os.Bundle;
import android.view.MenuItem;
import android.view.View;
import android.widget.Button;
import android.widget.PopupMenu;

import com.google.android.gms.maps.GoogleMap;
import com.google.android.gms.maps.MapFragment;
import com.google.android.gms.maps.OnMapReadyCallback;


public class MapsActivity extends Activity implements
    OnMapReadyCallback {


    MapFragment mapFragment;
```

```
GoogleMap map;
Button button;
PopupMenu popup;

@Override
protected void onCreate(Bundle savedInstanceState) {
    super.onCreate(savedInstanceState);
    setContentView(R.layout.activity_maps);
    button = (Button)findViewById(R.id.button);
    mapFragment = ((MapFragment)
      getFragmentManager().findFragmentById(R.id.map));
    mapFragment.getMapAsync(this);
}

@Override
public void onMapReady(GoogleMap googleMap) {
    map = googleMap;
    map.setMapType(GoogleMap.MAP_TYPE_NONE);
    button.setOnClickListener(new View.OnClickListener() {
        @Override
        public void onClick(View v) {
        showPopup();
        }
    });
}

public void showPopup(){
    if (popup == null) {
        popup = new PopupMenu(MapsActivity.this, button);
        popup.getMenuInflater().inflate(R.menu.popup,
          popup.getMenu());
    }
    popup.setOnMenuItemClickListener(new
      PopupMenu.OnMenuItemClickListener() {
        @Override
        public boolean onMenuItemClick(MenuItem item) {
            if (item.getItemId() == R.id.action_normal) {
                map.setMapType(GoogleMap.MAP_TYPE_NORMAL);
                button.setText("Normal");
            }else if (item.getItemId() ==
              R.id.action_satellite) {
                map.setMapType(GoogleMap.MAP_TYPE_SATELLITE);
                button.setText("Satellite");
```

```
            }else if (item.getItemId() == R.id.action_hydrid) {
                map.setMapType(GoogleMap.MAP_TYPE_HYBRID);
                button.setText("Hybrid");
            }else if (item.getItemId() == R.id.action_terrain) {
                map.setMapType(GoogleMap.MAP_TYPE_TERRAIN);
                button.setText("Terrain");
            }
            return true;
        }
    });
    popup.show();


    }
}
```

MapsActivity.java

Now, let's see what the preceding code does. We attach OnClickListener() to a button to trigger a callback. A PopupMenu object is created using the constructor. We attach OnMenuItemClickListener() to the PopupMenu object to handle the callback when an item from the pop-up menu is clicked. The showPopup() method has all the code to create the pop-up menu object and to handle pop-up item click events. When the button is clicked, the showPopup() method is called.

Then, we use an if-else condition to display the respective map when a corresponding item is clicked on. You can also use the switch statement instead of the if-else statement.

The show() method in the PopupMenu object is used to display the popup. Now, you can finally run the application. You will see a empty grid rendered like this:

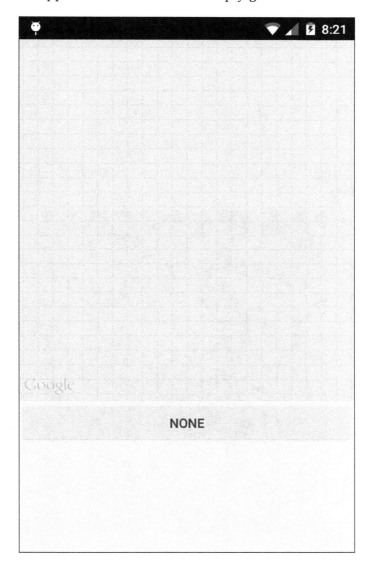

Now, when you press the button, you will see a pop-up list:

When you select any of the maps from the pop-up list, the application will render the corresponding map:

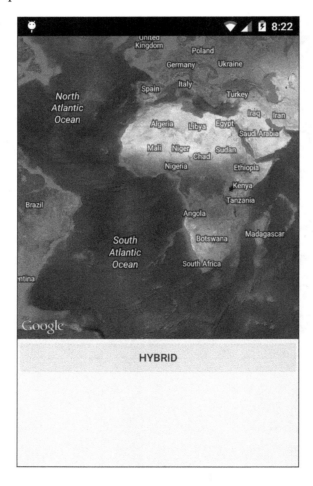

Working with indoor maps

Google provides indoor maps for some important places, such as airports, transit systems, sports venues, shopping malls, large retail stores, and so on. Such maps are activated at higher zoom levels. These maps are enabled by default and are only displayed as normal and satellite maps. To check the availability of indoor maps, visit `https://support.google.com/gmm/answer/1685827`.

The indoor map is normally shown with a level selector, which shows different maps for different floors. Here is the indoor map of a shopping mall:

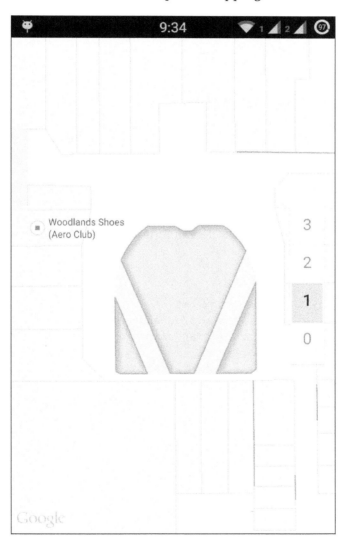

The overlay, which is shown on the right-hand side with numbers, is called a level selector as well as a floor selector.

If you do not wish to show the indoor map, you can easily disable it. Use the setIndoorEnabled() method to do this. This method should be called on a GoogleMap object by passing a Boolean value. In the preceding code, add the following line to disable indoor maps:

```
map.setIndoorEnabled(false);
```

If you need to disable the level picker, call the following:

```
map.getUiSettings().setIndoorLevelPickerEnabled(false);
```

We will learn more advanced concepts in later chapters.

Using the lite mode

The lite mode can be used to display a map as a static image. You cannot zoom or pan an image while using the lite mode. This is helpful in cases where you need to display less information. Now, let's see how to use this mode in an Android application.

The lite mode can be easily enabled from the XML MapFragment layout. Use the liteMode attribute of a namespace map. The map namespace should be specified initially. To set the zoom level, use the cameraZoom attribute. To display a map for a particular latitude and longitude, use the cameraTargetLat and cameraTargetLng attribute.

Here is the code for our layout:

```xml
<?xml version="1.0" encoding="utf-8"?>
<fragment xmlns:android="http://schemas.android.com/apk/res/android"
    xmlns:map="http://schemas.android.com/apk/res-auto"
    android:id="@+id/map"
    android:layout_width="match_parent"
    android:layout_height="match_parent"
    android:name="com.google.android.gms.maps.MapFragment"
    map:cameraZoom="17"
    map:cameraTargetLat="8.17597"
    map:cameraTargetLng="77.40734"
    map:liteMode="true" />
```

activity_maps.xml

Here, I am displaying a custom latitude and longitude. You can also change the map type in our layout by using the `mapType` attribute or programmatically, as we've seen earlier.

By default, a toolbar is displayed in the bottom right, which opens the Google maps application when clicked on. You can disable this by calling this code:

```
map.getUiSettings().setMapToolbarEnabled(false);
```

By default, when you tap the map, it opens the Google map application. You can override it by attaching `setOnMapClickListener()` with the `GoogleMap` object.

When you run the application, you will see a screen similar to this:

Map types and constants

The following table lists the map types and constants:

Map type	Constant
Normal	MAP_TYPE_NORMAL
Satellite	MAP_TYPE_SATELLITE
Hybrid	MAP_TYPE_HYBRID
Terrain	MAP_TYPE_TERRAIN
None	MAP_TYPE_NONE

Self-test questions

Q1. How many types of maps do we have?

1. 5
2. 4
3. 6

Q2. Which map does not display labels?

1. Terrain
2. Satellite
3. Normal

Q3. Which method should be called to set the type of a map?

1. setMap()
2. setMapType()
3. setmap()

Q4. The setIndoorEnabled() method is called to change the indoor map behavior.

1. True
2. False

Q5. The `liteMode` attribute is used to enable the lite mode.

1. True
2. False

Q6. Lite mode renders a static image map.

1. True
2. False

Summary

In this chapter, we learned how to work with different types of maps. We saw how to use normal, satellite, hybrid, and terrain maps with our application. We also developed a custom application that displays all these four types of maps. Finally, we learned about using indoor maps and the lite mode in our application.

In next chapter, we will gain a deeper insight into Google maps.

4
Adding Information to Maps

In the previous chapter, we learned about how to work with different types of maps, and also developed an application that displays the four different types of maps. In this chapter, we are going to learn a bit more about Android Google maps. This chapter delivers a clear idea on how to add additional information to a map using markers, overlays, information windows, and shapes. Now, let's start.

In this chapter, we will cover the following topics:

- Importance of adding information to a map
- Adding information with markers
- Expanding markers with information windows
- Working with shapes
- Using overlays

Importance of adding information to a map

A plain map without any information in it is useless. There is no meaning in displaying this kind of a map. For example, consider a situation where in your office, you are given the task of developing an Android app that displays employee addresses on a map. In this situation, you need to use the following method to accomplish your task. Let's learn about the various methods of adding information to a map with the help of various topics.

Adding information with markers

Markers can be used to indicate a particular location on a map. A marker can be customized by changing its color or using a custom image instead of a marker icon. This image is an example of a marker:

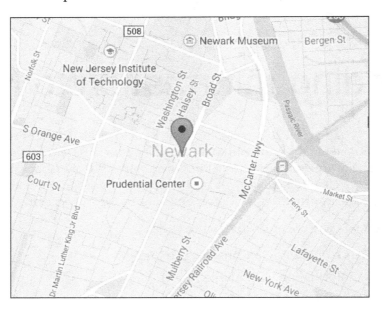

How to add a marker?

We need to use a `Marker` object to work with markers. A new marker can be added with the following method:

```
GoogleMap.addMarker()
```

This code takes the parameter as the `MarkerOptions` object. The latitude and longitude are set for the map using a `LatLng` object. The latitude and longitude can also be set as follows

```
MarkerOptions().position()
```

This method takes the `LatLng` object as a parameter. Now, let's create a sample app that displays a marker in Newark city. Let's see how we can code it. The code for our main layout is the same as the one we used in our previous chapters.

```
<?xml version="1.0" encoding="utf-8"?>
<fragment xmlns:android="http://schemas.android.com/apk/res/android"
    android:id="@+id/map"
```

```
android:layout_width="match_parent"
android:layout_height="match_parent"
android:name="com.google.android.gms.maps.MapFragment" />
```

activity_maps.xml

Next, we proceed to our activity:

```java
package com.raj.map;

import android.app.Activity;
import android.os.Bundle;

import com.google.android.gms.maps.GoogleMap;
import com.google.android.gms.maps.MapFragment;
import com.google.android.gms.maps.OnMapReadyCallback;
import com.google.android.gms.maps.model.LatLng;
import com.google.android.gms.maps.model.MarkerOptions;

public class MapsActivity extends Activity implements
OnMapReadyCallback {

    static final LatLng NEWARK = new LatLng(40.735188, -74.172414);


    @Override
    protected void onCreate(Bundle savedInstanceState) {
        super.onCreate(savedInstanceState);
        setContentView(R.layout.activity_maps);
        MapFragment mapFragment = (MapFragment)getFragmentManager().
findFragmentById(R.id.map);
        mapFragment.getMapAsync(this);

    }
    @Override
    public void onMapReady(GoogleMap map) {

        map.addMarker(new MarkerOptions().position(NEWARK));

    }
}
```

MapsActivity.java

Let's try to understand what the preceding code does. A new `LatLng` object is created and the latitude and longitude of Newark city is passed as the parameter. The new marker is created on a callback method using the `addMarker()` method, which takes `MarkerOptions` as a parameter. The position of the marker is set using a position marker, which takes the `LatLng` object as a parameter. Now, execute the program, and you will see output similar to what is shown in this screenshot:

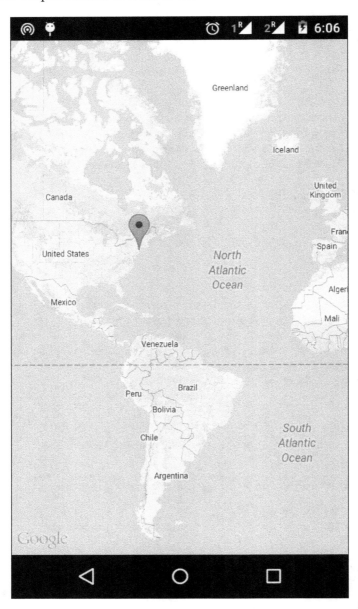

The new marker can also be assigned to the `Marker` object to perform more operations. The code for this would be as follows:

```
Marker newark = map.addMarker(new MarkerOptions().position(NEWARK));
```

Customizing the marker

In this section, we are going to learn how to customize the marker by changing its color, opacity, icon, and some other factors.

Changing the marker color

The marker color can be easily changed using the method `icon()`, which takes the parameter's `BitmapDescriptorFactory.defaultMarker()` object. The hue float value should be passed to the `defaultMarker()` object. The values have a range between 0 and 360. You can use predefined colors from the `BitmapDescriptorFactory` object. The predefined color constants are as follows:

- HUE_AZURE
- HUE_BLUE
- HUE_CYAN
- HUE_GREEN
- HUE_MAGENTA
- HUE_ORANGE
- HUE_RED
- HUE_ROSE
- HUE_VIOLET
- HUE_YELLOW

Now, let us change the color of the marker to red in our sample application. Change the code in the `onMapReady()` callback method to the following code:

```
BitmapDescriptor descriptor = BitmapDescriptorFactory.defaultMarker(Bi
tmapDescriptorFactory.HUE_RED);
 MarkerOptions options = new MarkerOptions().position(NEWARK).
icon(descriptor);
 map.addMarker(options);
```

You will see output similar to what is shown in this image:

Changing the marker opacity

The opacity value of a marker can be changed by calling the `alpha()` method on the `MarkerOptions` object, which takes float values between 0.0 and 1.0.

Float value	Opacity
0.0	Fully transparent
1.0	Fully opaque

Now, in our sample application, change the code in the `onMapReady()` callback to the following code:

```
map.addMarker(new MarkerOptions().position(NEWARK).alpha(0.5f));
```

Execute the application; you will see a partially transparent marker:

Using a custom image as a marker

In the previous topics, we saw how to change the appearance of the default marker. Now, we are going to use a custom image or icon as a marker. The custom icon can be set using the methods from the BitmapDescriptorFactory class. This icon should be passed to the icon() method. Let's see the methods and their functions:

Method	Parameter	Function
fromAsset()	String assetName	This loads a marker image from the assets directory
fromBitmap()	Bitmap image	This loads a marker image from Bitmap
fromPath()	String path	This loads a marker image from the absolute path of the file
fromResource()	Int resourceId	This loads a marker image from a resource

Next, in our sample application, change the code in the onMapReady() callback to the following code:

```
BitmapDescriptor descriptor = BitmapDescriptorFactory.fromResource(R.
drawable.ic_info);
MarkerOptions options = new MarkerOptions().position(NEWARK).
icon(descriptor);
map.addMarker(options);
```

In this example, we've placed the `ic_info.png` icon file in the `drawable` folder. This is the output we've got:

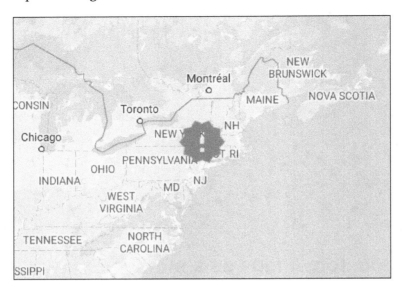

Let's load an image from the internal storage of a device. Here, we can use the `fromPath()` method to load the image from the root of the internal storage. Now, in our sample application, change the code in the `onMapReady()` callback to the following code:

```
BitmapDescriptor descriptor = (BitmapDescriptorFactory.
fromPath(Environment.getExternalStorageDirectory().
getAbsolutePath()+"/ic_info.png"));
MarkerOptions options = new MarkerOptions().position(NEWARK).
icon(descriptor);
map.addMarker(options);
```

Here, we've placed the `ic_info.png` file in the root of the internal storage. If you run the application, you will see output similar to the previous output.

Flattening a marker

Generally, marker icons are displayed with respect to the screen. For example, tilting, rotating, zooming, a map will not change its orientation. To change the orientation of a marker, call the marker's `flat()` method and pass Boolean value `true`.

Let me show you some examples. A normal rotated map will show a marker similar to the following image:

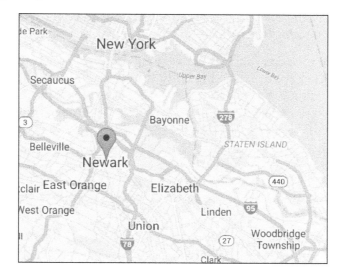

Now, in our sample application, change the code in the onMapReady() callback to the following code:

```
map.addMarker(new MarkerOptions().position(NEWARK).flat(true);
```

Next, run the application. The output will be similar to the preceding output with the marker icon rotated with respect to the map.

Rotating a marker

In this section, we are going to learn about how to rotate a marker. The marker can be rotated by calling the `rotate()` method by passing an angle in degrees. This will rotate the marker in a clockwise direction.

Another important property, anchor, is essential to rotate a marker. It sets the position of the marker according to the latitude and longitude mentioned on the map. It can be set using the `anchor()` method by passing position coordinates. If we use values, such as (0.5,0.5), the output will be such that the center of the marker image is placed on the latitude and longitude position.

Now, let's rotate the marker to 180 degrees in a clockwise direction with respect to the center.

In our sample application, change the code in the `onMapReady()` callback to the following:

```
map.addMarker(new MarkerOptions().position(NEWARK).
anchor(0.5f,0.5f).rotation(180.0f));
```

If you execute the code, you will get output with a marker that's rotated to 180 degrees.

The following image shows all the anchor scenarios with values, such as (0,0), (0.5,0.5), (1,1) and a default value when the anchor is not specified:

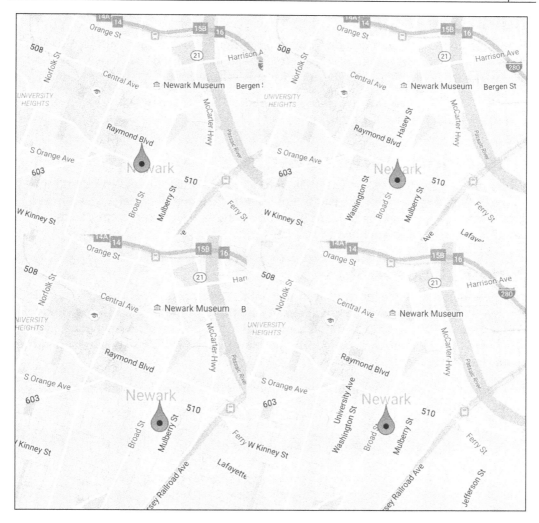

The image in the first quarter has anchor values of (0,0), followed by (0.5,0.5) in the second quarter, (1,1) in the third quarter, and a default value in the last quarter.

Hiding a marker

There may be a case when you don't need a marker anymore and want to hide it. The following code shows you an easy way to do this. Just call the `visible()` method by passing the Boolean as `false`. The code for this is as follows:

```
        map.addMarker(new MarkerOptions().position(NEWARK).
visible(false));
```

Employing marker events

In the previous sections, we saw how to add a marker, customize it by changing its color, changing its visibility, rotating it, and using a custom image as a marker. In this section, we are going to learn about working with marker events, such as dragging a marker and clicking on it.

Marker click events

To handle marker click events, we can use `OnMarkerClickListener()`. To enable this, call the `setOnMarkerClickListener()` method on the `GoogleMap` object, which takes `OnMarkerClickListener()` as a parameter. When you click on a marker, the `onMarkerClick()` method is called. In this example, we will display a toast and hide the marker when the user clicks on it.

The following code performs these operations. Here is the code in the `onMapReady()` callback method:

```
@Override
    public void onMapReady(GoogleMap map) {

        map.addMarker(new MarkerOptions().position(NEWARK));
        map.setOnMarkerClickListener(new GoogleMap.
OnMarkerClickListener() {
            @Override
            public boolean onMarkerClick(Marker marker) {
                marker.setVisible(false);
                Toast.makeText(getApplicationContext(),"You clicked
the marker",Toast.LENGTH_LONG).show();
                return false;
            }
        });

    }
```

In the preceding code, I have attached `OnMarkerClickListener()` to the `GoogleMap` object to handle marker click events.

When the user clicks on the marker, the `onMarkerClick()` method is called. Here, the marker is hidden and a toast is displayed. The following screenshot shows the initial screen as soon as the app is executed:

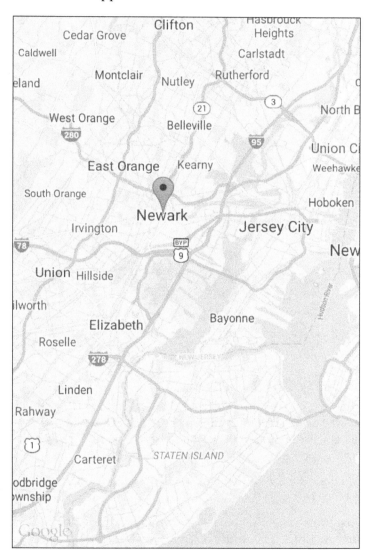

This screenshot shows the output when the marker is clicked on:

Marker drag events

By default, the marker is not draggable. You can set a marker to be draggable by calling the `draggable()` method on the `MarkerOptions` object, which takes a Boolean value as true or false as a parameter. To drag a marker, just long press the marker and drag it. The following code makes this possible:

```
map.addMarker(new MarkerOptions().position(NEWARK).
draggable(true));
```

Now, you can just long press the marker and make it drag. Next, we will learn some more functions. To handle the marker drag events, we must attach `OnMarkerDragListener()` to the `GoogleMap` object.

There are three methods in marker drag events. They are as follows:

- onMarkerDragStart()
- onMarkerDrag()
- onMarkerDragEnd()

The methods and functions are summarized in the following table:

Method	Function
onMarkerDragStart()	This is called initially
onMarkerDrag()	This is called constantly when a marker is being dragged
onMarkerDragEnd()	This is called when a user releases a marker.

The following example code shows the functions of each method. The code in the onMapReady() callback method is as follows:

```java
@Override
public void onMapReady(GoogleMap map) {

    map.addMarker(new MarkerOptions().position(NEWARK).
draggable(true));
        map.setOnMarkerDragListener(new GoogleMap.
OnMarkerDragListener() {
        @Override
        public void onMarkerDragStart(Marker marker) {
            Toast.makeText(getApplicationContext(),"Drag
started",Toast.LENGTH_SHORT).show();

        }

        @Override
        public void onMarkerDrag(Marker marker) {
            Toast.makeText(getApplicationContext(),"Dragging",Toa
st.LENGTH_SHORT).show();

        }

        @Override
        public void onMarkerDragEnd(Marker marker) {
```

```
                    Toast.makeText(getApplicationContext(),"Drag
    ended",Toast.LENGTH_SHORT).show();


            }
        });
    }
```

Now, execute the application. When you long press the marker, it becomes draggable. At this time, the onMarkerDragStart() method is called and a toast is displayed initially, which displays a **Drag Started** message. This method is called only once.

When the dragging process continues, the onMarkerDrag() method is called, and it is called constantly until you stop dragging. At this time, a toast is displayed, which displays a **Dragging** message.

When you stop dragging, onMarkerDragEnd() is called once, and also displays a toast message.

Now, let's make the marker a bit more complex. In our next example, we will find the latitude and longitude on the marker drag event and display it in a toast.

First, let's proceed with the code, and then we can see the explanation for it. The code in the onMapReady() callback method is as follows:

```
    @Override
    public void onMapReady(GoogleMap map) {

            map.addMarker(new MarkerOptions().position(NEWARK).
    draggable(true));
            map.setOnMarkerDragListener(new GoogleMap.
    OnMarkerDragListener() {
                @Override
                public void onMarkerDragStart(Marker marker) {
                    Log.d("Drag","Drag Started");

                }

                @Override
```

```
public void onMarkerDrag(Marker marker) {
    Log.d("Drag","Dragging");

}

@Override
public void onMarkerDragEnd(Marker marker) {
    Log.d("Drag","Drag ended");

    LatLng latLng = marker.getPosition();
    Double latitude = latLng.latitude;
    Double longitude = latLng.longitude;
    Toast.makeText(getApplicationContext(),"Latitude :
"+latitude+"\nLongitude : "+longitude,Toast.LENGTH_LONG).show();

        }
    });
}
```

In the preceding code, calling `getPosition()` on the marker object returns `LatLng`. From this, we obtain latitude and longitude values and display these in a toast. Run the application and watch logcat. You will see output similar to this:

```
02-23 19:57:42.038    14876-14876/com.raj.map D/Drag: Drag Started
02-23 19:57:42.805    14876-14876/com.raj.map D/Drag: Dragging
02-23 19:57:42.822    14876-14876/com.raj.map D/Drag: Dragging
02-23 19:57:42.844    14876-14876/com.raj.map D/Drag: Dragging
02-23 19:57:42.855    14876-14876/com.raj.map D/Drag: Dragging
02-23 19:57:42.872    14876-14876/com.raj.map D/Drag: Dragging
02-23 19:57:43.760    14876-14876/com.raj.map D/Drag: Drag ended
```

In a device, you will see output similar to what is shown in this screenshot:

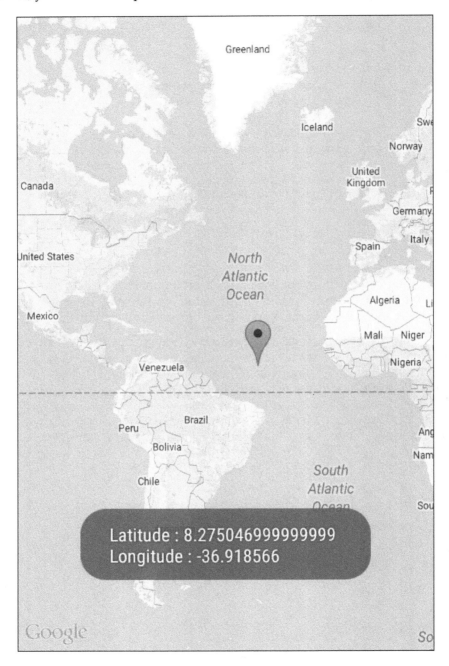

Expanding markers with information windows

Information windows are used to display additional information on a map, such as text and images. The information windows are supported by markers. Normally, information windows are displayed when a marker is tapped.

 You can display only one information window at a time. When another marker is clicked on, the current window is hidden and other windows pop up.

The following image is an example of an information window:

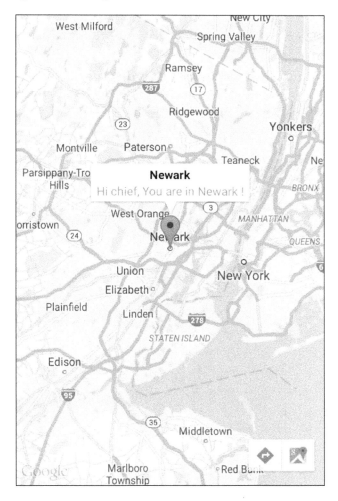

The information box that is displayed above the marker is the information window. The text that is displayed in bold is called a Title and the text that is displayed below the title is the called a Snippet.

How to add an information window?

An information window can be added by calling the `title()` and `snippet()` method on the `MarkerOptions()` object, which takes a string as an argument.

The following code makes this possible. We have predefined the `LatLng` values of a location, such as London, using this code:

```
static final LatLng LONDON= new LatLng(51.519029, -0.130094);
```

The code in the `onMapReady()` callback method is as follows:

```
map.addMarker(new MarkerOptions().position(LONDON).title("London").
snippet("Hi chief, Welcome to London !"));
```

In the preceding code, the text within the title is displayed in bold, and the text within the snippet is displayed below the title. Now let us run the code. It shows output similar to what is shown in the following image.

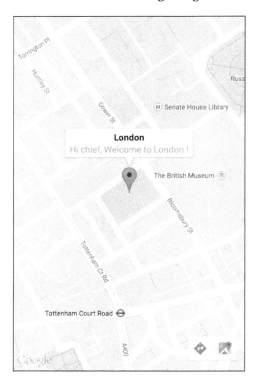

Showing/hiding an information window programmatically

By default, information windows are shown only when you tap a marker. You can override this by calling the showInfoWindow() method on the marker object.

Similarly, you can hide an information window by calling the hideInfoWindow() method on the marker object.

The code in the onMapReady() callback method is as follows:

```
map.addMarker(new MarkerOptions().position(LONDON).title("London").
snippet("Hi chief, Welcome to London !")).showInfoWindow();
```

When you execute this code, you will see that the information window is displayed by default.

Creating custom information windows

In the previous section, we took a look at how to add a normal information window with the help of a title and snippet. In this section, we are going to learn how to create a custom information window through images and text.

To display a custom information window, we must implement the InfoWindowAdapter interface. This can be done through two methods:

- getInfoWindow (Marker)
- getInfoContents (Marker)

At first, the getInfoWindow() method is called. If it returns null, the second method, getInfoContents(), is called. If the second method returns null, the default information window is displayed.

Now, we will create a custom information window that displays a country's flag as an icon, and we will also display a title, snippet, latitude, and longitude as text.

The first step is to create a layout resource file that is rendered on our custom information window. Here, I've created a layout called info_window.xml, which has LinearLayout as a parent and ImageView and TextView as child elements.

The code for `info_window.xml` is as follows:

```xml
<?xml version="1.0" encoding="utf-8"?>
<LinearLayout xmlns:android="http://schemas.android.com/apk/res/
android"
    android:layout_width="wrap_content"
    android:layout_height="wrap_content"
    android:orientation="vertical">

    <ImageView
        android:id="@+id/icon"
        android:layout_gravity="center"
        android:layout_width="80sp"
        android:layout_height="80sp" />
    <TextView
        android:id="@+id/title"
        android:layout_gravity="center"
        android:textStyle="bold"
        android:layout_width="wrap_content"
        android:layout_height="wrap_content" />
    <TextView
        android:id="@+id/snippet"
        android:layout_width="wrap_content"
        android:layout_height="wrap_content" />

    <TextView
        android:id="@+id/lat"
        android:layout_width="wrap_content"
        android:layout_height="wrap_content" />

    <TextView
        android:id="@+id/lng"
        android:layout_width="wrap_content"
        android:layout_height="wrap_content" />

</LinearLayout>
```

`info_window.xml`

The code for the activity layout is the same as the one we used earlier.

Here, we're going to display two markers: one at Newark and other at London. We've placed the flag icons for USA and UK in drawable folders named `us.png` and `uk.png`, respectively. You can use your own icons.

The complete code for `MapsActivity` is as follows:

```
package com.raj.map;

import android.app.Activity;
import android.os.Bundle;
import android.view.View;
import android.widget.ImageView;
import android.widget.TextView;

import com.google.android.gms.maps.GoogleMap;
import com.google.android.gms.maps.MapFragment;
import com.google.android.gms.maps.OnMapReadyCallback;
import com.google.android.gms.maps.model.LatLng;
import com.google.android.gms.maps.model.Marker;
import com.google.android.gms.maps.model.MarkerOptions;

public class MapsActivity extends Activity implements
OnMapReadyCallback {

    static final LatLng LONDON= new LatLng(51.519029, -0.130094);
    static final LatLng NEWARK = new LatLng(40.735188, -74.172414);


    @Override
    protected void onCreate(Bundle savedInstanceState) {
        super.onCreate(savedInstanceState);
        setContentView(R.layout.activity_maps);
        MapFragment mapFragment = (MapFragment)getFragmentManager().
findFragmentById(R.id.map);
        mapFragment.getMapAsync(this);

    }
    @Override
    public void onMapReady(GoogleMap map) {

        map.addMarker(new MarkerOptions().position(LONDON).
title("London").snippet("Hi chief, Welcome to London !"));
        map.addMarker(new MarkerOptions().position(NEWARK).
title("Newark").snippet("Hi chief, Welcome to Newark !"));

        map.setInfoWindowAdapter(new GoogleMap.InfoWindowAdapter() {
            @Override
            public View getInfoWindow(Marker marker) {
                return null;
```

```
            }

            @Override
            public View getInfoContents(Marker marker) {

                View v = getLayoutInflater().inflate(R.layout.info_
window, null);

                LatLng latLng = marker.getPosition();
                ImageView icon = (ImageView)v.findViewById(R.id.icon);
                TextView title = (TextView)v.findViewById(R.id.title);
                TextView snippet = (TextView)v.findViewById(R.
id.snippet);

                TextView lat = (TextView) v.findViewById(R.id.lat);
                TextView lng = (TextView) v.findViewById(R.id.lng);

                title.setText(marker.getTitle());
                snippet.setText(marker.getSnippet());
                if(marker.getTitle().equals("London")){
                    icon.setImageResource(R.drawable.uk);
                }else if(marker.getTitle().equals("Newark")){
                    icon.setImageResource(R.drawable.us);
                }

                lat.setText("Latitude: " + latLng.latitude);
                lng.setText("Longitude: "+ latLng.longitude);

                return v;
            }
        });

    }

}
```

MapsActivity.java

Here, we've declared the latitude and longitude coordinates of London and Newark as static variables.

Then, we implement the InfoWindowAdapter interface on the GoogleMap object which has two methods. The first method — getInfoWindow() — implemented by the interface returns null as the View object.

In the second method, we create a View object using LayoutInflator from a layout resource file called info_window.xml.

We can obtain the title, snippet, latitude, and longitude from a marker object and display them in the `TextView`. The `getTitle()` method on the marker object returns the title text, and the `getSnippet()` method returns the snippet text.

Finally, we need to display a suitable icon for the marker. So, we obtain the title text of the marker and display the flag icon according to the text.

We then execute the program. The output shown will be similar to what is shown in the following image:

Similar to the preceding image, another information window is shown at Newark.

Also, you can use many complex layouts, such as using buttons and other widgets.

Working with shapes

Google Maps for Android allows us to add custom shapes in our map application. The three ways supported are as follows:

- Polyline
- Polygon
- Circle

Let's understand these methods now.

Polyline

Polyline is a set of points where line segments are drawn between consecutive points. For example, you can give a set of latitude, longitude coordinates as input, and lines are drawn connecting these points.

The following image is an example of a polyline that connects two points:

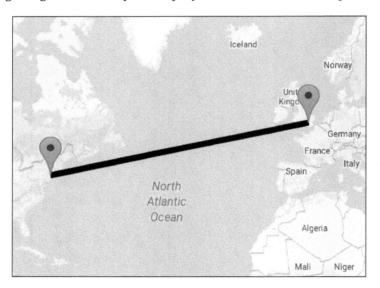

The `Polyline` object consists of a set of latitude, longitude coordinates and it connects the points to each other.

Creating a polyline

A polyline can be created using a PolylineOptions object. By calling the add() method on the PolylineOptions object, you can add latitude, longitude coordinates to the polyline. The add() method takes the LatLng object as a parameter. The polyline can be added to the Google map by calling the addPolyline() method on the GoogleMap object, which takes the PolylineOptions object as a parameter.

Now, let us draw a polyline connecting New York, Paris, and Madrid.

The LatLng value of the three cities are defined as static variables in this way:

```
static final LatLng PARIS = new LatLng(48.8588589,2.3470599);
static final LatLng NEWYORK = new LatLng(40.7033127,-73.979681);
static final LatLng MADRID = new LatLng(40.4378271,-3.6795367);
```

The code for the onMapReady() callback method is as follows:

```
PolylineOptions polylineOptions = new PolylineOptions().add(PARIS).
add(NEWYORK).add(MADRID);
map.addPolyline(polylineOptions);
```

In the preceding code, we've created a new PolylineOptions object and added the LatLng values of New York, Madrid, and Paris.

Then, the polyline is added to our Google map by calling the addPolyline() method on the GoogleMap object. It can be assigned to the Polyline object.

Now, execute the program; you will see output similar to what is shown in the following image:

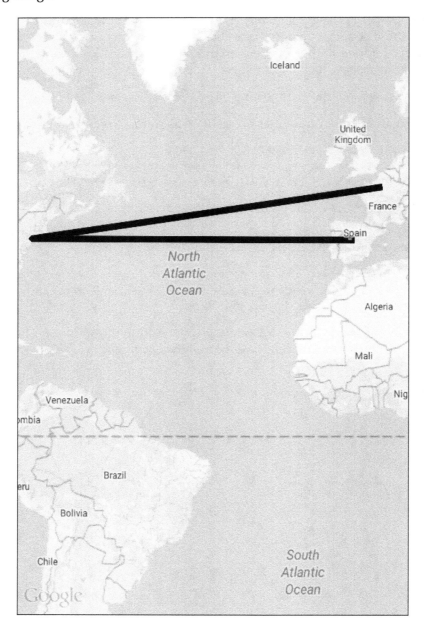

Similarly, you can add a list of the `LatLng` values that are defined in a class, such `ArrayList`, using the `addAll()` method. Here is another way to do this, and it gives you the same output:

```
ArrayList<LatLng> coordinates = new ArrayList<>();
coordinates.add(PARIS);
coordinates.add(NEWYORK);
coordinates.add(MADRID);

PolylineOptions polylineOptions = new PolylineOptions().
addAll(coordinates);
map.addPolyline(polylineOptions);
```

In the preceding code, we declare the `ArrayList` object of the `LatLng` type. Then, we add the `LatLng` elements using the `add()` method. By calling the `addAll()` method in the `PolylineOptions` object, we can add the list of coordinates to the polyline.

Next, execute the code; you will get the same output as you did previously.

To alter the polyline after adding, you can call the `setPoints()` method on the `Polyline` object, which takes a list of points as parameters.

Polygons

Polygons are similar to polylines; they connect a series of points. A polyline is open-ended, and a polygon is closed.

This image is an example of a polygon connecting four coordinates:

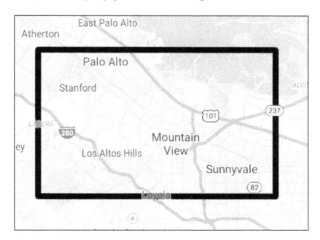

Creating a polygon

Similar to a polyline, you can create a polygon using a `PolygonOptions` object. By calling the `add()` method on the `PolygonOptions` object, you can add the latitude, longitude coordinate to the polygon. The `add()` method takes the `LatLng` object as a parameter. The polygon can be added to the Google map by calling the `addPolygon()` method on the `GoogleMap` object, which takes the `PolygonOptions` object as a parameter.

Now, let us draw a polygon connecting three cities in India. The `LatLng` values of the three cities are defined as follows:

```
static final LatLng CHENNAI = new LatLng(13.0475604,80.2089535);
static final LatLng BENGALURU = new LatLng(12.9539974,77.6309395);
static final LatLng HYDERABAD = new LatLng(17.4123487,78.4080455);
```

The code for the `onMapReady()` callback method is as follows:

```
PolygonOptions polygonOptions = new  PolygonOptions().add(CHENNAI).
add(BENGALURU).add(HYDERABAD);
map.addPolygon(polygonOptions);
```

With the help of the preceding code, I can create a new `PolygonOptions` object and add the `LatLng` values of three cities: Chennai, Bengaluru, and Hyderabad.

Then, the polygon is added to our Google map by calling the `addPolygon()` method on the `GoogleMap` object. It can be assigned to the `Polygon` object.

Next, execute the program; you will see output similar to what is shown in the following image:

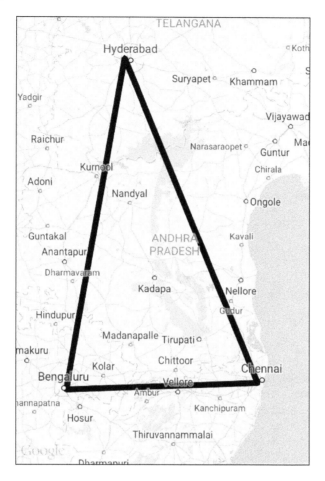

To alter the polygon after adding, you can call the `setPoints()` method on the `Polygon` object, which takes a list of points as parameters.

Creating a hollow polygon

You can draw a polygon within a polygon. The `fillColor()` method in the `PolygonOptions` object fills up an enclosed area with a custom color. You can draw an inner hole in the polygon by calling the `addHole()` method which takes a list of points as parameters. By doing this, the inner area enclosed by the polygon is left out and is transparent in color.

Let's draw a hollow polygon for the Bay of Bengal.

The outer coordinates are defined as follows:

```
static final LatLng Outer1 = new LatLng(13.079624, 80.332285);
static final LatLng Outer2 = new LatLng(13.079624, 80.462747);
static final LatLng Outer3 = new LatLng(12.939798, 80.475794);
static final LatLng Outer4 = new LatLng(12.941806, 80.315119);
```

Similarly, the inner coordinates are defined as follows:

```
static final LatLng Inner1 = new LatLng(13.060896, 80.350137);
static final LatLng Inner2 = new LatLng(13.061565, 80.413995);
static final LatLng Inner3 = new LatLng(12.985969, 80.413995);
static final LatLng Inner4 = new LatLng(12.985969, 80.334345);
```

The code in the `onMapReady()` callback method is as follows:

```
ArrayList<LatLng> outerCoordinates = new ArrayList<>();
ArrayList<LatLng> innerCoordinates = new ArrayList<>();
outerCoordinates.add(Outer1);
outerCoordinates.add(Outer2);
outerCoordinates.add(Outer3);
outerCoordinates.add(Outer4);
innerCoordinates.add(Inner1);
innerCoordinates.add(Inner2);
innerCoordinates.add(Inner3);
innerCoordinates.add(Inner4);

PolygonOptions polygonOptions = new PolygonOptions().
addAll(outerCoordinates).addHole(innerCoordinates).fillColor(Color.
GREEN);
map.addPolygon(polygonOptions);
```

In the preceding code, we can add the inner and outer coordinates to `ArrayList` of the `LatLng` type. The `addHole()` method makes the polygon hollow. The `fillColor()` method fills the polygon with a color. Execute the code; you will see output similar to what is shown in the following image:

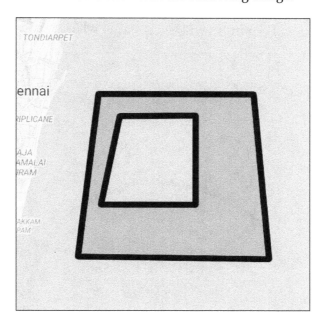

Circles

Similar to polygons, Google Maps' API provides us with a way to draw circles on a map. To draw a circle, we must specify two properties:

- Latitude and longitude
- Radius

Creating a circle

Similar to the shapes we've seen already, we can create a circle using a `CircleOptions` object. Calling a `center()` method in the `CircleOptions` sets the `LatLng` coordinate as the center of the circle. The radius of the circle must be set by calling a `radius()` method, which takes the radius in meters as a parameter.

In the following example, we will draw a circle by keeping New York as its center with a radius of 10 m.

The code for the `onMapReady()` callback method is as follows:

```
CircleOptions circleOptions = new CircleOptions().
center(NEWYORK).radius(10);
    map.addCircle(circleOptions);
```

Now, execute the code. The output will be similar to what is shown in this image:

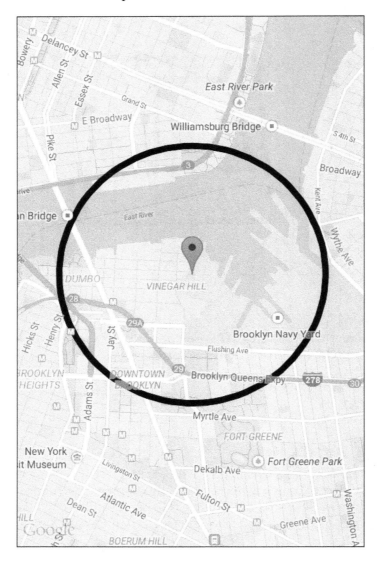

To alter the shape of the circle dynamically, you can call `setRadius()` and `setCenter()` on the `Circle` object.

Customizing the appearance of shapes

In the previous sections, we learned how to create simple shapes. Now we will learn how to customize these shapes according to our needs.

Changing the stroke color

Changing the stroke color of a shape is simple. All you need to do is call a `strokeColor()` method on the shape's `Options` object. For example, to change the stroke color of a circle, I would call `CircleOptions().strokeColor()`. The `strokeColor` method would take the color constant as a parameter.

To change the stroke color of the circle to blue, we can use the following code:

```
CircleOptions circleOptions = new CircleOptions().center(NEWYORK).
radius(1000).strokeColor(Color.BLUE);
```

For a polyline, we can call the `color()` method on the `PolylineOptions` object.

Using a fill color

A fill color can be only applied to closed shapes, such as polygons and circles. To change the fill color, we need to call the `fillColor()` method on a shape's `Options` object. The default color is transparent.

To change the fill color of a circle to blue, we can use the following code:

```
CircleOptions circleOptions = new CircleOptions().center(NEWYORK).
radius(1000).fillColor(Color.BLUE);
```

The output will be similar to what is shown here:

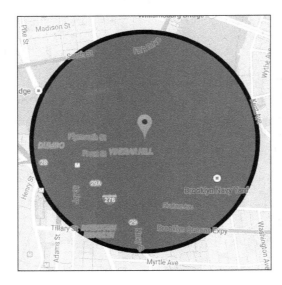

Changing the stroke width

The default width of a stroke is 10 pixels. The width of a stroke can be changed by calling the strokeWidth() method on a shape's Options object.

For a polyline, we need to call the width() method instead of strokeWidth().

Geodesic segments

Geodesic segments determine how line segments are drawn between coordinates. By default, line segments are straight. By enabling geodesic segments, line segments follow curved paths along the spherical surface of the Earth. However, this is only applicable to polylines and polygons.

These can be enabled by calling the geodesic() method on a shape's Options object, which takes a Boolean as a parameter. In such a case, true indicates that geodesic should be enabled.

Previously, we drew a polyline between three cities: New York, Madrid, and Paris. Now, lets enable geodesic in the code.

Change the code to the following:

```
PolylineOptions polylineOptions = new PolylineOptions().
addAll(coordinates).geodesic(true);
```

Let's see how the output differs from the original:

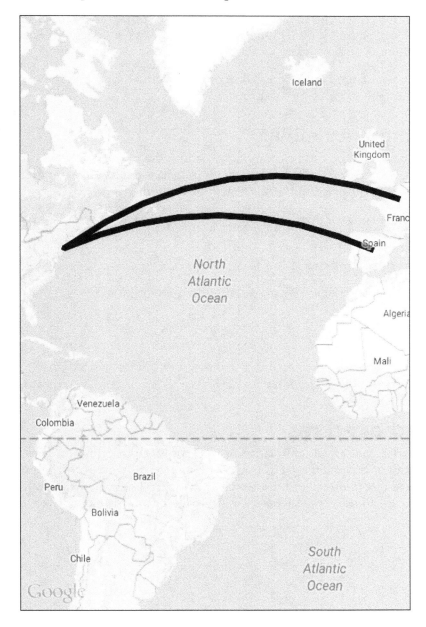

As seen in the preceding image, the lines are curved when compared to the original image.

Z-Index

Z-Index specifies the order of a shape with respect to other overlays. By default, the Z-Index is 0. Shapes with a higher Z-Index are drawn above those with a lower Z-Index.

Z-Index can be changed by calling the `zIndex()` method on the shape's `Options` object. It takes a float value as a parameter.

Changing the visibility

The visibility of a shape can be changed by calling the `visible()` method on the shape's `Options` object. The `true` parameter indicates that the shape will be drawn, whereas `false` indicates that the shape will be hidden.

To permanently remove the shape, call the `remove()` method on the shape.

Using overlays

Overlays are images that are displayed on top of the original Google map. There are two types of overlays:

- Ground overlays
- Tile overlays

Let's discuss both of these in detail.

Ground overlays

Ground overlays are attached to latitude and longitude coordinates. They move when we drag or zoom a map. Ground overlays are really helpful when we wish to display a single image over the surface of the map. The following image is an example of a ground overlay, where the Android logo is displayed over the map:

Adding a ground overlay

A ground overlay can be added using a `GroundOverlayOptions` object. By calling the `image()` method, you can set an image as an overlay. It takes `BitmapDescriptor` as a parameter. You can use methods from the `BitmapDescriptorFactory` class to select the image. Refer to the *Using a custom image as a marker* section. We can call the `position()` method to position the image at a particular location and adjust its width. We must pass the `LatLng` coordinates and width as a float value to the `position()` method.

Here, we're going to display the Android logo over the city of Madrid.

The coordinates we've used is as follows:

```
static final LatLng MADRID = new LatLng(40.4378271,-3.6795367);
```

The code for the `onMapReady()` callback method is as follows:

```
GroundOverlayOptions groundOverlayOptions = new
GroundOverlayOptions().image(BitmapDescriptorFactory.fromResource(R.
drawable.android)).position(MADRID,200f,200f);
map.addGroundOverlay(groundOverlayOptions);
```

In this example, we've placed the image in the `drawable` folder and chosen an image using the `fromResource()` method from the `BitmapDescriptorFactory` class. We've set the position as `Madrid`, and have also specified the width and height values as float values. Finally, the ground overlay is added by calling the `addGroundOverlay()` method on the `GoogleMap` object. We can assign this to the `GroundOverlay` object.

You will get output similar to what is shown here:

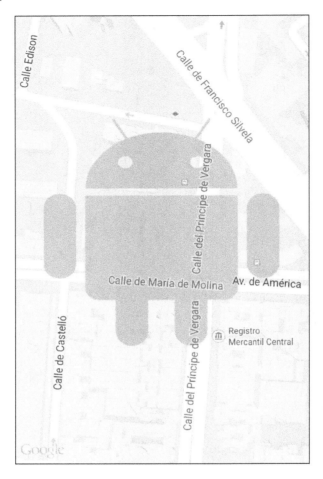

The overlay can be removed by calling the `remove()` method on the `GroundOverlay` object. To remove the image, we can modify the code as shown here:

```
GroundOverlay groundOverlay = map.addGroundOverlay(groundOverlayOpti
ons);
groundOverlay.remove();
```

The overlay image can be changed by calling the `setImage()` method on the `GroundOverlay` object similar to the previous example, which took `BitmapDescriptor` as a parameter.

Positioning a ground overlay

We have previously learned to use the `anchor()` method to position a marker. We can use the same method to position an image in a map by calling the `anchor()` method in a `GroundOverlayOptions` object.

Another way to position the image is by using `LatLngBounds`. It is used to set the north-east and south-west corners of the image.

A `LatLngBounds` object should be created and the coordinates for the south-west and north-east corners should be passed. You can then call the `positionFromBounds()` method on the `GroundOverlayOptions` object. Next, pass the `LatLngBounds` object to the `positionFromBounds()` method.

Now, we're going to display an image in Madrid. We can define the `LatLng` coordinates for the south-west and north-east corners as follows:

```
static final LatLng NE = new LatLng(40.461341, -3.688721);
static final LatLng SW = new LatLng(40.435998, -3.717903);
```

The code in the `onMapReady()` callback method is given as follows:

```
LatLngBounds latLngBounds = new LatLngBounds(SW,NE);
GroundOverlayOptions groundOverlayOptions = new
GroundOverlayOptions().image(BitmapDescriptorFactory.fromResource(R.
drawable.android)).positionFromBounds(latLngBounds);
map.addGroundOverlay(groundOverlayOptions);
```

When you run the program, you will see the Android logo set as an overlay in Madrid.

Tile overlays

In the previous section, we learned about using ground overlays in which we can display a single image over a surface. Now, how do we display multiple images to cover a large area? This can be done using tile overlays, which we can use to display a collection of images over base map tiles.

Tile coordinates and zoom levels

The image that renders in the Google map is a set of tiles arranged in a grid. For each zoom level, the corresponding tile for a grid renders. For example, for a Google map that is set to zoom level 0, only one tile will be rendered, which is represented by (0,0) coordinates. For each zoom level, the tiles increase by a factor of two.

For zoom level 1, four tiles with coordinates of (0,0), (1,0), (0,1), (1,1) will be rendered.

Similarly, for zoom level 2, 16 tiles will be rendered. So, I need 16 images to support zoom level 2.

The size of the images should be 256 x 256 px. For higher resolution devices, the images should be 512 x 512 px.

The most common way is to load and render images from URLs. So, we need to place a URL in our web servers. Let's see how we can implement this.

Here, we're going to use tile overlays for zoom level 2. Therefore, we need 16 images to be placed in our server.

The images we've placed are as follows:

- `images/2/0/0.jpg,1.jpg,2.jpg,3.jpg`
- `images/2/1/0.jpg,1.jpg,2.jpg,3.jpg`
- `images/2/2/0.jpg,1.jpg,2.jpg,3.jpg`
- `images/2/3/0.jpg,1.jpg,2.jpg,3.jpg`

The `images` directory can be created in the root of our servers. The first directory is named `2`, which corresponds to the zoom level 2. The second-level directories are named `0,1,2,3`, which correspond to the x coordinate. In the third level, four files are placed `0.jpg,1.jpg,2.jpg,3.jpg`, which correspond to the y coordinate. There are a total of 16 JPEG images.

Now, let's take a look at the coding.

We need to define `UrlTileProvider` to load an image from a URL, which is a partial implementation of the `TileProvider` class. Then, we need to override the `getTileUrl()` method. Next, the URL string is formatted to load a particular tile for the specified zoom level.

Then, a tile overlay is created by using the `TileOverlayOptions` object. The `tileProvider()` method is called on the `TileOverlayOptions` object and the `TileProvider` object is passed.

Finally, the tile overlay is added to a map by calling the `addTileOverlay()` method on the `GoogleMap` object that takes the `TileOverlayOptions` object as a parameter.

The code for the `onMapReady()` callback method is as follows:

```
map.setMapType(GoogleMap.MAP_TYPE_NORMAL);

    TileProvider tileProvider = new UrlTileProvider(256, 256) {
        @Override
```

```
public URL getTileUrl(int x, int y, int zoom) {

        String s = String.format("http://192.168.43.253/
images/%d/%d/%d.jpg",
                zoom, x, y);

        try {
            return new URL(s);
        } catch (MalformedURLException e) {
            throw new AssertionError(e);
        }
    }
};
TileOverlayOptions tileOverlayOptions = new
TileOverlayOptions().tileProvider(tileProvider);
    map.addTileOverlay(tileOverlayOptions);
```

We've used the same texture for 16 tiles, so we'd get output similar to what is shown here:

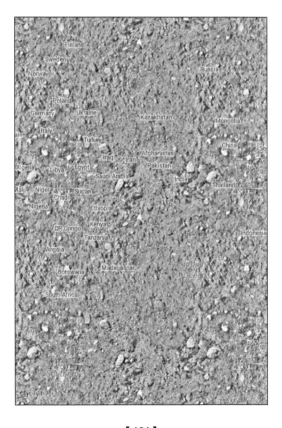

These tiles are loaded for the zoom level 2. For further zoom levels, normal Google maps are loaded.

Removing a tile overlay

A tile overlay can be removed by calling the `remove()` method on a `TileOverlay` object.

We can modify the code to do this as follows:

```
TileOverlay tileOverlay =  map.addTileOverlay(tileOverlayOptions);
  tileOverlay.remove();
```

Clearing the cache

If the tile being used is no longer new and we need to refresh it, we can clear the cache by calling the `clearTileCache()` method on the `GoogleMap` object.

Self-test questions

Q1. By default, markers are draggable.

1. True
2. False

Q2. Which method should be called on a `MarkerOptions` object to change opacity?

1. `Alpha()`
2. `Flat()`
3. `Anchor()`

Q3. Which method should be called to set the title for an information window?

1. `Snippet()`
2. `Title()`
3. `Icon()`

Q4. Which method should be called on a shape's `Options` object to change the fill color of a shape?

1. `fillColor()`
2. `strokeColor()`
3. `strokeWidth()`

Q5. What are the types of overlays used in Google maps?

1. 4
2. 5
3. 2

Q6. Multiple images can be used in ground overlays.

1. True
2. False

Q7. How many image tiles are needed to support a zoom level of 2 in Google maps?

1. 4
2. 9
3. 16

Summary

In this chapter, we learned about so much more stuff to make our Google map awesome.

We explored the concept of markers, adding and customizing markers, and making a marker draggable. We then proceeded with learning more about information windows and their creation. Next, we took a look at shapes, polylines, polygons, circles, and how to customize them. Finally, we finished the chapter by exploring concepts, such as ground and tile overlays.

In the next chapter, we will learn how to interact with the help of maps.

5
Interacting with a Map

In the last chapter, we learned how to add additional information to a map using markers, overlays, information windows, and shapes. In this chapter, we will learn how to interact with map using events, gestures, controls, and toolbars. Let's start!

In this chapter, we will cover the following topics:

- Need for interaction with a map
- Working with UI controls
- Working with a map toolbar
- Working with gestures
- Disabling/enabling UI controls and gestures with XML attributes
- Working with events
- Using projections
- Custom applications

Need for interaction with a map

An application with no user interaction will be boring and won't be user-friendly. A real-time application needs a considerable amount of user interaction to make it intuitive, interesting, and fun. To make our map application more interesting and fun, we have arrived to this chapter.

Working with UI controls

The Google map's API provides some inbuilt UI controls to make our task easier. The UI controls that can be enabled or disabled are as follows:

- Zoom controls
- Compass
- My Location button
- Level picker

Let's learn about these UI controls in more detail.

Zoom controls

Zoom controls are normally used for zoom-in and zoom-out functions. These buttons are disabled by default. The new version of the Google Maps application has removed these controls. It is up to you to display or disable them in your application.

These zoom controls are enabled or disabled using the `UiSettings` class, which can be obtained by calling the `getUiSettings()` method on the `GoogleMap` object. Then, call the `setZoomControlsEnabled()` method on the obtained `UiSettings` class, which takes a Boolean value as a parameter. The `true` parameter indicates that zoom controls should be displayed.

Let's now code for this requirement.

The layout code for `MapsActivity` is as follows:

```xml
<?xml version="1.0" encoding="utf-8"?>
<fragment xmlns:android="http://schemas.android.com/apk/res/android"
    android:id="@+id/map"
    android:layout_width="match_parent"
    android:layout_height="match_parent"
    android:name="com.google.android.gms.maps.MapFragment" />
```

activity_maps.xml

To enable the zoom controls, we can use the following code in the `onMapReady()` callback method:

```
map.getUiSettings().setZoomControlsEnabled(true);
```

The complete code for MapsActivity is as follows:

```java
package com.raj.map;

import android.app.Activity;
import android.os.Bundle;

import com.google.android.gms.maps.GoogleMap;
import com.google.android.gms.maps.MapFragment;
import com.google.android.gms.maps.OnMapReadyCallback;

public class MapsActivity extends Activity implements
OnMapReadyCallback {


    @Override
    protected void onCreate(Bundle savedInstanceState) {
        super.onCreate(savedInstanceState);
        setContentView(R.layout.activity_maps);
        MapFragment mapFragment =
           (MapFragment)getFragmentManager().findFragmentById(R.
id.map);
        mapFragment.getMapAsync(this);

    }
    @Override
    public void onMapReady(GoogleMap map) {

        map.getUiSettings().setZoomControlsEnabled(true);

    }
}
```

MapsActivity.java

In the preceding code, we've called the `getUiSettings()` method on the `GoogleMap` object. Then, we've called the `setZoomControlsEnabled()` method and passed the Boolean `true` to enable the zoom controls. Now, let's execute our project.

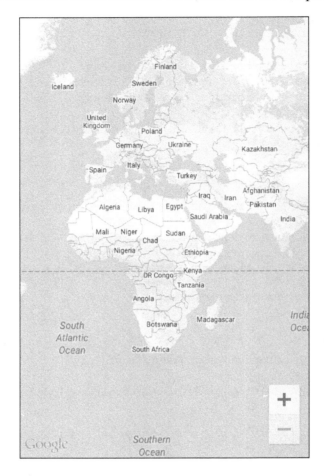

In the preceding image, the zoom controls are displayed in the bottom right-hand corner.

Compass

The Google map's API provides a compass to reorient a map when it is tilted. The compass is enabled by default. This is displayed in the top left-hand corner. This compass is displayed whenever you tilt the map. When you tap the compass, the map returns to its original orientation and the compass fades away.

This compass can be enabled or disabled using the `UiSettings` class, which is similar to zoom controls. Call the `setCompassEnabled()` method on the obtained `UiSettings` class, which takes a Boolean value as a parameter.

The Boolean value `true` indicates that the compass should be enabled, and `false` indicates it should be disabled.

To disable the compass, we can use the following code snippet in the `onMapReady()` callback method:

```
map.getUiSettings().setCompassEnabled(false);
```

By executing the preceding code, the compass is not displayed even if you tilt the map.

The following image is an example of a compass displayed in a map:

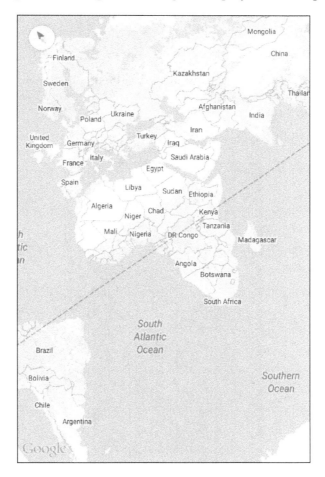

In the preceding image, the compass is displayed in the top left-hand corner and the map is tilted. If you tap the compass, the map will come back to its original orientation.

The My Location button

The **My Location** button is used to set a user's location on a map. This button is displayed in the top right-hand corner of the map. When you tap this button, the camera will zoom to the user's location if GPS is enabled.

The **My Location** button is usually disabled by default. To enable this button, the my location layer should be enabled. This can be enabled by calling the setMyLocationEnabled() method on the GoogleMap object which takes Boolean as a parameter.

To enable the **My Location** button, use the following code snippet in the onMapReady() callback method:

```
map.setMyLocationEnabled(true);
```

If you want to disable the **My Location** button but leave the my location layer enabled, call the setMyLocationButtonEnabled() method in the UiSettings class and pass the Boolean value as false.

The following image will display the **My Location** button:

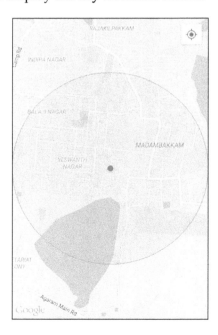

In the preceding image, the **My Location** button is displayed in the top right-hand corner. When you tap the button, it zooms to your current location and the blue dot denotes your location.

We can also attach `ClickListener` to the **My Location** button. It gets triggered when you tap the **My Location** button.

This can be done by the `GoogleMap.OnMyLocationButtonClickListener` interface, which is similar to what we do with buttons. The `onMyLocationButtonClick()` method is executed when a user clicks the button.

Here, let's display a toast when you click the **My Location** button:

The complete code for the `onMapReady()` callback method is as follows:

```
@Override
public void onMapReady(GoogleMap map) {
    map.setMyLocationEnabled(true);
    map.setOnMyLocationButtonClickListener(new
      GoogleMap.OnMyLocationButtonClickListener() {
        @Override
        public boolean onMyLocationButtonClick() {
            Toast.makeText(getApplicationContext(),"Location
              Button clicked",Toast.LENGTH_LONG).show();
            return false;
        }
    });
}
```

In the preceding code, we set the `GoogleMap.`
`OnMyLocationButtonClickListener()` interface on the GoogleMap object by calling the `setOnMyLocationButtonClickListener()` method. The code in the `onMyLocationButtonClick()` method gets executed when the button is clicked. Here, we're displaying a toast. Run the code and you will get output similar to what is shown here:

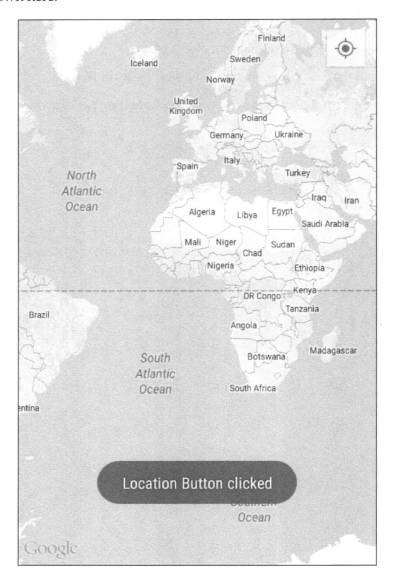

Level picker

A Level picker is another UI control that is displayed when you view an indoor map. It is used to select the map for a particular floor. You can enable or disable by calling the setIndoorLevelPickerEnabled() method on the UiSettings class, which takes Boolean as a parameter. We took a look at indoor maps in *Chapter 3, Working with Different Map Types*.

The code for the onMapReady() callback method to disable the level picker is as follows:

```
map.getUiSettings().setIndoorLevelPickerEnabled(false);
```

The following image displays a level picker in an indoor map:

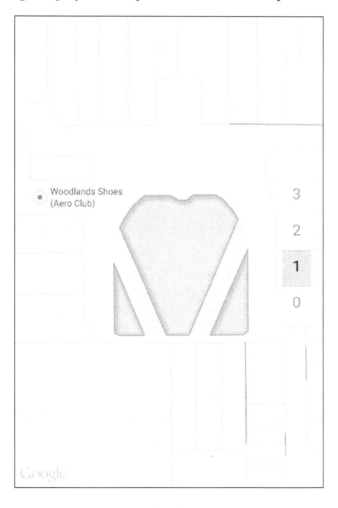

In the preceding image, the toolbar that is shown to the right is the level picker. It has four levels: 0, 1, 2, and 3. These are displayed in a indoor map.

Custom applications

Now, we are going to create a custom application that asks preferences from the user about the type of which control that should be displayed. These preferences are asked in a dialog box when the application is launched. Then, it displays UI controls according to a user's preference from this dialog.

Let's start with a layout. The code for MapsActivity is the same as the one we've used before. The code is as follows:

```xml
<?xml version="1.0" encoding="utf-8"?>
<fragment xmlns:android="http://schemas.android.com/apk/res/android"
    android:id="@+id/map"
    android:layout_width="match_parent"
    android:layout_height="match_parent"
    android:name="com.google.android.gms.maps.MapFragment" />
```

activity_maps.xml

The complete code for MapsActivity is as follows:

```java
package com.raj.map;

import android.app.Activity;
import android.app.AlertDialog;
import android.content.DialogInterface;
import android.os.Bundle;

import com.google.android.gms.maps.GoogleMap;
import com.google.android.gms.maps.MapFragment;
import com.google.android.gms.maps.OnMapReadyCallback;

public class MapsActivity extends Activity implements
  OnMapReadyCallback {

    CharSequence mapSettings[] = { "Zoom Controls", "Compass",
      "My Location button","Level Picker" };
    boolean bl[] = new boolean[mapSettings.length];
    boolean zoom = false;
    boolean compass = false;
```

```
boolean location = false;
boolean level = false;

AlertDialog.Builder alert;
GoogleMap map;


@Override
protected void onCreate(Bundle savedInstanceState) {
    super.onCreate(savedInstanceState);
    setContentView(R.layout.activity_maps);
    initDialog();
    MapFragment mapFragment =
      (MapFragment)getFragmentManager().findFragmentById(R.id.map);
    mapFragment.getMapAsync(this);
}
@Override
public void onMapReady(GoogleMap googleMap) {
    map = googleMap;
    googleMap.setMyLocationEnabled(true);
    alert.show();
}

public void initDialog(){
    alert = new AlertDialog.Builder(this);
    alert.setTitle("Map Settings");
    alert.setMultiChoiceItems(mapSettings, bl, new
      DialogInterface.OnMultiChoiceClickListener() {
        @Override
        public void onClick(DialogInterface dialog, int which,
          boolean isChecked) {
            if (which == 0) {
                zoom = isChecked;
            } else if (which == 1) {
                compass = isChecked;
            } else if (which == 2) {
                location = isChecked;
            } else if (which == 3) {
                level = isChecked;
            }
        }
    });
```

```
            alert.setPositiveButton("Save", new
             DialogInterface.OnClickListener() {
                 @Override
                 public void onClick(DialogInterface dialog, int which) {
                     if (zoom) {
                         map.getUiSettings().setZoomControlsEnabled(true);
                     } else {
                         map.getUiSettings().setZoomControlsEnabled(false);
                     }
                     if (compass) {
                         map.getUiSettings().setCompassEnabled(true);
                     } else {
                         map.getUiSettings().setCompassEnabled(false);
                     }
                     if (location) {
                         map.getUiSettings().setMyLocationButtonEnabled(tr
ue);
                     } else {
                         map.getUiSettings().setMyLocationButtonEnabled(fa
lse);
                     }
                     if (level) {
                         map.getUiSettings().setIndoorLevelPickerEnabled(t
rue);
                     } else {
                         map.getUiSettings().setIndoorLevelPickerEnabled(f
alse);
                     }
                     dialog.dismiss();
                 }
             });
            alert.setNegativeButton("Cancel", new
              DialogInterface.OnClickListener() {
                 @Override
                 public void onClick(DialogInterface dialog, int which) {
                     dialog.dismiss();
                 }
             });
        }
    }

MapsActivity.java
```

Now, let's discuss what this code does.

An alert dialog is created using the `AlertDialog.Builder` class, which is displayed initially when the app is launched. `AlertDialog` has four checkboxes that are set using the `setMultiChoiceItems()` method. The chosen item click is handled using the `DialogInterface.OnMultiChoiceClickListener` interface.

When the **SAVE** button is pressed, the checkboxes are checked whether they are enabled or not. If they're enabled, the corresponding UI control is displayed.

If the **CANCEL** button, is pressed the dialog is dismissed. It can be done by calling the `dismiss()` method on the `Dialog` object.

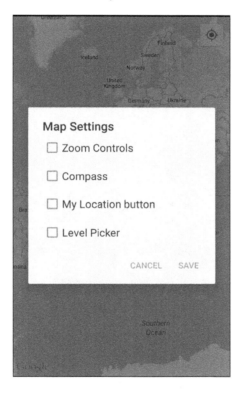

The preceding screen is displayed when you open the application. When you enable the checkboxes and select **SAVE**, the UI controls are displayed.

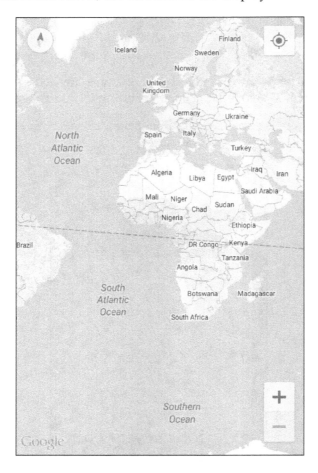

The preceding image displays the UI controls we've selected from the dialog.

Working with the map toolbar

In the previous chapters, we worked with markers and a lite map. While working with markers, you may have noticed that when you click on one, two icons appear at the bottom right-hand corner. This is the map toolbar. When you click on the map toolbar, it opens the Google Maps application. The map toolbar disappears when the marker is out of focus.

This toolbar also appears in the lite mode by default.

The following screenshot displays the map toolbar in the bottom right-hand corner as the marker is clicked on:

If we do not want to display the map toolbar, we can disable it by calling the setMapToolbarEnabled() method on the UiSettings class by passing the Boolean value as false.

The code for the onMapReadyCallback() method is as follows:

```
map.getUiSettings().setMapToolbarEnabled(false)
```

Working with gestures

A map application created with the Google Maps API supports all the gestures supported by the Google Maps app. It is up to you to choose whether you need all the gestures or would like to disable some.

As with UI controls, we can enable/disable gestures from the `UiSettings` class.

The various gestures that are supported are as follows:

- Zoom gestures
- Scroll gestures
- Tilt gestures
- Rotate gestures

Let's discuss these gestures in detail.

Zoom gestures

There are four types of zoom gestures available. Let's discuss them in detail.

Double tap

This refers to double tapping on the surface of a map which increases the zoom level by 1 (that is, zoom in).

Two finger tap

This refers to a two finger tap on the surface of a map which decreases the zoom level by 1 (that is, zoom out).

Two finger pinch/stretch (pinch to zoom)

This refers to pinching the surface of a map with two fingers which decreases the zoom level (that is, zoom out).

This refers to stretching the surface of the map with two fingers which increases the zoom level (that is, zoom in).

One finger zoom

This refers to double tapping but not releasing the second tap, and then sliding a finger to zoom in / zoom out.

By default, these zoom gestures are enabled.

We can disable them if needed by calling the `setZoomGesturesEnabled()` method on the `UiSettings` class by passing a Boolean value as `false`.

The code in the `OnMapReady()` callback method is as follows:

```
map.getUiSettings().setZoomGesturesEnabled(false);
```

Scroll gestures

Scroll gestures can be used to move a map around, dragging the surface of the map with finger pans or scrolls.

As with the gestures seen previously, we can disable scroll gestures by calling the `setScrollGesturesEnabled()` method on the `UiSettings` class and passing the Boolean value as `false`.

The code for the `onMapReady()` callback method is as follows:

```
map.getUiSettings().setScrollGesturesEnabled(false);
```

Tilt gestures

Tilt gestures are used to change the tilt angle of a map. This can be done by placing two fingers on the map and dragging up/down to increase/decrease the tilt angle.

As with the gestures seen previously, we can disable tilt gestures by calling the `setTiltGesturesEnabled()` method on the `UiSettings` class and passing the Boolean value as `false`.

The code for the `onMapReady()` callback method is as follows:

```
map.getUiSettings().setTiltGesturesEnabled(false);
```

Take a look at the following image. The left-hand side corresponds to the tilted part of the image, and the right-hand side corresponds to the normal part of the image.

Rotate gestures

Rotate gestures are used to rotate a map. This can be done by placing two fingers on the map and rotating it.

The preceding image is an example of an image that's been rotated.

As with the gestures seen previously, this rotate gesture can be easily disabled by calling the `setRotateGesturesEnabled()` method on the `UiSettings` class and passing the Boolean value as `false`.

The code for the `onMapReady()` callback method is as follows:

```
map.getUiSettings().setRotateGesturesEnabled(false);
```

Disabling/Enabling UI controls and gestures with XML attributes

Until now, we have learned how to disable UI controls and gestures programmatically using the `UiSettings` class. Now, let's take a look at how we can disable these UI controls using the XML attributes in our layout file.

Till this point, we've used the following layout code:

```xml
<?xml version="1.0" encoding="utf-8"?>
<fragment xmlns:android="http://schemas.android.com/apk/res/android"
    android:id="@+id/map"
    android:layout_width="match_parent"
    android:layout_height="match_parent"
    android:name="com.google.android.gms.maps.MapFragment" />
```

To use the XML attributes, we need to add a namespace declaration:

```xml
xmlns:map="http://schemas.android.com/apk/res-auto"
```

To disable the zoom controls, we can use the `uiZoomControls` attribute of the namespace map. The value of this attribute should be Boolean. To disable it, set it as `false`.

Similarly, the attributes for other UI controls and gestures are as follows:

Property	Attribute
Zoom controls	uiZoomControls
Compass	uiCompass
Zoom gestures	uiZoomGestures
Scroll gestures	uiScrollGestures
Rotate gestures	uiRotateGestures
Tilt gestures	uiTiltGestures

The complete `activity_maps.xml` layout code that we use to disable the UI controls and gestures is as follows:

```xml
<?xml version="1.0" encoding="utf-8"?>
<fragment xmlns:android="http://schemas.android.com/apk/res/android"
    xmlns:map="http://schemas.android.com/apk/res-auto"
    android:id="@+id/map"
    android:layout_width="match_parent"
    android:layout_height="match_parent"
    android:name="com.google.android.gms.maps.MapFragment"
    map:uiZoomControls="false"
    map:uiCompass="false"
    map:uiZoomGestures="false"
    map:uiScrollGestures="false"
    map:uiRotateGestures="false"
    map:uiTiltGestures="false"/>
```

`activity_maps.xml`

Now, run the project; you will see that all the preceding UI controls and gestures are disabled. By doing this, there is no need to disable the `onMapReady()` callback method programmatically.

Disabling/enabling the UI controls and gestures with the GoogleMapOptions object

Until now, we've added `MapFragment` directly in our layout and used the `UiSettings` class to change the controls. In *Chapter 2, Configuring an API Key and Creating Our First Map Application*, we learned how to add `MapFragment` dynamically in `FrameLayout`. Let's now discuss how to disable UI controls and gestures using the `GoogleMapOptions` object for a dynamically added fragment.

Our layout code is as follows:

```xml
<LinearLayout xmlns:android="http://schemas.android.com/apk/res/
android"
    android:layout_width="match_parent"
    android:layout_height="match_parent"
    android:orientation="horizontal">
    <FrameLayout
```

```
        android:id="@+id/content_frame"
        android:layout_width="match_parent"
        android:layout_height="match_parent" />
</LinearLayout>
```

activity_maps.xml

Next, in MapsActivity, we are going to replace the contents of FrameLayout with MapFragment.

To construct MapFragment, we can call the newInstance() method on the MapFragment class. The defined GoogleMapOptions object should be passed to the newInstance() method to configure custom options.

The GoogleMapOptions object is defined as follows:

```
GoogleMapOptions options = new GoogleMapOptions();
```

By default, the zoom controls are disabled. To enable the zoom controls, call the zoomControlsEnabled() method on the GoogleMapOptions object by passing the Boolean value as true.

Similarly, the methods for other UI controls and gestures are as follows:

Property	Method	Parameter
Zoom controls	zoomControlsEnabled()	Boolean
Compass	compassEnabled()	Boolean
Zoom gestures	zoomGesturesEnabled()	Boolean
Scroll gestures	scrollGesturesEnabled()	Boolean
Rotate gestures	rotateGesturesEnabled()	Boolean
Tilt gestures	tiltGesturesEnabled()	Boolean

The complete MapsActivity.java code to disable the controls and gestures is as follows:

```
package com.raj.map;

import android.app.Activity;
import android.app.Fragment;
import android.app.FragmentTransaction;
import android.os.Bundle;

import com.google.android.gms.maps.GoogleMapOptions;
```

```java
import com.google.android.gms.maps.MapFragment;

public class MapsActivity extends Activity {
    Fragment mapFragment;

    @Override
    protected void onCreate(Bundle savedInstanceState) {
        super.onCreate(savedInstanceState);
        setContentView(R.layout.activity_maps);

        GoogleMapOptions options = new GoogleMapOptions();
        options.compassEnabled(false);
        options.zoomControlsEnabled(true);
        options.zoomGesturesEnabled(false);
        options.scrollGesturesEnabled(false);
        options.tiltGesturesEnabled(false);
        options.rotateGesturesEnabled(false);

        mapFragment = MapFragment.newInstance(options);
        FragmentTransaction fragmentTransaction =
getFragmentManager().beginTransaction();
        fragmentTransaction.add(R.id.content_frame, mapFragment);
        fragmentTransaction.commit();

    }}
```

MapsActivity.java

In the preceding code, we create a new `GoogleMapOptions` object. We can then call the methods on the `GoogleMapOptions` object to disable/enable the controls and gestures.

Next, we construct `MapFragment` using the `newInstance()` method, and pass the `GoogleMapsOptions` object to configure the controls and gestures used in the map. Finally, we replace the contents of `FrameLayout` with `MapFragment`.

As we learned earlier, we should use `SupportMapFragment` to support devices with a lower API.

Now, run the code; we will see a map where all the gestures are disabled and only the zoom controls are enabled:

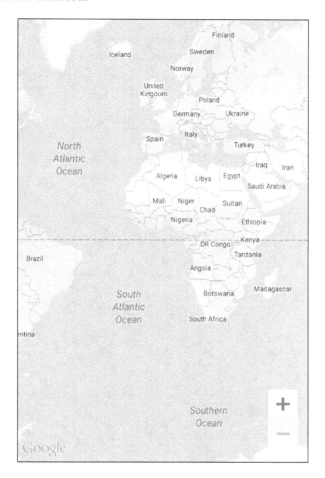

Working with map events

The Google Map's API allows us to listen for events on a map similar to those that we listen to on buttons and other views. The events that are available for this purpose are:

- Map click / long click events
- Camera change events
- Indoor map events

Let's discuss these events in detail.

Map click/long click events

To handle map click events, we should use the `OnMapClickListener` interface on the `GoogleMap` object. To enable this, call the `setOnMapClickListener()` method on the `GoogleMap` object, which takes the `GoogleMap.OnMapClickListener()` interface as a parameter. When you click anywhere on a map, the `onMapClick()` method is called. In this example, we shall display a toast that shows the latitude and longitude of the location that has been clicked on. Now, we are going to display the output similar to the following screenshot:

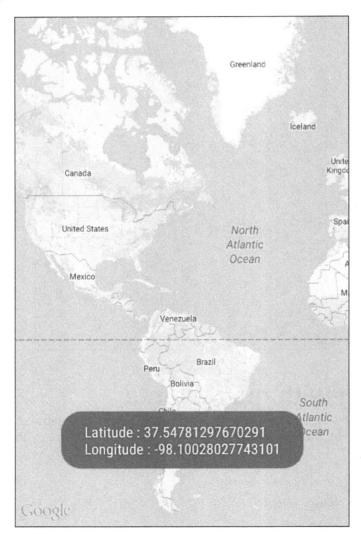

The complete code for the onMapReady() callback method is as follows:

```
@Override
    public void onMapReady(GoogleMap map) {

        map.setOnMapClickListener(new GoogleMap.OnMapClickListener() {
            @Override
            public void onMapClick(LatLng latLng) {
                Toast.makeText(getApplicationContext(), "Latitude :
" + latLng.latitude +"\nLongitude : "+latLng.longitude, Toast.LENGTH_
LONG).show();
            }
        });

    }
```

In the preceding code, we use the OnMapClickListener interface to handle the click. When the map is clicked on, the onMapClick(LatLng latLng) method is called. After this, we obtain the latitude and longitude of the location from the LatLng object and display it in a toast.

Next, execute the code, and you will see output similar to what is shown in the preceding image.

Similarly, you can use the OnMapLongClickListener interface to handle long click events on the map.

Camera change events

The camera position of a map changes when you pan, zoom, tilt, and rotate it. These events can be handled using the OnCameraChangeListener interface on the GoogleMap object. To enable it, call the setCameraChangeListener() method on the GoogleMap object, which takes the GoogleMap.OnCameraChangeListener() interface as a parameter. In this example, we will print the bearing angle, tilt angle, zoom level, latitude, and longitude of the location where the camera is pointed.

The complete code for the onMapReady() callback method is as follows:

```
@Override
    public void onMapReady(GoogleMap map) {

        map.setOnCameraChangeListener(new GoogleMap.
OnCameraChangeListener() {
            @Override
            public void onCameraChange(CameraPosition cameraPosition)
{
```

```
                    Toast.makeText(getApplicationContext(),"Camera
changed",Toast.LENGTH_LONG).show();
                    Log.d("Latitude ", String.valueOf(cameraPosition.
target.latitude));
                    Log.d("Longitude ",String.valueOf(cameraPosition.
target.longitude));
                    Log.d("Bearing",String.valueOf(cameraPosition.
bearing));
                    Log.d("Tilt",String.valueOf(cameraPosition.tilt));
                    Log.d("Zoom",String.valueOf(cameraPosition.zoom));


            }
        });


    }
```

In the preceding code, we use the `OnCameraChangeListener` interface to handle the callback. When the camera changes, the `onCameraChange(CameraPosition cameraPosition)` method is called.

Next, we obtain the latitude, longitude, bearing angle, tilt angle, zoom level, and then print them in a log. A toast is also displayed when the camera is changed.

The message printed in the log will be similar to this:

```
03-23 18:11:58.421    18426-18426/com.raj.map D/Latitude:
10.404233320043707
03-23 18:11:58.421    18426-18426/com.raj.map D/Longitude:
83.65944061428308
03-23 18:11:58.421    18426-18426/com.raj.map D/Bearing: 335.49707
03-23 18:11:58.421    18426-18426/com.raj.map D/Tilt: 21.014008
03-23 18:11:58.421    18426-18426/com.raj.map D/Zoom: 4.0
03-23 18:11:58.730    18426-18426/com.raj.map D/Latitude:
10.404233320043707
03-23 18:11:58.730    18426-18426/com.raj.map D/Longitude:
83.65944061428308
03-23 18:11:58.731    18426-18426/com.raj.map D/Bearing: 335.49707
03-23 18:11:58.731    18426-18426/com.raj.map D/Tilt: 30.0
03-23 18:11:58.731    18426-18426/com.raj.map D/Zoom: 4.0
```

Take a look at the following screenshot. The preceding values are printed for the camera position in this screenshot:

Indoor map events

Similar to click and camera change events, we can handle indoor map events as well. These events can be handled using the OnIndoorStateChangeListener interface on the GoogleMap object. To enable, call the setOnIndoorStateChangeListener method on the GoogleMap object, which takes the GoogleMap. OnIndoorStateChangeListener interface as a parameter.

It has two methods. The onIndoorBuildingFocused() method is called when an indoor map enabled building comes into focus.

The onIndoorLevelActivated() method is called when a level in a particular building changes. In this simple example, we will display a toast when the building is focused on and the level is changed.

The code for the onMapReady() callback is as follows:

```java
@Override
public void onMapReady(GoogleMap map) {

        map.setOnIndoorStateChangeListener(new GoogleMap.
OnIndoorStateChangeListener() {
    @Override
    public void onIndoorBuildingFocused() {
        Toast.makeText(getApplicationContext(),"Building
Focused",Toast.LENGTH_LONG).show();
    }

    @Override
    public void onIndoorLevelActivated(IndoorBuilding
indoorBuilding) {
        Toast.makeText(getApplicationContext(),"Level Activated : "
+indoorBuilding.getActiveLevelIndex(),Toast.LENGTH_LONG).show();

    }
});

}
```

In the preceding code, we display a toast when the indoor map-enabled building is in focus. We also display another toast that shows the activated level of the building when the level is changed.

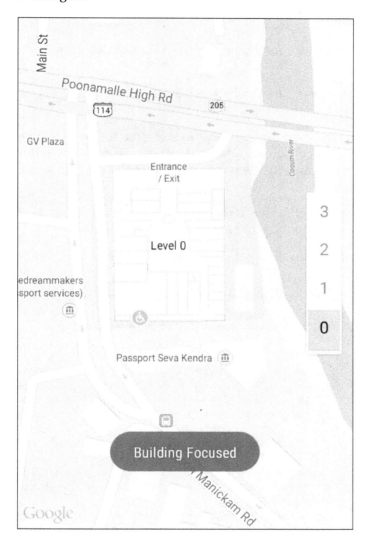

Take a look at the preceding image. It displays the map of an indoor map-enabled shopping mall. When it is focused on, a toast is displayed.

Similarly, when the level is changed, another toast is displayed along with the level index.

Using a Projection class

Google maps provides a `Projection` class, which has some useful methods. The `fromScreenLocation()` method converts screen pixels in point coordinates to `LatLng` coordinates.

The `toScreenLocation()` method converts the `LatLng` coordinates to the screen pixel point coordinates.

The `getVisibleRegion()` method returns the `VisibleRegion` object from which we can obtain `LatLngBounds`.

Let's see an example where we are going to convert a screen pixel Point coordinate, (100,100), to a `LatLng` coordinate when the camera changes. From this, we get the visible region and display the north-east and south-west corners of the `LatLng` coordinate.

Then, when the map is clicked on, we obtain the `LatLng` coordinate of the clicked location and convert it to the screen pixels point coordinate.

The complete code for the `onMapReady()` callback method is as follows:

```
@Override
    public void onMapReady(final GoogleMap map) {

        map.setOnCameraChangeListener(new GoogleMap.
OnCameraChangeListener() {
            @Override
            public void onCameraChange(CameraPosition cameraPosition)
{
                Projection projection = map.getProjection();
                LatLng latLng = projection.fromScreenLocation(new
Point(100, 100));
                VisibleRegion visibleRegion = projection.
getVisibleRegion();
                Log.d("Projection","North East : "+visibleRegion.
latLngBounds.northeast.latitude + ","+visibleRegion.latLngBounds.
northeast.longitude);
                Log.d("Projection","South West : "+visibleRegion.
latLngBounds.southwest.latitude + ","+visibleRegion.latLngBounds.
southwest.longitude);
                Log.d("Projection","Point 100, 100 :"+latLng.latitude
+ ","+latLng.longitude);


            }
        });
        map.setOnMapClickListener(new GoogleMap.OnMapClickListener() {
```

```
        @Override
        public void onMapClick(LatLng latLng) {
            Projection projection = map.getProjection();
            Point point = projection.toScreenLocation(latLng);
            Log.d("Projection","X : "+point.x +",Y : "+point.y);
        }
    });

}
```

In the preceding code, when the camera position changes, we can convert the `Point` coordinate to the `LatLng` coordinate and print it in a log. We also get `LatLngBounds` of the visible region and print the `LatLng` coordinates of the north-east and south-west corners.

Finally, when the map is clicked on, we convert the `LatLng` coordinate of the location that is clicked on to the `Point` coordinate and print it in the log.

The output will be similar to:

```
Projection: North East : 23.36584530915385,61.439662724733346
Projection: South West : -60.055697911923716,-1.8416228145360949
Projection: Point 100, 100 :12.22912947888171,9.877133779227734
Projection: X : 418,Y : 596
```

Next, we will create a custom map application with some more functionalities.

Creating a custom application

We are now going to create a custom map application. When we tap anywhere on a map, a dialog is shown, which takes text for **Title** and **Snippet** for a marker as input. The marker is placed on the clicked location along with an information window.

We can add as many markers as we need and remove a marker by tapping on the information window. Let's proceed!

Our activity layout code is the same as the one we've used before:

```xml
<?xml version="1.0" encoding="utf-8"?>
<fragment xmlns:android="http://schemas.android.com/apk/res/android"
    android:id="@+id/map"
    android:layout_width="match_parent"
    android:layout_height="match_parent"
    android:name="com.google.android.gms.maps.MapFragment" />
```

activity_maps.xml

Next, we need to create a custom dialog to add the marker. It has two `EditText` widgets and two button widgets. The `EditText` widgets are used to get the title and snippet text as input. One button is used to add the marker, the other is to cancel it. The dialog layout code is as follows:

```xml
<?xml version="1.0" encoding="utf-8"?>
<LinearLayout xmlns:android="http://schemas.android.com/apk/res/
android"
    android:orientation="vertical"
    android:layout_width="250sp"
    android:layout_height="match_parent">

    <EditText
        android:id="@+id/title"
        android:hint="Title"
        android:layout_width="match_parent"
        android:layout_height="wrap_content" />
    <EditText
        android:id="@+id/snippet"
        android:hint="Snippet"
        android:layout_width="match_parent"
        android:layout_height="wrap_content" />
    <Button
        android:id="@+id/btn_add"
        android:text="Add Marker"
        android:layout_width="match_parent"
        android:layout_height="wrap_content" />
    <Button
        android:id="@+id/btn_cancel"
        android:text="Cancel"
        android:layout_width="match_parent"
        android:layout_height="wrap_content" />

</LinearLayout>
```

dialog_add.xml

Next, let's proceed to `MapsActivity`. Let's first take a look at the code for it and then its explanation:

```java
package com.raj.map;

import android.app.Activity;
import android.app.AlertDialog;
import android.app.Dialog;
import android.content.DialogInterface;
```

```
import android.os.Bundle;
import android.view.View;
import android.widget.Button;
import android.widget.EditText;
import android.widget.Toast;

import com.google.android.gms.maps.GoogleMap;
import com.google.android.gms.maps.MapFragment;
import com.google.android.gms.maps.OnMapReadyCallback;
import com.google.android.gms.maps.model.LatLng;
import com.google.android.gms.maps.model.Marker;
import com.google.android.gms.maps.model.MarkerOptions;

public class MapsActivity extends Activity implements
OnMapReadyCallback {

    Dialog dialog;
    EditText title,snippet;
    Button add,cancel;
    AlertDialog.Builder alertDialog;


    @Override
    protected void onCreate(Bundle savedInstanceState) {
        super.onCreate(savedInstanceState);
        setContentView(R.layout.activity_maps);
        initAddMarkerDialog();
        initRemoveMarkerDialog();
        MapFragment mapFragment = (MapFragment) getFragmentManager().
findFragmentById(R.id.map);
        mapFragment.getMapAsync(this);

    }
    @Override
    public void onMapReady(GoogleMap map) {
        initInfoWindowClick(map);
        initMapClick(map);
    }

    public void initAddMarkerDialog(){
        dialog = new Dialog(this);
        dialog.setTitle("Add marker !");
        dialog.setContentView(R.layout.dialog_add);
        title = (EditText)dialog.findViewById(R.id.title);
```

```
            snippet = (EditText)dialog.findViewById(R.id.snippet);
            add = (Button)dialog.findViewById(R.id.btn_add);
            cancel = (Button)dialog.findViewById(R.id.btn_cancel);
    }

    public void initRemoveMarkerDialog(){
        alertDialog = new AlertDialog.Builder(this);
        alertDialog.setTitle("Delete Marker !");
        alertDialog.setMessage("Do you want to delete the Marker !");
    }

    public  void initInfoWindowClick(GoogleMap googleMap){
        googleMap.setOnInfoWindowClickListener(new GoogleMap.
OnInfoWindowClickListener() {
            @Override
            public void onInfoWindowClick(final Marker marker) {
                alertDialog.setPositiveButton("Yes", new
DialogInterface.OnClickListener() {
                    @Override
                    public void onClick(DialogInterface dialog, int
which) {
                        marker.remove();
                    }
                });
                alertDialog.setNegativeButton("No", new
DialogInterface.OnClickListener() {
                    @Override
                    public void onClick(DialogInterface dialog, int
which) {
                        dialog.dismiss();
                    }
                });
                alertDialog.show();
            }
        });
    }
    public void initMapClick(final GoogleMap googleMap){
        googleMap.setOnMapClickListener(new GoogleMap.
OnMapClickListener() {
            @Override
            public void onMapClick(final LatLng latLng) {
                title.setText("");
                snippet.setText("");
                dialog.show();
```

```
                        add.setOnClickListener(new View.OnClickListener() {
                            @Override
                            public void onClick(View v) {
                                if (title.getText().toString().isEmpty() ||
            snippet.getText().toString().isEmpty()) {
                                    Toast.makeText(getApplicationContext(),
            "Text fields cannot be empty", Toast.LENGTH_SHORT).show();
                                } else {
                                    googleMap.addMarker(new MarkerOptions().
            position(latLng).title(title.getText().toString()).snippet(snippet.
            getText().toString()));
                                    dialog.dismiss();
                                }
                            }
                        });
                        cancel.setOnClickListener(new View.OnClickListener() {
                            @Override
                            public void onClick(View v) {
                                dialog.dismiss();
                            }
                        });
                    }
                });
            }
        }
```

MapsActivity.java

Now, let's try to understand what this code does. Initially, we create a new `Dialog` object by passing the context to the constructor. By calling the `setTitle()` method on the `Dialog` object, we can define a custom title for our dialog. By calling the `setContentView()` method, we set the layout resource file as content for `Dialog`.

In the `onMapClick()` method, we can display the dialog. Then, when you press the **ADD** button, a new marker is added with the `LatLng` object as the position, and the text obtained from the `EditText` widgets from the dialog is set as the title and snippet.

When the **CANCEL** button is pressed, the dialog is dismissed.

Next, we attach the `OnInfoWindowClickListener()` interface to the map. When the information window is clicked on, an alert dialog is shown, which decides whether to delete the marker or not. The alert dialog is created using the `AlertDialog.Builder` class. Then, a new `AlertDialog.Builder` object is created as follows:

```
AlertDialog.Builder alertDialog = new AlertDialog.Builder(this);
```

We can add a positive button to the alert dialog using the `setPositiveButton()` method. Similarly, the title and message on the alert dialog are set using the `setTitle()` and `setMessage()` methods. When the positive button is pressed, the marker is removed.

The preceding dialog is displayed when you tap anywhere on the map.

The following image shows the added marker with the information window consisting of the title and snippet:

When you tap on the information window, an alert dialog is displayed that confirms whether you want to delete the marker or not:

Self-test questions

Q1. The `UiSettings` class can be obtained by calling the `getUiSettings` method on the `GoogleMap` object.

1. True
2. False

Q2. By default, zoom controls are disabled.

1. True
2. False

Q3. The XML attribute disables compass control.

1. `uiCompass`
2. `uiSettings`
3. `uiZoom`

Q4. Tilt gestures can be disabled/enabled by this method.

1. `setTiltGesturesEnabled()`
2. `setTiltEnabled()`
3. `setTiltGestures()`

Q5. How many values can be obtained from the `CameraPosition` object?

1. 4
2. 5
3. 6

Q6. Which method is used to convert screen pixels to `LatLng` coordinates?

1. `fromScreenLocation()`
2. `toScreenLocation()`

Q7. The `OnMapClickListener` interface is used to handle map click events.

1. True
2. False

Summary

In this chapter, we learned a lot about user interaction.

We explored the disabling/enabling of UI controls, gestures, and a map toolbar with the help of XML attributes and programmatically. Then, we learned about map click events, camera change events, indoor map change events, and the usage of projections. Finally, we finished the chapter by creating a custom map application that includes some complex features.

In the next chapter, we will learn about custom views.

6
Working with Custom Views

In the previous chapter, we learned how to interact with maps with events, gestures, controls, and toolbars. In this chapter, we are moving a bit further. We will learn about implementing different camera views. Let's start!

In this chapter, we will cover the following topics:

- The need for different camera views
- Working with camera positions
- Moving the camera
- Animating the camera
- Map padding

The need for different camera views

The normal map displayed in Google Maps is flat and from the top view. Let's consider some real scenarios. If you need to display a 3D building, you will need to adjust the tilt to display its 3D projection. We have already used tilt and bearing in the previous chapter. Another scenario would be to adjust the camera dynamically in a navigation application, following a particular route. In the following sections, we will learn about different camera views.

Working with camera positions

The position of the camera is based on the following parameters:

- Target
- Zoom
- Bearing
- Tilt

Let's discuss these parameters in detail.

Target

The target is a visible area on the map, which is specified by the latitude and longitude. Take a look at the following image:

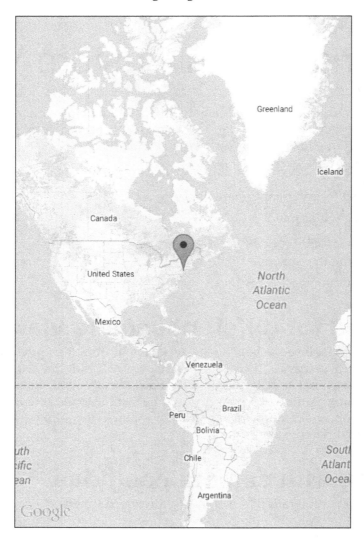

In the image, the target is (40.735188, -74.172414), which are the coordinates for Newark City. The target is centered in the map.

Zoom

As the zoom level increases, the level of detail increases. Zoom can be used to display more accurate information to the user.

The image given in the previous section is a camera view with zoom level 2. However, the level of detail is very less. In order to display more detail, we will increase the zoom level. The following image is an example of this:

The zoom level of the image is 12.

As the zoom level increases by a factor of n, the width increases by a factor of 2^n.

Bearing

The term "bearing" is also called orientation. For a normal map, the bearing is zero degrees. It is the angle at which the map is rotated anticlockwise. A bearing of 180 degrees turns the map upside down, as shown in the following image:

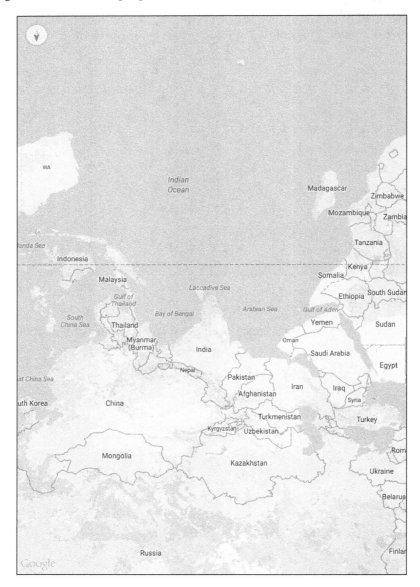

This image is the world map displayed with a bearing of 180 degrees. The image is rotated anticlockwise at a angle of 180 degrees.

Tilt

Tilt can also be called the viewing angle. When the tilt angle is increased, more area on the top of the map is visible. This can be shown with an example.

Consider an arc drawn over the visible surface of a map. For the normal view, the camera is placed at the center of the map. For a tilt angle of 45 degrees, the camera moves halfway along the arc.

Take a look at the following image:

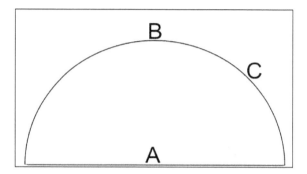

In the preceding image, the location targeted is A. B is the normal position of the camera. For a tilt angle of 45 degrees, the camera moves to position C and it still targets A.

The tilt angle range is from zero degrees to 90 degrees:

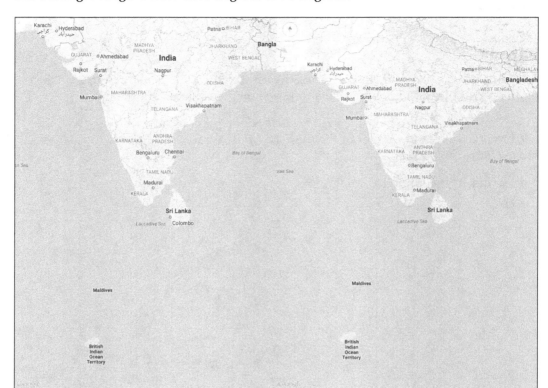

Take a look at the preceding image. The image placed on the left-hand side is the normal one and it has a tilt angle of 60 degrees.

You can see that the areas not visible on the map on the left are visible on the map on the right.

Moving the camera

The Google Maps API helps us to move from one visible region to another. This can be done by changing the camera view.

The camera view changing from one location to another can be animated. The duration of the animation can also be controlled.

To achieve this, we need to obtain the `CameraUpdate` object from the `CameraUpdateFactory` class.

The different ways to animate the camera views are as follows:

- Changing zoom levels in the current position
- Changing the camera position
- Setting boundaries for the view
- Panning the map

Changing the zoom level in the current position

Let's discuss the different methods used to change the zoom level. These methods should be called on the `CameraUpdateFactory` class to obtain the `CameraUpdate` object:

Method	Parameter	Function
`zoomIn()`	None	This increases the zoom level by 1. Other properties remain the same.
`zoomOut()`	None	This decreases the zoom level by 1. Other properties remain the same.
`zoomTo()`	Zoom level in float	This changes the zoom level to the given value. Other properties remain the same.
`zoomBy()`	Zoom level in float; X and Y coordinates as Point	This increases or decreases the zoom level by the given value by fixing focus at the defined Point (this method can also be invoked without a second parameter).

Let's see this with an example. Our layout code is the same as the one we used earlier and is shown as follows:

```xml
<?xml version="1.0" encoding="utf-8"?>
<fragment xmlns:android="http://schemas.android.com/apk/res/android"
    android:id="@+id/map"
    android:layout_width="match_parent"
    android:layout_height="match_parent"
    android:name="com.google.android.gms.maps.MapFragment" />
```

activity_maps.xml

The camera can be moved by calling the `moveCamera()` method on the Google Maps object. It takes the `CameraUpdate` object as a parameter. The code for this activity is as follows:

```java
package com.raj.map;

import android.app.Activity;
import android.graphics.Point;
import android.os.Bundle;

import com.google.android.gms.maps.CameraUpdateFactory;
import com.google.android.gms.maps.GoogleMap;
import com.google.android.gms.maps.MapFragment;
import com.google.android.gms.maps.OnMapReadyCallback;

public class MapsActivity extends Activity implements
OnMapReadyCallback {


    @Override
    protected void onCreate(Bundle savedInstanceState) {
        super.onCreate(savedInstanceState);
        setContentView(R.layout.activity_maps);
        MapFragment mapFragment = (MapFragment) getFragmentManager()
                .findFragmentById(R.id.map);
        mapFragment.getMapAsync(this);

    }
    @Override
    public void onMapReady(GoogleMap map) {

        map.moveCamera(CameraUpdateFactory.zoomBy(6,new
Point(1050,800)));
    }
}
```

MapsActivity.java

Here, we obtain the `CameraUpdate` object by calling the `zoomBy()` method on the `CameraUpdateFactory` class. It is passed to the `moveCamera()` method and is denoted as follows:

```java
CameraUpdateFactory.zoomBy(6,new Point(1050,800);
```

Here, the second parameter is `Point`, in which the *X* and *Y* coordinates are stored.

This makes the camera focus on the point. The *X* and *Y* coordinates denote the screen pixels. This focused location changes according to the display resolution of the device.

While executing the code, we obtained the following screenshot. This was tested on ASUS Nexus 7 with a resolution of 1920 x 1200 pixels.

The camera focuses on a location in India. This varies if you execute the code on other devices.

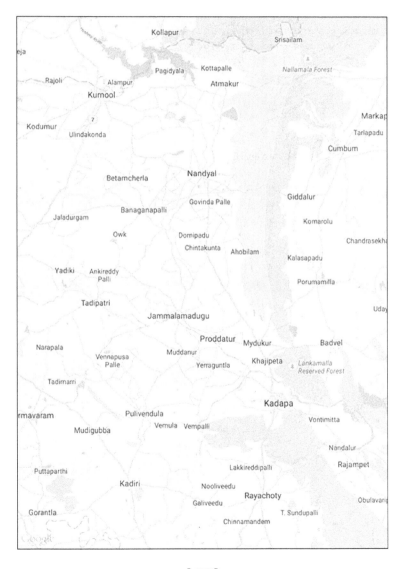

If you do not want to perform this in the onMapReady() callback method, you can use code similar to it. We are performing this in the onCreate() method. The MapsActivity code is as follows:

```
package com.raj.map;

import android.app.Activity;
import android.graphics.Point;
import android.os.Bundle;

import com.google.android.gms.maps.CameraUpdateFactory;
import com.google.android.gms.maps.GoogleMap;
import com.google.android.gms.maps.MapFragment;

public class MapsActivity extends Activity {



    @Override
    protected void onCreate(Bundle savedInstanceState) {
        super.onCreate(savedInstanceState);
        setContentView(R.layout.activity_maps);
        MapFragment mapFragment = (MapFragment) getFragmentManager()
                .findFragmentById(R.id.map);

        GoogleMap map = mapFragment.getMap();
        if (map != null) {
        map.moveCamera(CameraUpdateFactory.zoomBy(6,new
Point(1050,800)));
        }
    }

}

MapsActivity.java
```

Changing the camera position

In the previous section, we learned how to change the camera view in the current position using zoom. In this section, we are going to learn how to change the camera position from one location to another. The methods used are as follows:

Method	Parameter	Function
newLatLng()	Latitude and Longitude coordinates as the LatLng object.	The camera moves the center of the screen to the new latitude and longitude.
newLatLngZoom()	Latitude and Longitude coordinates as the LatLng object. Zoom level in float.	The camera moves the center of the screen to the new latitude and longitude with the specified zoom level.

Let's proceed with an example. The layout code consists of MapFragment with a button, which helps in moving the camera to another location. The code is given by:

```
<LinearLayout xmlns:android="http://schemas.android.com/apk/res/
android"
    xmlns:tools="http://schemas.android.com/tools"
    android:layout_width="match_parent"
    android:layout_height="match_parent"
    android:orientation="vertical"
    tools:context=".MapsActivity">
    <fragment
        android:id="@+id/map"
        android:layout_width="match_parent"

        android:layout_height="0dp"
        android:layout_weight="1"
        android:name="com.google.android.gms.maps.MapFragment"/>
    <Button
        android:id="@+id/button"
        android:layout_width="match_parent"
        android:layout_height="wrap_content"
        android:text="Move Camera" />
</LinearLayout>
```

activity_maps.xml

In our activity, when the button is pressed, we just move the camera to a new location with the specified zoom level:

```java
package com.raj.map;

import android.app.Activity;
import android.os.Bundle;
import android.view.View;
import android.widget.Button;

import com.google.android.gms.maps.CameraUpdateFactory;
import com.google.android.gms.maps.GoogleMap;
import com.google.android.gms.maps.MapFragment;
import com.google.android.gms.maps.OnMapReadyCallback;
import com.google.android.gms.maps.model.LatLng;

public class MapsActivity extends Activity implements
OnMapReadyCallback {
    static final LatLng NEWARK = new LatLng(40.735188, -74.172414);
    Button btn;


    @Override
    protected void onCreate(Bundle savedInstanceState) {
        super.onCreate(savedInstanceState);
        setContentView(R.layout.activity_maps);
        MapFragment mapFragment = (MapFragment) getFragmentManager().
findFragmentById(R.id.map);
        mapFragment.getMapAsync(this);
        btn = (Button)findViewById(R.id.button);

    }
    @Override
    public void onMapReady(final GoogleMap map) {

        btn.setOnClickListener(new View.OnClickListener() {
            @Override
            public void onClick(View v) {
                map.moveCamera(CameraUpdateFactory.
newLatLngZoom(NEWARK,4));
            }
        });

    }
}

MapsActivity.java
```

Here, we use the target location as Newark with a zoom level of 4. The `newLatLngZoom()` method is then called. This code yields the following result:

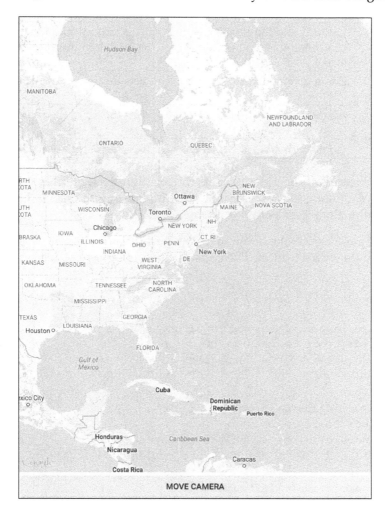

Using the CameraPosition class

To make the process more simple and flexible, the Google Maps API provides the `CameraPosition` class. We need to pass the `CameraPosition` object to the `newCameraPosition()` method on the `CameraUpdateFactory` class.

A builder can be created using the following code:

```
new CameraPosition.Builder()
```

The methods that can be called on the `CameraPosition.Builder` class are as follows:

Method	Parameter	Function
`target()`	Latitude and longitude coordinates as the `LatLng` object.	This latitude and longitude is centered on the map.
`zoom()`	Zoom level in float.	Sets the zoom level of the camera view.
`tilt()`	Angle in degrees. Ranges from 0 to 90 degrees.	Sets the tilt of the camera view.
`bearing()`	Angle in degrees.	Sets the orientation of the camera.

Let's design a custom application that sets the location we long pressed as the target. Also, it displays a dialog that takes zoom, tilt, and bearing as inputs. The layout is the same as the one we used before with `MapFragment`.

Now, we need a dialog to take zoom, bearing, and tilt as inputs. It consists of three `EditText` widgets with a button. The code for the dialog layout is as follows:

```xml
<?xml version="1.0" encoding="utf-8"?>
<LinearLayout xmlns:android="http://schemas.android.com/apk/res/
android"
    android:layout_width="match_parent"
    android:layout_height="match_parent"
    android:orientation="vertical">

    <EditText
        android:id="@+id/zoom"
        android:hint="Zoom"
        android:layout_width="match_parent"
        android:layout_height="wrap_content" />
    <EditText
        android:id="@+id/bearing"
        android:hint="Bearing"
        android:layout_width="match_parent"
        android:layout_height="wrap_content" />
    <EditText
        android:id="@+id/tilt"
        android:hint="Tilt"
        android:layout_width="match_parent"
        android:layout_height="wrap_content" />

    <Button
```

```
android:id="@+id/button"
android:text="Move Camera"
android:layout_width="match_parent"
android:layout_height="wrap_content" />

</LinearLayout>

dialog_camera.xml
```

We are using some of the concepts used in the previous chapters. When we long press the map, the dialog is displayed. The touch location is taken as the new target.

The zoom, tilt, and bearing are obtained from the dialog as inputs. When the user presses the **MOVE CAMERA** button, the camera is moved to the new location. The code for activity is as follows:

```
package com.raj.map;

import android.app.Activity;
import android.app.Dialog;
import android.os.Bundle;
import android.util.Log;
import android.view.View;
import android.widget.Button;
import android.widget.EditText;


import com.google.android.gms.maps.CameraUpdateFactory;
import com.google.android.gms.maps.GoogleMap;
import com.google.android.gms.maps.MapFragment;
import com.google.android.gms.maps.OnMapReadyCallback;
import com.google.android.gms.maps.model.CameraPosition;
import com.google.android.gms.maps.model.LatLng;

public class MapsActivity extends Activity implements
OnMapReadyCallback {

    Dialog cameraDialog;
    EditText zoom,tilt,bearing;
    Button move_camera;
    LatLng lngClick;



    @Override
```

```java
protected void onCreate(Bundle savedInstanceState) {
    super.onCreate(savedInstanceState);
    setContentView(R.layout.activity_maps);
    initDialog();
    MapFragment mapFragment = (MapFragment)
      getFragmentManager().findFragmentById(R.id.map);
    mapFragment.getMapAsync(this);
}
@Override
public void onMapReady(GoogleMap map) {
    initMapLongClick(map);
    moveCamera(map);
}

public void initDialog(){
    cameraDialog = new Dialog(this);
    cameraDialog.setTitle("Move Camera");
    cameraDialog.setContentView(R.layout.dialog_camera);

    zoom = (EditText) cameraDialog.findViewById(R.id.zoom);
    tilt = (EditText)cameraDialog.findViewById(R.id.tilt);
    bearing = (EditText)cameraDialog.findViewById(R.id.bearing);
    move_camera = (Button)cameraDialog.findViewById(R.id.button);
}
public void initMapLongClick(GoogleMap googleMap){
    googleMap.setOnMapLongClickListener(new
      GoogleMap.OnMapLongClickListener() {
        @Override
        public void onMapLongClick(LatLng latLng) {
            cameraDialog.show();
            lngClick = latLng;
        }
    });
}

public void moveCamera(final GoogleMap googleMapmap){
    move_camera.setOnClickListener(new View.OnClickListener() {
        @Override
        public void onClick(View v) {
            String zoomText = zoom.getText().toString();
            String tiltText = tilt.getText().toString();
            String bearingText = bearing.getText().toString();
```

```
                    if(!(zoomText.isEmpty() || tiltText.isEmpty() ||
                      bearingText.isEmpty() )){

                   try {
                       CameraPosition cameraPosition =
                        new CameraPosition.Builder().
    target(lngClick).zoom(Float.valueOf(zoomText)).tilt(Float.
    valueOf(tiltText)).bearing(Float.valueOf(bearingText)).build();
                           googleMapmap.moveCamera(CameraUpdateFactory.ne
    wCameraPosition(cameraPosition));
                           cameraDialog.dismiss();
                   } catch (NumberFormatException nfe) {
                       Log.d("Map","Number Format Error");
                   }
               }
           }
       });
   }
}
```

MapsActivity.java

We are using a `CameraPosition.Builder` class to create a `CameraPosition` object. By calling the `zoom()`, `bearing()`, and `tilt()` methods, we are passing the obtained values from the dialog.

The `CameraPosition` object is passed to the `newCameraPosition()` method on the `CameraUpdateFactory` class to obtain the `CameraUpdate` class. This is passed to the `moveCamera()` method.

When we execute the program and long press on the map, we will see a dialog similar to the following screenshot:

Here, I have long pressed a location in India. I have set the zoom level to 4 and the tilt angle to 45 degrees. The output will be similar to the next image:

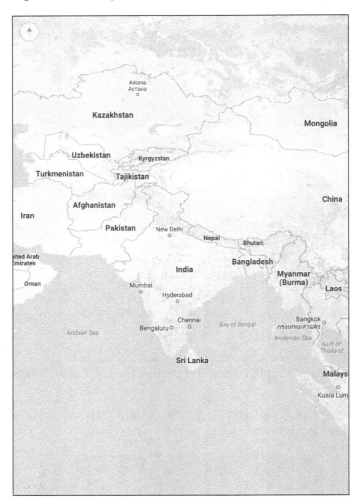

Setting boundaries

There may be a situation; sometimes, you may need to display a particular region at the maximum possible zoom level. For example, you may need to display the complete view of a shopping mall on the map. You can do this by creating the LatLngBounds object of the particular location. This LatLngBounds object is passed to the newLatLngBounds() method on the CameraUpdatefactory class.

Padding should be specified; the width and height of the region can also be specified.

This `newLatLngBounds(LatLngBounds latlngBounds, int padding)` method should not be called until it has undergone layout or it will throw an error. Or, we can preferably use the method with width and height:

```
newLatLngBounds(LatLngBounds latlngBounds,int width,int height, int padding)
```

In this example, I have set `LatLngBounds` as a region around Madrid. The code in `MapsActivity` is as follows:

```
package com.raj.map;

import android.app.Activity;
import android.os.Bundle;

import com.google.android.gms.maps.CameraUpdateFactory;
import com.google.android.gms.maps.GoogleMap;
import com.google.android.gms.maps.MapFragment;
import com.google.android.gms.maps.OnMapReadyCallback;
import com.google.android.gms.maps.model.LatLng;
import com.google.android.gms.maps.model.LatLngBounds;

public class MapsActivity extends Activity implements
OnMapReadyCallback {

    static final LatLng NE = new LatLng(40.461341, -3.688721);
    static final LatLng SW = new LatLng(40.435998, -3.717903);


    @Override
    protected void onCreate(Bundle savedInstanceState) {
        super.onCreate(savedInstanceState);
        setContentView(R.layout.activity_maps);
        MapFragment mapFragment =
          (MapFragment)getFragmentManager().findFragmentById(R.id.map);
        mapFragment.getMapAsync(this);

    }
    @Override
    public void onMapReady(GoogleMap map) {

        LatLngBounds latLngBounds = new LatLngBounds(SW,NE);
```

```
        map.moveCamera(CameraUpdateFactory.newLatLngBoun
ds,600,600,20));

    }
}
```

MapsActivity.java

Here, in this example, I set the north east and south west boundaries as the `LatLng` coordinates. Then, I created a new `LatLngBounds` object with the defined values.

The `LatLngBounds` object, along with the width, height, and padding, is passed to the `newLatLngBounds()` method.

Width is set as 600 px. Height is set as 600 px. Padding is set as 20 px.

One important point to note: the bearing and tilt of the target view is 0.

When you execute the code, the output obtained will be similar to the next screenshot:

If we do not want to display the entire region but center the region bounded by the boundaries, do as follows.

The center of LatLngBounds can be obtained by calling the getCenter() method on the LatLngBounds object. The code in the onMapReady() callback method is as follows:

```
@Override
    public void onMapReady(GoogleMap map) {

        LatLngBounds latLngBounds = new LatLngBounds(SW,NE);
        map.moveCamera(CameraUpdateFactory.newLatLngZoom(latLngBounds.
getCenter(),8));

    }
```

When we execute the code, the output will be similar to the following image:

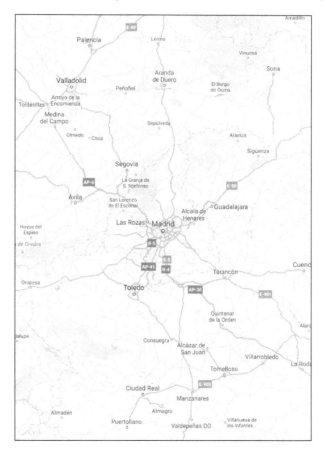

Panning the map

This can be also called scrolling. By calling the `scrollBy()` method on the `CameraUpdatefactory` class, we can pan the map in a certain direction. It takes *x* and *y* float values as parameters:

- Positive x value makes the map to move right
- Negative x value makes the map to move left
- Positive y value makes the map to move down
- Negative y value makes the map to move up

Let's create a simple map with controls for the four directions, which on being pressed pan 10 pixels in that direction which is pressed.

Our main layout consists of `MapFragment` with four buttons to pan in the respective directions. The layout code is as follows:

```
<LinearLayout xmlns:android="http://schemas.android.com/apk/res/
android"
    xmlns:tools="http://schemas.android.com/tools"
    android:layout_width="match_parent"
    android:layout_height="match_parent"
    android:orientation="vertical"
    tools:context=".MapsActivity">
    <fragment
        android:id="@+id/map"
        android:layout_width="match_parent"

        android:layout_height="0dp"
        android:layout_weight="1"
        android:name="com.google.android.gms.maps.MapFragment"/>
    <Button
        android:id="@+id/btn_up"
        android:layout_width="match_parent"
        android:layout_height="wrap_content"
        android:text="Up" />
    <Button
        android:id="@+id/btn_down"
        android:layout_width="match_parent"
        android:layout_height="wrap_content"
        android:text="Down" />
    <Button
        android:id="@+id/btn_left"
        android:layout_width="match_parent"
```

```
            android:layout_height="wrap_content"
            android:text="Left" />
    <Button
            android:id="@+id/btn_right"
            android:layout_width="match_parent"
            android:layout_height="wrap_content"
            android:text="Right" />
</LinearLayout>
```

activity_maps.xml

The code for activity is as follows:

```
package com.raj.map;

import android.app.Activity;
import android.os.Bundle;
import android.view.View;
import android.widget.Button;

import com.google.android.gms.maps.CameraUpdateFactory;
import com.google.android.gms.maps.GoogleMap;
import com.google.android.gms.maps.MapFragment;
import com.google.android.gms.maps.OnMapReadyCallback;


public class MapsActivity extends Activity implements
OnMapReadyCallback {
    Button up,down,left,right;


    @Override
    protected void onCreate(Bundle savedInstanceState) {
        super.onCreate(savedInstanceState);
        setContentView(R.layout.activity_maps);
        MapFragment mapFragment =
          (MapFragment)getFragmentManager().findFragmentById(R.id.map);
        mapFragment.getMapAsync(this);

        up = (Button)findViewById(R.id.btn_up);
        down = (Button)findViewById(R.id.btn_down);
        left = (Button)findViewById(R.id.btn_left);
        right = (Button)findViewById(R.id.btn_right);

    }
```

```
        @Override
        public void onMapReady(final GoogleMap map) {



            up.setOnClickListener(new View.OnClickListener() {
                @Override
                public void onClick(View v) {
                    map.moveCamera(CameraUpdateFactory.scrollBy(0,-10));
                }
            });
            down.setOnClickListener(new View.OnClickListener() {
                @Override
                public void onClick(View v) {
                    map.moveCamera(CameraUpdateFactory.scrollBy(0,10));


                }
            });

            left.setOnClickListener(new View.OnClickListener() {
                @Override
                public void onClick(View v) {
                    map.moveCamera(CameraUpdateFactory.scrollBy(-10,0));


                }
            });
            right.setOnClickListener(new View.OnClickListener() {
                @Override
                public void onClick(View v) {
                    map.moveCamera(CameraUpdateFactory.scrollBy(10,0));


                }
            });
        }
    }
```

MapsActivity.java

When one of the four direction the button is pressed, we pass the CameraUpdate object obtained by calling the scrollBy() method on the CameraUpdateFactory method to the moveCamera() method on the GoogleMap object:

```
map.moveCamera(CameraUpdateFactory.scrollBy(10,0));
```

This line moves the camera by 10 pixels on the x axis (that is, the camera pans right).

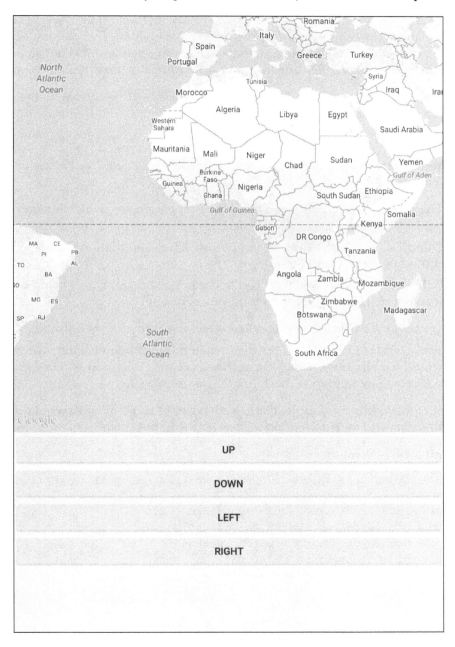

Animating the camera

In the previous sections, we used the moveCamera() method on the GoogleMap object. It changes the camera and updates the view immediately. You may have noted that, during the transformation, there is no animation and it is not smooth. So, in order to make smoother transformations, we need to use animations.

Using animation is very simple. Replace the moveCamera() method with the animateCamera() method. It would be similar to:

```
map.animateCamera(CameraUpdateFactory.scrollBy(10,0));
```

To get more control over the animation, we can use the same animateCamera() method with more parameters. They are as follows:

- **The CameraUpdate object**: This is the first parameter, which is same as the one used in the moveCamera() method.

- **Duration**: This is the time interval for which the animation should exist. It should be specified as the integer type.

- **Callback**: A callback method is called when the animation is being executed. It is optional. The callback methods are given by:

  onFinish(): This method is called when the animation is finished.

  OnCancel(): This method is called when the animation is interrupted. This would usually occur when the stopAnimation() method is called on the GoogleMap object when the animation is progressing.

Let's look at this with an example. Here, we have MapFragment with two buttons in the layout's start and stop animation to start and stop the animation.

The layout code is as follows:

```
<LinearLayout xmlns:android="http://schemas.android.com/apk/res/
android"
    xmlns:tools="http://schemas.android.com/tools"
    android:layout_width="match_parent"
    android:layout_height="match_parent"
    android:orientation="vertical"
    tools:context=".MapsActivity">
    <fragment
        android:id="@+id/map"
        android:layout_width="match_parent"
        android:layout_height="0dp"
```

```
        android:layout_weight=!"1"

        android:name="com.google.android.gms.maps.MapFragment"/>
    <Button
        android:id="@+id/btn_start"
        android:layout_width="match_parent"
        android:layout_height="wrap_content"
        android:text="Start Animation" />
    <Button
        android:id="@+id/btn_stop"
        android:layout_width="match_parent"
        android:layout_height="wrap_content"
        android:text="Stop Animation" />
</LinearLayout>
```

activity_maps.xml

In our activity, we defined the LatLng coordinates of London. When the **START ANIMATION** button is pressed, the camera performs a smooth animation transition toward London.

When the **STOP ANIMATION** button is pressed, the animation pauses and a message is printed in log. When the animation is successfully completed, a message is printed in log.

The activity code is as follows:

```
package com.raj.map;

import android.app.Activity;
import android.os.Bundle;
import android.util.Log;
import android.view.View;
import android.widget.Button;

import com.google.android.gms.maps.CameraUpdateFactory;
import com.google.android.gms.maps.GoogleMap;
import com.google.android.gms.maps.MapFragment;
import com.google.android.gms.maps.OnMapReadyCallback;
import com.google.android.gms.maps.model.CameraPosition;
import com.google.android.gms.maps.model.LatLng;


public class MapsActivity extends Activity implements
OnMapReadyCallback {
```

```java
    static final LatLng LONDON= new LatLng(51.519029, -0.130094);
    Button start,stop;




    @Override
    protected void onCreate(Bundle savedInstanceState) {
        super.onCreate(savedInstanceState);
        setContentView(R.layout.activity_maps);
        MapFragment mapFragment =
            (MapFragment)getFragmentManager().findFragmentById(R.
id.map);
        mapFragment.getMapAsync(this);

        start = (Button)findViewById(R.id.btn_start);
        stop = (Button)findViewById(R.id.btn_stop);


    }
    @Override
    public void onMapReady(final GoogleMap map) {

    final CameraPosition cameraPosition = new CameraPosition.
Builder().
                target(LONDON).
                zoom(8).
                build();
        start.setOnClickListener(new View.OnClickListener() {
            @Override
            public void onClick(View v) {


                map.animateCamera(CameraUpdateFactory.newCameraPositio
n(cameraPosition),
2000, new GoogleMap.CancelableCallback() {
                    @Override
                    public void onFinish() {
                        Log.d("Map", "Animation finished");
                    }

                    @Override
                    public void onCancel() {
```

```
                    Log.d("Map", "Animation interrupted");
                }
            });
        }
    });
    stop.setOnClickListener(new View.OnClickListener() {
        @Override
        public void onClick(View v) {
            map.stopAnimation();
        }
    });
    }
}
```

MapsActivity.java

We are creating a CameraPosition object with its target as the LanLng coordinates of London and a zoom level of 8.

Then, we call the map.animateCamera() method on the onClick() method, which will be called when the **START** button is pressed.

The animation's duration is defined as 2,000 milliseconds. Next, the GoogleMap.CancelableCallback() interface is implemented for the animation.

A log message is printed when the animation is finished or interrupted.

When you execute the program, you will see a smooth animation.

The log message, which will be printed when interrupted, is similar to:

```
D/Map: Animation interrupted
```

The log message, which will be printed when the animation is finished, is as follows:

```
D/Map: Animation finished
```

When you run the project you will find a screen similar to the following:

Map padding

In general, Google Maps fills the entire container and its controls are displayed at the edges. They are as follows:

- Zoom controls are displayed in the bottom right corner
- My location button is displayed in the top right corner
- Compass controls are displayed in the top left corner

Other than these, the Google Maps copyright information is displayed in the bottom-left corner.

There may be situations where you may have to display other information in place of these elements. To make this possible, you can pad the elements in the corners.

This can be done by calling the setPadding() method on the GoogleMap object. It takes pixels as an integer value to pad the left, top, right, and bottom edges.

It would be called as follows:

```
map.setPadding(400, 100, 100, 0);
```

This means that 400 pixels are padded in the left corner and 100 pixels are padded in the top and right corners.

Let's discuss this with an example. The code for the layout remains the same as we used in the beginning with MapFragment.

The code in the onMapReady() callback method is:

```
@Override
public void onMapReady(final GoogleMap map) {
    LatLng center = map.getCameraPosition().target;
    map.addMarker(new MarkerOptions().position(center));
    map.setMyLocationEnabled(true);
    map.getUiSettings().setZoomControlsEnabled(true);
    map.setPadding(400, 100, 100, 0);
    map.setOnMapLongClickListener(new
      GoogleMap.OnMapLongClickListener() {
        @Override
        public void onMapLongClick(LatLng latLng) {
            LatLng center = map.getCameraPosition().target;
            map.addMarker(new
              MarkerOptions().position(center).
icon(BitmapDescriptorFactory.
            defaultMarker(BitmapDescriptorFactory.HUE_GREEN)));


        }
    });
}
```

The center of the region before the padding is obtained by:

```
LatLng center = map.getCameraPosition().target;
```

Then, a marker is added with the target as the obtained center.

We enable the zoom controls and the **My Location** button. Then, we pad the map 400 pixels left and 100 pixels top and right.

When we long press the map, the center of the padded region is obtained. A new marker is added with the green color.

When you run the program, you will see a red marker placed at the center before you pad the normal region. When you long press the map, a green marker is added at the center of the padded region.

You can see that all the UI controls are moved according to the padding pixels. The Google logo is moved right.

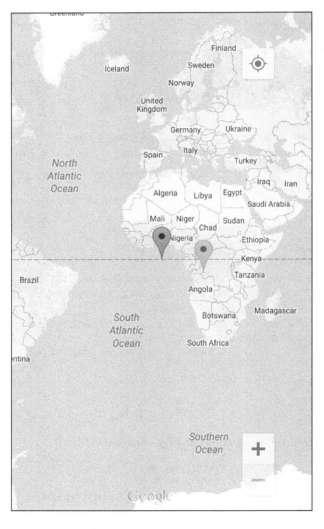

While padding, the Google logo should be visible and it should not be removed according to the terms.

Self-test questions

Q1. The tilt angle ranges between 0 and 180 degrees.

1. True
2. False

Q2. A bearing angle of 90 degrees rotates the map 90 degrees clockwise.

1. True
2. False

Q3. The `zoomIn()` method increases zoom level by?

1. 1
2. 2
3. 3
4. 4

Q4. In the `scrollBy(float x, float y)` method, the positive value of x moves the map in which direction?

1. Left
2. Right
3. Up
4. Down

Q5. Which method is called when the animation is finished?

1. `onFinish()`
2. `onCancel()`

Summary

In this chapter, we learned about different camera views. We covered different camera perspectives such as target, zoom, tilt, and bearing. Then, we learned how to move the camera view from one location to another by panning the camera. We also learned how to implement cool animations. We concluded with how to pad a map.

In next chapter, we will learn about integrating location data with maps.

7
Working with Location Data

In our previous chapter, we learned how to work with custom camera views by changing zoom, bearing, and tilt. Also, we learned how to set the initial camera position and design a custom application. In this chapter, we are going to learn about working with real-time location data (GPS data). Let's start!

In this chapter, we will cover the following topics:

- Need for location data
- Prerequisites
- Working with the Android Location API
- Working with the Google Play services Location API
- Integrating location data with maps

The need for location data

Let's start with an example. You may have used the app Uber, which is a GPS-based taxi booking service. It relies on your real-time GPS data. Another great example is Waze, which is a GPS-based social map application. Location data (or GPS data) helps us build complex applications such as map-based navigation applications.

This screenshot shows the Uber app, which uses GPS data to determine our current location. This makes the task easier for the Uber driver to locate you. Let's discuss the process in detail in the coming sections.

Prerequisites

The first important step before proceeding is to specify the required permissions to access GPS data. Two new permissions are required. They are:

- `android.permission.ACCESS_COARSE_LOCATION`
- `android.permission.ACCESS_FINE_LOCATION`

Let's discuss what these permissions are for:

ACCESS_COARSE_LOCATION

This permission is used to retrieve the approximate location from cell phone towers and Wi-Fi.

ACCESS_FINE_LOCATION

This permission is used to retrieve the accurate location from GPS satellites, cell phone towers, and Wi-Fi.

We have learned about permissions in *Chapter 2*, *Configuring an API Key and Creating Our First Map Application*. Similarly, we add the permissions to the `AndroidManifest.xml` file.

The permissions are added as follows:

```
<uses-permission android:name="android.permission.ACCESS_COARSE_
LOCATION"/>
<uses-permission android:name="android.permission.ACCESS_FINE_
LOCATION"/>
```

There are three ways we can work with location data:

- Using the my location layer
- Using the Android Location API
- Using the Google Play services Location API

Using the my location layer

We have already worked with the my location layer in *Chapter 5*, *Interacting with a Map*. This can only be used to display the user location on the map. It does not provide any data.

When the location layer is enabled, the **My Location** button is displayed in the top right corner of the map. When a user presses the button, the current location of the user is displayed on the map.

To retrieve GPS data such as latitude and longitude, we must use the Android Location API or Google Play services Location API.

Using the Android Location API

The Android framework provides the Location API to add location awareness to our app. It is provided in the `android.location` package. We need to implement the `LocationListener` interface to access the API.

Using the Google Play services Location API

Google recommends that we use the Google Play services Location API over the Android framework Location API. The Google Play services Location API provides several new features over the Android Location API.

Some of the features are:

- Get the current location
- Get periodic location updates
- Get the address from the location
- Geofences

Working with the Android Location API

The Android framework has an inbuilt `android.location` package, which helps us retrieve the user's current location.

It can be implemented by using the `LocationListener` interface. It provides four methods. They are:

- `onLocationChanged()`
- `onStatusChanged()`
- `onProviderEnabled()`
- `onProviderDisabled()`

The `onLocationChanged()` method is called when the location is changed (when the user moves). The `onStatusChanged()` method is executed when the status of the provider is changed (the provider may be unavailable initially and available after some time). The `onProviderEnabled()` and `onProviderDisabled()` methods are called when the location provider is enabled and disabled.

Then, we should use the `LocationManager` class to get access to the system's location services. This class can be instantiated by:

```
LocationManager locationManager = (LocationManager)
getSystemService(Context.LOCATION_SERVICE);
```

Here, `locationManager` is the object created from the `LocationManager` class. The `getSystemService` method is the context method. The types of location providers are as follows:

Location provider type	Description
GPS provider	This determines the location using satellites.
Network provider	This determines the location using Wi-Fi and cell phone towers.
Passive provider	This provider determines the location passively. It returns locations determined by other providers.

By calling the `isProviderEnabled()` method on the `LocationManager` object with the parameter of the `LocationProvider` string, we can determine whether a provider is enabled or not.

By calling the `requestLocationUpdates()` method on the `LocationManager` object, we can request location updates for a time interval and distance. It takes the parameters as the `LocationProvider` string, the minimum time interval between updates in milliseconds, the minimum distance between location updates in meters, and also `LocationListener`.

Let's create an example project.

I have created a new project with the package named `com.raj.map`, the layout named `activity_main`, and the activity as `MainActivity`.

I have added the two permissions to `AndroidManifest.xml`. The complete manifest is as follows:

```
<?xml version="1.0" encoding="utf-8"?>
<manifest xmlns:android="http://schemas.android.com/apk/res/android"
    package="com.raj.map" >
    <uses-permission android:name="android.permission.ACCESS_COARSE_
LOCATION"/>
```

```
    <uses-permission android:name="android.permission.ACCESS_FINE_
LOCATION"/>

    <application
        android:allowBackup="true"
        android:icon="@mipmap/ic_launcher"
        android:label="@string/app_name"
        android:theme="@style/AppTheme" >


        <activity
            android:name=".MainActivity"
            android:label="@string/app_name" >
            <intent-filter>
                <action android:name="android.intent.action.MAIN" />

                <category android:name="android.intent.category.
LAUNCHER" />
            </intent-filter>
        </activity>
    </application>

</manifest>
```

AndroidManifest.xml

Our main layout consists of nothing more than a LinearLayout. We are going to display information only using toast. The main layout is as follows:

```
<LinearLayout xmlns:android="http://schemas.android.com/apk/res/
android"
    xmlns:tools="http://schemas.android.com/tools"
    android:layout_width="match_parent"
    android:layout_height="match_parent"
    tools:context=".MainActivity">
    </LinearLayout>
```

activity_main.xml

Next, we can proceed to MainActivity. Let's take a look at the code first and then proceed with the explanation. The code for the activity is:

```
package com.raj.map;

import android.app.Activity;
import android.content.Context;
```

```
import android.location.Location;
import android.location.LocationListener;
import android.location.LocationManager;
import android.os.Bundle;
import android.util.Log;
import android.widget.Toast;


public class MainActivity extends Activity implements
LocationListener{

    LocationManager locationManager;
    double latitude;
    double longitude;

    @Override
    protected void onCreate(Bundle savedInstanceState) {
        super.onCreate(savedInstanceState);
        setContentView(R.layout.activity_main);

        locationManager = (LocationManager)getSystemService(Context.
LOCATION_SERVICE);
        if(locationManager.isProviderEnabled(LocationManager.GPS_
PROVIDER)){
            locationManager.requestLocationUpdates(LocationManager.
GPS_PROVIDER,1000,1,this);
        }else{
            Toast.makeText(getApplicationContext(),"Enable GPS",Toast.
LENGTH_LONG).show();

        }
    }


    @Override
    public void onLocationChanged(Location location) {

        latitude = location.getLatitude();
        longitude = location.getLongitude();

        Toast.makeText(getApplicationContext(),"Latitude :
"+latitude+"\nLongitude : "+longitude,Toast.LENGTH_SHORT).show();


    }

    @Override
```

```java
    public void onStatusChanged(String s, int i, Bundle bundle) {
        Log.d("Updates",s+" Changed");

    }

    @Override
    public void onProviderEnabled(String s) {
        Log.d("Updates",s+" Enabled");

    }

    @Override
    public void onProviderDisabled(String s) {
        Log.d("Updates",s+" Disabled");

    }
}
```

MainActivity.java

Initially, we implemented the LocationListener interface; it has four methods. In this example project, we are using only the GPS provider.

In our onCreate() method, we are checking whether the GPS provider is enabled or not. If it is enabled, we will request a location update from the GPS provider using the LocationManager class.

In the requestLocationUpdates() method, 1,000 milliseconds is the update interval (the minimum time interval between the location updates is 1 second) and the next parameter 1 denotes the minimum distance between the location update is 1 meter.

A toast alert is displayed when the GPS is disabled. The onLocationChanged() method is called when the location changes. By using the getLatitude() and getLongitude() method on the Location object, we obtain the latitude and longitude. The obtained latitude and longitude is displayed in a toast.

When the GPS is enabled or disabled, the onProviderEnabled() and onProviderDisabled() methods are called. Log is printed. It is similar to:

```
D/Updates: gps Disabled
D/Updates: gps Enabled
```

The latitude and longitude displayed in the toast is similar to the following screenshot:

If you are trying to get location data when the GPS provider is disabled, a toast message will be displayed to enable GPS. It will be similar to the next screenshot:

Now, we have learned to obtain the latitude and longitude using the inbuilt Android framework Location API.

We can also obtain the last known location with the help of the Android framework Location API by using the `getLastKnownLocation()` method on the `LocationManager` object by passing the name of location provider.

For example, if I need to get the last known location using a network provider, I would use:

```
Location location = locationManager.getLastKnownLocation(LocationManag
er.NETWORK_PROVIDER);
```

Similarly, we can use the GPS provider or passive provider.

Google recommended us to use the Google Play services Location API over this. We shall learn about it in the next section.

Working with the Google Play services Location API

We already looked at the features of Google Play services. Let's see some of the initial steps before we proceed:

- Make sure you have set up Google Play services for our Android project
- Check whether you have added the suitable permissions required

Getting the last known location

Using the Google Play services Location API, we can also request the last known location of the device. In most cases, the current location will be equal to the last known location.

We use the fused location provider to retrieve the last known location. It is present in Google Play services. It provides a simple API and it also helps in optimizing the device's battery power.

We must implement the GoogleApiClient.ConnectionCallbacks interface, which provides a callback when the client is connected or disconnected. It provides two methods: the onConnected() method is called when the connect request is successfully completed and the onConnectionSuspended() method is called when the client is temporarily in a disconnected state.

The GoogleApiClient.OnConnectionFailedListener interface should be implemented so that it provides a callback when the connection attempt fails. It provides a onConnectionFailed() method, which is called when there is an error while connecting. By calling the getErrorCode() method on the ConnectionResult object, we can obtain the error code. For example, an error code of 1 denotes that the Google Play services is missing on the device. We can also use the ConnectionResult object to resolve the error. The resolution can be started by calling the startResolutionForResult() method on the ConnectionResult object with the Activity and Request code as integers for its parameter. If the error is resolved, the client should again connect on the onActivityResult() method. It is given in the following code.

Then, we must instantiate the `GoogleApiClient` class, which is the entry point of Google Play services using its `GoogleApiClient.Builder` nested class. This should be done in the `onCreate()` method. This can be done by:

```
GoogleApiClient googleApiClient = new GoogleApiClient.Builder(this)
                .addConnectionCallbacks(this)
                .addOnConnectionFailedListener(this)
                .addApi(LocationServices.API)
                .build();
```

The client can connect to the service by calling the `connect()` method on the `GoogleApiClient` object.

By calling `getLastLocation()` in the fused location provider, the most recent location can be obtained.

Let's perform this with an example. I have added a button to the layout to display the location dialog. The layout code is as follows:

```
<LinearLayout xmlns:android="http://schemas.android.com/apk/res/
android"
    xmlns:tools="http://schemas.android.com/tools"
    android:layout_width="match_parent"
    android:layout_height="match_parent"
    android:orientation="vertical"
    android:gravity="center"
    tools:context=".MainActivity">

    <Button
        android:id="@+id/btn"
        android:layout_gravity="center"
        android:text="Get Recent Location"
        android:layout_width="wrap_content"
        android:layout_height="wrap_content" />

</LinearLayout>
```

`activity_main.xml`

The complete main activity code is:

```
package com.raj.map;

import android.app.Activity;
import android.app.AlertDialog;
import android.content.DialogInterface;
```

```
import android.location.Location;
import android.os.Bundle;
import android.view.View;
import android.widget.Button;

import com.google.android.gms.common.ConnectionResult;
import com.google.android.gms.common.api.GoogleApiClient;
import com.google.android.gms.location.LocationServices;


public class MainActivity extends Activity implements
        GoogleApiClient.ConnectionCallbacks, GoogleApiClient.
OnConnectionFailedListener {


    GoogleApiClient googleApiClient;
    Location location;
    AlertDialog.Builder alertDialog;
    Button button;
    double latitude;
    double longitude;

    @Override
    protected void onCreate(Bundle savedInstanceState) {
        super.onCreate(savedInstanceState);
        setContentView(R.layout.activity_main);
        googleApiClient = new GoogleApiClient.Builder(this)
                .addConnectionCallbacks(this)
                .addOnConnectionFailedListener(this)
                .addApi(LocationServices.API)
                .build();
        googleApiClient.connect();

        alertDialog = new AlertDialog.Builder(this);
        alertDialog.setTitle("Location");
        alertDialog.setPositiveButton("OK", new DialogInterface.
OnClickListener() {
            @Override
            public void onClick(DialogInterface dialogInterface, int
i) {
                dialogInterface.dismiss();
            }
        });
        button = (Button)findViewById(R.id.btn);
```

```java
button.setOnClickListener(new View.OnClickListener() {
    @Override
    public void onClick(View view) {

        if (latitude != 0 && longitude != 0) {
            alertDialog.show();
        }

    }
});
}


@Override
public void onConnected(Bundle bundle) {
    location = LocationServices.FusedLocationApi.getLastLocation(
            googleApiClient);
    if (location != null) {
        latitude = location.getLatitude();
        longitude = location.getLongitude();
        alertDialog.setMessage("Latitude :" + latitude + "\
nLongitude :" + longitude);


    }
}

@Override
public void onConnectionSuspended(int i) {
    Log.d("Connection","Code : "+i);
}

@Override
public void onConnectionFailed(ConnectionResult connectionResult)
{
    Log.d("Connection","Code :"+connectionResult.getErrorCode());
    try {
        connectionResult.startResolutionForResult(MapsActivity.
this, 1000);
    } catch (IntentSender.SendIntentException e) {
        e.printStackTrace();
    }

}
@Override
protected void onActivityResult(int requestCode, int resultCode,
Intent data){
```

```
        if (requestCode == 1000) {
            if (resultCode == RESULT_OK) {
                if (!googleApiClient.isConnected()){
                    googleApiClient.connect();
                }
            }
        }

    }
}
```

MainActivity.java

We obtained the last known location from the fused location provider. When the user presses the button, we display the obtained latitude and longitude coordinates in a dialog, which is constructed using AlertDialog.Builder.

While executing the app, the initial screen should be similar to the following screenshot:

When you press the **GET RECENT LOCATION** button, an alert dialog is displayed that shows the latitude and longitude. The next screenshot shows this:

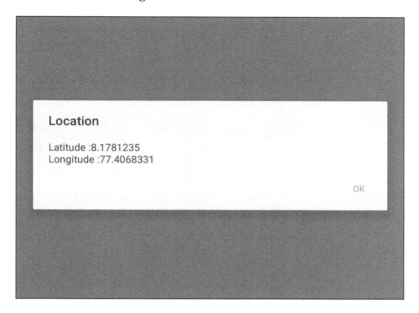

Location updates

In our previous section, we learned how to retrieve the last known location using a fused location provider. What if you need location updates for every *t* seconds? What if you need less power consumption while retrieving updates? Well, this is what we are going to see now. These location updates can also be retrieved from a fused location provider.

The accuracy of the location depends on the type of the location provider.

As in the previous section, we need to instantiate the `GoogleApiClient` class and connect to the service. We use the `LocationRequest` class to get periodic location updates. Let's see some of the methods that should be called on the `LocationRequest` object and what it does:

Method	Parameter	Function
`setInterval()`	`long` (time in milliseconds)	The time interval in which our app prefers to receive location updates
`setFastestInterval()`	`long` (time in milliseconds)	The fastest rate in which our app can handle location updates
`setPriority()`	`int` (constant value)	Determines which location source to use

The constant values defined in the `LocationRequest` class for priority is given in the following table:

Constant value	Feature
`PRIORITY_BALANCED_POWER_ACCURACY`	It provides an accuracy of about 100 meters. The device likely uses Wi-Fi and cell phone towers to determine the location.
`PRIORITY_HIGH_ACCURACY`	It retrieves the location using GPS.
`PRIORITY_LOW_POWER`	It has an accuracy of about 10 kilometers. It consumes less power.
`PRIORITY_NO_POWER`	It has negligible effect on power consumption. It uses location updates retrieved by other apps.

Location updates can be requested by calling the `requestLocationUpdates()` method on the fused location provider. Location updates can be stopped by calling the `removeLocationUpdates()` method on the fused location provider.

The `LocationListener` interface should be implemented. It has a `onLocationChanged()` method, which is called when the location is changed.

Let's see this with an example in which the UI has two buttons, start and stop, which triggers and stops location updates. The code for the layout is as follows:

```
<LinearLayout xmlns:android="http://schemas.android.com/apk/res/
android"
    xmlns:tools="http://schemas.android.com/tools"
    android:layout_width="match_parent"
    android:layout_height="match_parent"
    android:orientation="vertical"
```

```
        android:gravity="center"
        tools:context=".MainActivity">

        <Button
            android:id="@+id/btn_start"
            android:layout_gravity="center"
            android:text="Start Updates"
            android:layout_width="wrap_content"
            android:layout_height="wrap_content" />
        <Button
            android:id="@+id/btn_stop"
            android:layout_gravity="center"
            android:text="Stop Updates"
            android:layout_width="wrap_content"
            android:layout_height="wrap_content" />

    </LinearLayout>
```

activity_main.xml

The complete code for the activity is:

```
    package com.raj.map;

    import android.app.Activity;
    import android.location.Location;
    import android.os.Bundle;
    import android.util.Log;
    import android.view.View;
    import android.widget.Button;

    import com.google.android.gms.common.ConnectionResult;
    import com.google.android.gms.common.api.GoogleApiClient;
    import com.google.android.gms.location.LocationListener;
    import com.google.android.gms.location.LocationRequest;
    import com.google.android.gms.location.LocationServices;


    public class MainActivity extends Activity implements
            GoogleApiClient.ConnectionCallbacks, GoogleApiClient.
    OnConnectionFailedListener, LocationListener {


        GoogleApiClient googleApiClient;
```

```
LocationRequest locationRequest;
Button start,stop;
double latitude;
double longitude;
Boolean update = false;

@Override
protected void onCreate(Bundle savedInstanceState) {
    super.onCreate(savedInstanceState);
    setContentView(R.layout.activity_main);
    googleApiClient = new GoogleApiClient.Builder(this)
            .addConnectionCallbacks(this)
            .addOnConnectionFailedListener(this)
            .addApi(LocationServices.API)
            .build();
    googleApiClient.connect();

    locationRequest = new LocationRequest();
    locationRequest.setInterval(2000);
    locationRequest.setFastestInterval(1000);
    locationRequest.setPriority(LocationRequest.PRIORITY_HIGH_
ACCURACY);

    start = (Button)findViewById(R.id.btn_start);
    stop = (Button)findViewById(R.id.btn_stop);
    start.setOnClickListener(new View.OnClickListener() {
        @Override
        public void onClick(View view) {

            update = true;
            LocationServices.FusedLocationApi.requestLocationUpdat
es(googleApiClient, locationRequest, MainActivity.this);

        }
    });

    stop.setOnClickListener(new View.OnClickListener() {
        @Override
        public void onClick(View view) {
            update = false;
            LocationServices.FusedLocationApi.removeLocationUpdate
s(googleApiClient, MainActivity.this);

        }
```

```
        });

    }

    @Override
    public void onConnected(Bundle bundle) {
        if(update)
        LocationServices.FusedLocationApi.requestLocationUpdates(googl
eApiClient, locationRequest, this);

    }

    @Override
    public void onLocationChanged(Location location) {

        if (location != null) {
            latitude = location.getLatitude();
            longitude = location.getLongitude();
            Log.d("Updates", "Latitude :" + latitude);
            Log.d("Updates","Longitude :" + longitude);
        }
    }

    @Override
    public void onConnectionSuspended(int i) {

    }

    @Override
    public void onConnectionFailed(ConnectionResult connectionResult)
    {

    }
}
```

MainActivity.java

In this example, we are printing the obtained latitude and longitude as log.
The output will be similar to:

```
D/Updates: Latitude :8.1781426
D/Updates: Longitude :77.4070431
D/Updates: Latitude :8.1781528
D/Updates: Longitude :77.4070236
```

The initial screen will be similar to:

Using reverse geocoding

Geocoding is the process of converting the address to latitude and longitude coordinates. Reverse geocoding is the inverse; it converts the coordinates into an address. Reverse geocoding will be useful to most users, because addresses provide more value than coordinates. This can be performed using the `Geocoder` class present in the `android.location` package.

The `Geocoder` object is created by passing the `Context` and `Locale` object as follows:

```
Geocoder geocoder = new Geocoder(this, Locale.getDefault());
```

The `Geocoder` class requires a backend service that is not included in the core Android framework. Use the `isPresent()` method to determine whether a geocoder implementation exists. The list of addresses can be retrieved by calling the `getFromLocation()` method on the `Geocoder` object, which takes the latitude, longitude and maximum number of results as a parameter. From this list, we obtain the first address and assign it to the `Address` object.

The `getAddressLine()`, `getLocality()`, `getCountryName()`, and `getPostalCode()` methods can be called on the `Address` object to retrieve the address line of the given index, locality of the address, country name, and postal code.

In this example, we are just modifying the example given in the *Getting the last known location* section.

We are creating a `getAddress()` function of the void type, which performs the reverse geocoding operation. It is given by:

```
public void getAddress(Location location){
      if(Geocoder.isPresent()) {
      Geocoder geocoder = new Geocoder(this, Locale.getDefault());
      List<Address> addresses = null;
      String addressText = null;
      latitude = location.getLatitude();
      longitude = location.getLongitude();
      try {
            addresses = geocoder.getFromLocation(latitude, longitude,
1);
      } catch (IOException | IllegalArgumentException e) {
            e.printStackTrace();
      }
      if (addresses != null && addresses.size() > 0) {
            Address address = addresses.get(0);
            addressText = String.format(
                  "%s, %s, %s, %s", address.getMaxAddressLineIndex()
> 0 ? address.getAddressLine(0) : "",
                  address.getLocality(),
                  address.getCountryName(),
                  address.getPostalCode());

      }
      alertDialog.setMessage(addressText);
} else {
            Toast.makeText(this, "Geocoder could not implemented",
Toast.LENGTH_LONG).show();
      }
   }
```

The code in the `onConnected()` callback method is as follows:

```
@Override
   public void onConnected(Bundle bundle) {
      location = LocationServices.FusedLocationApi.getLastLocation(g
oogleApiClient);

      if (location != null) {
         Thread thread = new Thread(new Runnable(){
            @Override
            public void run(){
```

```
                    getAddress(location);
            }
        });
        thread.start();

    }
}
```

When you execute the code, you will get the output address displayed in a dialog. Make sure you add the Internet permission to manifest.

Working with Geofences

Geofences helps us create and monitor fences. It helps us provide location-based applications. You can notify users when the they enter or exit the Geofence. For example, when a user enters a railway station, a notification can be sent to the user about the price and so on.

First, the client must be connected to the service. In order to handle the Geofence transitions, we need to use IntentService. It should be specified in the manifest.

The service to handle Geofence's transition service is as follows:

```
package com.raj.map;


import android.app.IntentService;
import android.content.Intent;
import android.util.Log;

import com.google.android.gms.location.Geofence;
```

```
import com.google.android.gms.location.GeofencingEvent;

public class GeofenceTransitionService extends IntentService{
    public GeofenceTransitionService() {
        super("GEO");
    }

    @Override
    public void onCreate() {
        super.onCreate();
    }
    @Override
    protected void onHandleIntent(Intent intent) {
        GeofencingEvent geofencingEvent = GeofencingEvent.
fromIntent(intent);

        if (geofencingEvent.hasError()) {

            Log.e("GEO","Error"+ geofencingEvent.getErrorCode());
        }
        int geofenceTransition = geofencingEvent.
getGeofenceTransition();
        if (geofenceTransition == Geofence.GEOFENCE_TRANSITION_ENTER )
{
            Log.d("Update", "Entered Geofence");
        }else if(
        geofenceTransition == Geofence.GEOFENCE_TRANSITION_EXIT){
            Log.d("Update", "Exited Geofence");

        }


    }
}
```

GeofenceTransitionService.java

In the earlier code, a message is printed in log when the user enters or leaves the Geofence. By calling the getGeofenceTransition() method on the GeofencingEvent object, we can find out whether it is an enter event or an exit event.

The Geofence list is defined in MainActivity as:

```
Geofence geofences = new ArrayList<Geofence>();
```

The Geofence is created by:

```
geofences.add(new Geofence.Builder().setRequestId("1")
                .setCircularRegion(
                        8.1780967, 77.4068884, 100f)
                .setExpirationDuration(20000)
                .setTransitionTypes(Geofence.GEOFENCE_TRANSITION_ENTER
 | Geofence.GEOFENCE_TRANSITION_EXIT)
                .build());
```

The circular region for Geofence is set by passing the latitude, longitude, and radius to the setCircularRegion() method. The expiration time of the Geofence is defined. The Geofence transition type is defined as well.

The PendingIntent item, which starts GeofenceTransitionService, is defined as:

```
private PendingIntent getGeofencePendingIntent() {
        if (geofencePendingIntent != null) {
            return geofencePendingIntent;
        }
        Intent intent = new Intent(this, GeofenceTransitionService.
class);
        return PendingIntent.getService(this, 0, intent,
PendingIntent.
                FLAG_UPDATE_CURRENT);
    }
```

How the Geofence events are triggered can be defined by the following code snippet:

```
private GeofencingRequest getGeofencingRequest() {
        GeofencingRequest.Builder builder = new GeofencingRequest.
Builder();
        builder.setInitialTrigger(GeofencingRequest.INITIAL_TRIGGER_
ENTER);
        builder.addGeofences(geofences);
        return builder.build();
    }
```

In the snippet, we have defined the initial trigger as INITIAL_TRIGGER_ENTER, which means that, if a user is already present in the Geofence, the enter transition will be triggered.

To add the geofence, the GeofencingApi.addGeofences() method is used. It processes the callback in the onResult() callback method. Similarly, Geofences can be removed by the removeGeofences() method.

The complete `MainActivity` code is as follows:

```java
package com.raj.map;

import android.app.Activity;
import android.app.PendingIntent;
import android.content.Intent;
import android.location.Location;
import android.os.Bundle;
import android.util.Log;
import android.view.View;
import android.widget.Toast;

import com.google.android.gms.common.ConnectionResult;
import com.google.android.gms.common.api.GoogleApiClient;
import com.google.android.gms.common.api.ResultCallback;
import com.google.android.gms.common.api.Status;
import com.google.android.gms.location.Geofence;
import com.google.android.gms.location.GeofencingRequest;
import com.google.android.gms.location.LocationServices;

import java.util.ArrayList;


public class MainActivity extends Activity implements
        GoogleApiClient.ConnectionCallbacks, GoogleApiClient.
OnConnectionFailedListener, ResultCallback<Status> {


    GoogleApiClient googleApiClient;
    protected ArrayList<Geofence> geofences;
    private PendingIntent geofencePendingIntent;
    Location location;


    @Override
    protected void onCreate(Bundle savedInstanceState) {
        super.onCreate(savedInstanceState);
        setContentView(R.layout.activity_main);
        googleApiClient = new GoogleApiClient.Builder(this)
                .addConnectionCallbacks(this)
                .addOnConnectionFailedListener(this)
                .addApi(LocationServices.API)
                .build();
```

```java
            googleApiClient.connect();

            geofences = new ArrayList<Geofence>();

            geofences.add(new Geofence.Builder().setRequestId("1")
                    .setCircularRegion(
                            8.1780967, 77.4068884, 100f
                    )
                    .setExpirationDuration(20000)
                    .setTransitionTypes(Geofence.GEOFENCE_TRANSITION_ENTER
| Geofence.GEOFENCE_TRANSITION_EXIT)
                    .build());

    @Override
    public void onConnected(Bundle bundle) {

            location = LocationServices.FusedLocationApi.getLastLocation(g
oogleApiClient);
            if(location != null){
            Log.d("Lat",location.getLatitude()+"");
            Log.d("Lng", location.getLongitude() + "");}



            LocationServices.GeofencingApi.addGeofences(
                    googleApiClient,
                    getGeofencingRequest(),
                    getGeofencePendingIntent()
            ).setResultCallback(this);

    }

    private PendingIntent getGeofencePendingIntent() {
        if (geofencePendingIntent != null) {
            return geofencePendingIntent;
        }
        Intent intent = new Intent(this, GeofenceTransitionService.
class);
        return PendingIntent.getService(this, 0, intent,
PendingIntent.
                FLAG_UPDATE_CURRENT);
    }

    private GeofencingRequest getGeofencingRequest() {
```

```
        GeofencingRequest.Builder builder = new GeofencingRequest.
    Builder();
        builder.setInitialTrigger(GeofencingRequest.INITIAL_TRIGGER_
    ENTER);
        builder.addGeofences(geofences);
        return builder.build();
    }
    @Override
    public void onConnectionSuspended(int i) {
    }

    @Override
    public void onConnectionFailed(ConnectionResult connectionResult)
    {
    }

    @Override
    public void onResult(Status status) {
        if (status.isSuccess()) {
            Toast.makeText(getApplicationContext(),"Geofence
    added",Toast.LENGTH_LONG).show();
        }
    }
}
```

`MainActivity.java`

A toast is displayed when the Geofence is added. While testing the code, if the user is present inside the Geofence or enters the Geofence, the log is printed similar to:

```
D/Update: Entered Geofence
```

Integrating location data with maps

In our previous sections, such as working with the Android Location API and working with the Google Play services Location API, we learned how to obtain location data in different ways. Integrating location data with the map makes it more interesting. Let's finish this chapter with a simple example that has location data integrated with maps.

In this example, I am going to display a marker in my last known location.

The layout code is as follows:

```xml
<?xml version="1.0" encoding="utf-8"?>
<fragment xmlns:android="http://schemas.android.com/apk/res/android"
    android:id="@+id/map"
    android:layout_width="match_parent"
    android:layout_height="match_parent"
    android:name="com.google.android.gms.maps.MapFragment" />
```

activity_maps.xml

The complete `MapsActivity` code is:

```java
package com.raj.map;

import android.app.Activity;
import android.location.Location;
import android.os.Bundle;


import com.google.android.gms.common.ConnectionResult;
import com.google.android.gms.common.api.GoogleApiClient;
import com.google.android.gms.location.LocationServices;
import com.google.android.gms.maps.GoogleMap;
import com.google.android.gms.maps.MapFragment;
import com.google.android.gms.maps.model.LatLng;
import com.google.android.gms.maps.model.MarkerOptions;

public class MapsActivity extends Activity implements GoogleApiClient.
ConnectionCallbacks, GoogleApiClient.OnConnectionFailedListener{

    GoogleApiClient googleApiClient;
    Location location;
    GoogleMap map;


    @Override
    protected void onCreate(Bundle savedInstanceState) {
        super.onCreate(savedInstanceState);
        setContentView(R.layout.activity_maps);
        googleApiClient = new GoogleApiClient.Builder(this)
                .addConnectionCallbacks(this)
                .addOnConnectionFailedListener(this)
                .addApi(LocationServices.API)
                .build();
```

```
        googleApiClient.connect();

        MapFragment mapFragment = (MapFragment)getFragmentManager().
findFragmentById(R.id.map);
        map = mapFragment.getMap();
    }

    @Override
    public void onConnected(Bundle bundle) {
        location = LocationServices.FusedLocationApi.getLastLocation(g
oogleApiClient);
        if(location != null)
            map.addMarker(new MarkerOptions().position(new
LatLng(location.getLatitude(),location.getLongitude()))).setTitle("My
Location");

    }

    @Override
    public void onConnectionSuspended(int i) {
    }

    @Override
    public void onConnectionFailed(ConnectionResult connectionResult)
{
    }
}
```

MapsActivity.java

When you execute the code, you will see a map with a marker at your current location.

Self-test questions

Q1. Which permission allows you to retrieve a location using GPS?

1. ACCESS_FINE_LOCATION
2. ACCESS_COARSE_LOCATION

Q2. Which of these has more accuracy?

1. GPS Satellite
2. Wi-Fi
3. Cell phone towers

Q3. Fused location providers can be used to retrieve the device's last known location.

1.   True
2.   False

Q4. Network providers determine the location using Wi-Fi and cell phone towers.

1.   True
2.   False

Q5. Geofence is provided by the Android framework Location API?

1.   True
2.   False

Summary

In this chapter, we learned about working with location data. We learned about the different ways of retrieving location data with the Android framework Location API and the Google Play services Location API. Then, we learned about location updates and the usage of Geofence. Finally, we finished the chapter with an example which integrated location data with a map.

In our next chapter, we will learn about Street View.

Know about the Street View

8

In our previous chapter, we learned how to work with location data. In this chapter, we are going to learn about Street View. For anyone who does not know about Street View, it provides a 360-degree view for roads and specific locations. Google provides an excellent API to integrate this with our application. Let's do it!

In this chapter, we will cover the following topics:

- About Google Street View
- Prerequisites
- Implementing StreetViewPanoramaFragment
- Customize StreetViewPanorama
- Using custom camera views
- Other functions

About Google Street View

Google Street View is a service launched by Google and it is used in Google Earth and Google Maps. It provides a 360-degree panoramic view across roads and some specific locations.

This image is an example of Street View at Hoover Dam. The street view makes it easy to learn about a particular location in detail. Let's learn about it in the forthcoming sections.

Prerequisites

The prerequisites for Google Street View are:

- Make sure you have properly configured Google Play services for the project
- Add the required permissions

Implementing StreetViewPanoramaFragment

Until now, we have used `MapFragment` to integrate Google Maps with our application. However, to integrate street view with our application, we need to use `StreetViewPanoramaFragment` instead of `MapFragment`.

Add the following code to your main activity's layout file:

```xml
<?xml version="1.0" encoding="utf-8"?>
<fragment xmlns:android="http://schemas.android.com/apk/res/android"
    android:id="@+id/map"
    android:layout_width="match_parent"
    android:layout_height="match_parent"
    android:name="com.google.android.gms.maps.
StreetViewPanoramaFragment" />
```

`activity_maps.xml`

The `android:name` attribute in the earlier fragment specifies the `StreetViewPanoramaFragment` class to instantiate the layout. The `android:id` attribute defines a unique ID for our fragment. This code only works for API 12 or greater (Honeycomb or later versions). To support lower versions of Android, you need to use `SupportStreetViewPanoramaFragment`.

Then, in our activity, we will need to implement the `OnStreetViewPanoramaReadyCallback` interface to use it with a callback method.

The `onStreetViewPanoramaReady()` callback method is executed when the Street View Panorama is ready. The `StreetViewPanoramaFragment` is instantiated by:

```java
StreetViewPanoramaFragment streetViewPanoramaFragment =
(StreetViewPanoramaFragment) getFragmentManager().findFragmentById(R.
id.map);
```

The `getStreetViewPanoramaAsync()` method is called on the `StreetViewPanoramaFragment` object to set the callback. It is executed in the main thread, as we have seen before for `MapFragment`.

In the callback method, we are setting the position of the panorama. The complete activity code is as follows:

```
package com.raj.map;

import android.app.Activity;
import android.os.Bundle;

import com.google.android.gms.maps.OnStreetViewPanoramaReadyCallback;
import com.google.android.gms.maps.StreetViewPanorama;
import com.google.android.gms.maps.StreetViewPanoramaFragment;
import com.google.android.gms.maps.model.LatLng;


public class MapsActivity extends Activity implements
OnStreetViewPanoramaReadyCallback {

    static final LatLng NEWARK = new LatLng(40.735188, -74.172414);


    @Override
    protected void onCreate(Bundle savedInstanceState) {
        super.onCreate(savedInstanceState);
        setContentView(R.layout.activity_maps);
        StreetViewPanoramaFragment streetViewPanoramaFragment =
(StreetViewPanoramaFragment) getFragmentManager().findFragmentById(R.
id.map);
        streetViewPanoramaFragment.getStreetViewPanoramaAsync(this);
    }

    @Override
    public void onStreetViewPanoramaReady(StreetViewPanorama panorama)
{
        panorama.setPosition(NEWARK);
    }
}
```

`MapsActivity.java`

Initially, we were implementing the `OnStreetViewPanoramaReadyCallback` interface. Then, we defined the `LatLng` coordinates for Newark.

Then, the `StreetViewPanoramaFragment` is instantiated and the callback method is set. In the callback, when the `StreetViewPanorama` is ready, the position will be set as `Newark` city. The position can be set by calling the `setPosition()` method on the `StreetViewPanorama` object. It is done as follows:

```
panorama.setPosition(NEWARK);
```

When we execute the code, the Street View of the location, Newark, will be rendered in our application with navigation controls.

The screenshot will be similar to the following:

You can take a look at the screenshot. The street name is displayed on the road and two arrows are displayed for navigation.

To support lower API, we need to use SupportStreetViewPanoramaFragment. Let's discuss how we can do it. The layout code is as follows:

```xml
<?xml version="1.0" encoding="utf-8"?>
<fragment xmlns:android="http://schemas.android.com/apk/res/android"
    android:id="@+id/map"
    android:layout_width="match_parent"
    android:layout_height="match_parent"
        android:name="com.google.android.gms.maps.
SupportStreetViewPanoramaFragment" />
```

activity_maps.xml

Here, the android:name attribute in the earlier fragment specifies the SupportStreetViewPanoramaFragment class to instantiate the layout.

The activity code is as follows:

```java
package com.raj.map;

import android.os.Bundle;
import android.support.v4.app.FragmentActivity;

import com.google.android.gms.maps.OnStreetViewPanoramaReadyCallback;
import com.google.android.gms.maps.StreetViewPanorama;
import com.google.android.gms.maps.SupportStreetViewPanoramaFragment;
import com.google.android.gms.maps.model.LatLng;


public class MapsActivity extends FragmentActivity implements
OnStreetViewPanoramaReadyCallback {

    static final LatLng NEWARK = new LatLng(40.735188, -74.172414);


    @Override
    protected void onCreate(Bundle savedInstanceState) {
        super.onCreate(savedInstanceState);
        setContentView(R.layout.activity_maps);
        SupportStreetViewPanoramaFragment streetViewPanoramaFragment
= (SupportStreetViewPanoramaFragment) getSupportFragmentManager().
findFragmentById(R.id.map);
```

```
        streetViewPanoramaFragment.getStreetViewPanoramaAsync(this);
    }

    @Override
    public void onStreetViewPanoramaReady(StreetViewPanorama panorama)
{
        panorama.setPosition(NEWARK);
    }
}
```

MapsActivity.java

Here, in the code, our activity extends to the FragmentActivity class. We use the SupportStreetViewPanorama class and support fragment manager. The rest remains the same. These are similar to the ones we used in *Chapter 2, Configuring an API Key and Creating Our First Map Application*. When we execute the code, we will get the same results.

In the previous example, we have used the OnStreetViewPanoramaReadyCallback interface. However, what if we do not want to implement the interface using a callback method?

The following code will do this:

```
package com.raj.map;

import android.app.Activity;
import android.os.Bundle;

import com.google.android.gms.maps.StreetViewPanorama;
import com.google.android.gms.maps.StreetViewPanoramaFragment;
import com.google.android.gms.maps.model.LatLng;


public class MapsActivity extends Activity{

    static final LatLng NEWARK = new LatLng(40.735188, -74.172414);


    @Override
    protected void onCreate(Bundle savedInstanceState) {
        super.onCreate(savedInstanceState);
        setContentView(R.layout.activity_maps);
```

```
        StreetViewPanoramaFragment streetViewPanoramaFragment =
    (StreetViewPanoramaFragment) getFragmentManager().findFragmentById(R.
    id.map);

        StreetViewPanorama panorama = streetViewPanoramaFragment.
    getStreetViewPanorama();
        panorama.setPosition(NEWARK);
    }
}
```

`MapsActivity.java`

In the earlier code, we made some small changes. We are not using the callback method. The `StreetViewPanorama` object is obtained by calling the `getStreetViewPanorama()` method on the `StreetViewPanoramaFragment` object.

Then, we call the `setPosition()` method on the `StreetViewPanorama` object to set Newark as the location.

Adding StreetViewPanoramaFragment programmatically

In this section, we are going to learn how to create the `StreetViewPanoramaFragment` dynamically and render the layout. The layout code is as follows:

```xml
<LinearLayout xmlns:android="http://schemas.android.com/apk/res/
android"
    android:layout_width="match_parent"
    android:layout_height="match_parent"
    android:orientation="horizontal">
    <FrameLayout
        android:id="@+id/content_frame"
        android:layout_width="match_parent"
        android:layout_height="match_parent" />
</LinearLayout>
```

`activity_maps.xml`

We are using `FrameLayout` in our layout and dynamically replacing replacing the `FrameLayout` content with `StreetViewPanoramaFragment`.

The activity code is as follows:

```
package com.raj.map;

import android.app.Activity;
import android.app.Fragment;
import android.app.FragmentTransaction;
import android.os.Bundle;

import com.google.android.gms.maps.StreetViewPanoramaFragment;
import com.google.android.gms.maps.StreetViewPanoramaOptions;
import com.google.android.gms.maps.model.LatLng;

public class MapsActivity extends Activity {
    static final LatLng NEWARK = new LatLng(40.735188, -74.172414);
    Fragment streetViewPanoramaFragment;

    @Override
    protected void onCreate(Bundle savedInstanceState) {
        super.onCreate(savedInstanceState);
        setContentView(R.layout.activity_maps);
        StreetViewPanoramaOptions streetViewPanoramaOptions = new
StreetViewPanoramaOptions();
        streetViewPanoramaOptions.position(NEWARK);

        streetViewPanoramaFragment = StreetViewPanoramaFragment.newIns
tance(streetViewPanoramaOptions);
        FragmentTransaction fragmentTransaction =
getFragmentManager().beginTransaction();
        fragmentTransaction.add(R.id.content_frame,
streetViewPanoramaFragment);
        fragmentTransaction.commit();

    }}
```

MapsActivity.java

In the earlier code, we are creating a StreetViewPanoramaOptions object.
The position of the street view is set by calling the position() method on
the StreetViewPanoramaOptions object by passing the LatLng coordinates
of Newark city.

Then, we are creating a new instance of StreetViewPanoramaFragment by calling
the newInstance() method with the StreetViewPanoramaOptions object.

We create `fragmentTransaction` as an object for the `FragmentTransaction` class. Then, we use the `add()` method to insert `StreetViewPanoramaFragment` in `FrameLayout`.

Finally, the `commit()` method is called to apply the changes.

The result obtained using this code will be similar to the one obtained in previous sections.

Customizing StreetViewPanorama

In this section, we are going to customize user-controlled features such as zoom gestures, pan gestures, navigation icons, and so on. We are going to learn about:

- Disabling/enabling pan gestures
- Disabling/enabling user navigation
- Disabling/enabling zoom gestures
- Disabling/enabling the street name
- Working with click events
- Listening to panorama change events

Disabling/enabling pan gestures

By default, pan gestures are enabled. These help us move around in the street view. To disable this, we can call the `setPanningGesturesEnabled()` method on the `StreetViewPanorama` object, which will take Boolean as a parameter. The code would be similar to:

```
panorama.setPanningGesturesEnabled(false);
```

In the earlier code, the panorama is the `StreetViewPanorama` object.

Disabling/enabling user navigation

By default, user navigation is enabled and directional arrows are visible for navigation. Take a look at the following image:

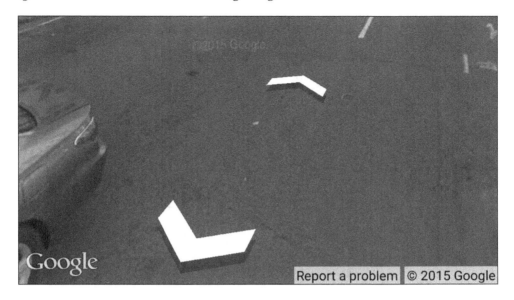

In the earlier image, you can see the two directional arrows displayed for navigation. To disable this, we can call the setUserNavigationEnabled() method on the StreetViewPanorama object, which will take Boolean as a parameter. The code would be similar to:

```
panorama.setUserNavigationEnabled(false);
```

Disabling/enabling zoom gestures

By default, zoom gestures are enabled. It helps us retrieve more detailed information. To disable this, we can call the setZoomGesturesEnabled() method on the StreetViewPanorama object, which will take a Boolean as a parameter. The code would be similar to:

```
panorama.setZoomGesturesEnabled(false);
```

Disabling/enabling the street name

By default, the street name of the corresponding street is displayed in the street view. Take a look at the following image:

In the earlier image, the street name is displayed along the road. To disable this, we can call the `setStreetNamesEnabled()` method on the `StreetViewPanorama` object, which will take Boolean as a parameter. The code would be similar to:

```
panorama.setStreetNamesEnabled(false);
```

Let's test this with an example. I am disabling all the user functions. The code in the callback method is as follows:

```
@Override
public void onStreetViewPanoramaReady(StreetViewPanorama panorama)
{
    panorama.setPosition(NEWARK);
    panorama.setPanningGesturesEnabled(false);
    panorama.setUserNavigationEnabled(false);
    panorama.setZoomGesturesEnabled(false);
    panorama.setStreetNamesEnabled(false);
}
```

In the earlier code, I am setting the position of `StreetViewPanorama` as `Newark` by calling the `setPosition()` method.

Disabling panning gestures by calling the `setPanningGesturesEnabled()` method.

Disabling user navigation by calling the `setUserNavigationEnabled()` method.

Disabling zoom gestures by calling the `setZoomGesturesEnabled()` method.

Disabling the street name by calling the `setStreetNamesEnabled()` method.

When we run the code, we will get the following output with all functions disabled:

Working with click events

Similar to the event listeners in normal Google Maps, we can also attach event listeners to StreetViewPanorama such as single tap and long press. To handle the click event, we must use the OnStreetViewPanoramaClickListener() method on the StreetViewPanorama object. To enable it, we can call the setOnStreetViewPanoramaClickListener() method on the GoogleMap object, which will take the StreetViewPanorama.OnStreetViewPanoramaClickListener() interface as a parameter. The code in the callback method is as follows:

```
@Override
    public void onStreetViewPanoramaReady(final StreetViewPanorama
panorama) {
        panorama.setPosition(NEWARK);
        panorama.setOnStreetViewPanoramaClickListener(new
StreetViewPanorama.OnStreetViewPanoramaClickListener() {
            @Override
            public void onStreetViewPanoramaClick(StreetViewPanoramaOr
ientation streetViewPanoramaOrientation) {

                float tilt = streetViewPanoramaOrientation.tilt;
                float bearing = streetViewPanoramaOrientation.bearing;
                Toast.makeText(getApplicationContext(),"Tilt :
"+tilt+" Bearing : "+bearing,Toast.LENGTH_SHORT).show();
            }
        });

    }
```

When you execute this code and tap on the location, it will display a toast with tilt and bearing.

Listening to panorama change events

We can listen to panorama change events (when you are navigating to another location using front or back). To achieve this, we need to use the OnStreetViewPanoramaChangeListener interface on the StreetViewPanorama object. The onStreetViewPanoramaChange() method is called when this occurs.

We can obtain the LatLng position from the StreetViewPanoramaLocation object. Also, we can obtain links. What are links? It is the other panorama that the current view is linked to.

The example code in the callback method is as follows:

```
@Override
 public void onStreetViewPanoramaReady(final StreetViewPanorama
panorama) {
     panorama.setPosition(NEWARK);
     panorama.setOnStreetViewPanoramaChangeListener(new
StreetViewPanorama.OnStreetViewPanoramaChangeListener() {
         @Override
         public void onStreetViewPanoramaChange(StreetViewPanoramaL
ocation streetViewPanoramaLocation) {
             LatLng location = streetViewPanoramaLocation.position;
             Log.d("Panorama Change","Location " +location +",
Links : "+streetViewPanoramaLocation.links.length );

         }
     });
 }
```

When the panorama is changed, a message is printed in log with the LatLng coordinates and the number of links.

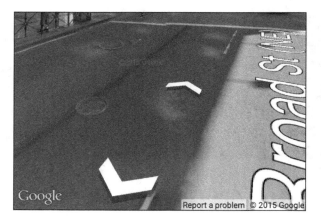

The corresponding message printed in log is:

```
D/Panorama Change: Location lat/lng: (40.735200999999996,-74.172422),
Links : 2
D/Panorama Change: Location lat/lng: (40.735285,-74.172375), Links :
2
D/Panorama Change: Location lat/lng: (40.735369999999996,-74.172328),
Links : 2
```

Here, the `LatLng` coordinates are printed along with the number of links. It is linked to two panoramas because navigation is only possible in two directions.

Take a look at the following image:

The earlier image indicates a view of a four-way crossroads, where it is possible to navigate in four directions. Here, the link is 4, since the view is linked to four panoramas. The corresponding log will be:

```
D/Panorama Change: Location lat/lng: (40.735603,-74.17219899999999),
Links : 4
D/Panorama Change: Location lat/lng: (40.735583,-74.172145), Links :
4
```

Using custom camera views

Until now, we have manually changed the camera view by panning and zooming. Let's see how we can do it programmatically.

To do this, we need to use the `StreetViewPanoramaCamera` object. Create a `StreetViewPanoramaCamera` object by using the nested `StreetViewPanoramaCamera.Builder` class. We can set the tilt, zoom, and bearing of the street view. The methods are as follows:

Method	Parameter	Function
`zoom()`	Zoom level in float	By default, the zoom level is 0. The maximum zoom level depends on the panorama. If the zoom level is specified in a negative value, it is set to 0.
`tilt()`	Tilt angle in float	Sets the tilt angle of the camera from the horizon of the panorama. The angle ranges between -90 and 90.
`bearing()`	Bearing angle in float	Sets the bearing angle. It fixes the camera in degrees clockwise from north.

To set a camera view with a zoom level of 2, and the bearing and tilt angle as 45 degrees, I would use the code:

```
StreetViewPanoramaCamera camera = new StreetViewPanoramaCamera.
Builder()
                    .zoom(2)
                    .bearing(45)
                    .tilt(45)
                    .build();
```

Here, I have created a `StreetViewPanoramaCamera` object named `camera` with the nested `StreetViewPanoramaCamera.Builder` class. By using the `zoom()`, `bearing()`, and `tilt()` methods, I have set the zoom level as 2, the bearing and tilt angle as 45 degrees.

Finally, to animate the camera from the current view to the new view, we need to use the `animateTo()` method on the `StreetViewPanorama` object. It takes the parameter as the `StreetCamera` object and the animation's duration in milliseconds.

The code will be similar to:

```
panorama.animateTo(camera,500);
```

Here, panorama is the StreetViewPanorama object and camera is the
StreetViewPanoramaCamera object. 500 is the duration in milliseconds.

Let's create an example application similar to what we created in *Chapter 6, Working
with Custom Views*. When you tap the panorama view anywhere, a dialog pops up
and asks for zoom, tilt, and bearing as input values. Then, it animates the camera to
the new view corresponding to the input values.

Our main layout is the same as the one we used before with
StreetViewPanoramaFragment. The code for the custom camera dialog is as follows:

```xml
<?xml version="1.0" encoding="utf-8"?>
<LinearLayout xmlns:android="http://schemas.android.com/apk/res/
android"
    android:layout_width="match_parent"
    android:layout_height="match_parent"
    android:orientation="vertical">

    <EditText
        android:id="@+id/zoom"
        android:hint="Zoom"
        android:inputType="number"
        android:layout_width="match_parent"
        android:layout_height="wrap_content" />
    <EditText
        android:id="@+id/bearing"
        android:hint="Bearing"
        android:inputType="number"
        android:layout_width="match_parent"
        android:layout_height="wrap_content" />
    <EditText
        android:id="@+id/tilt"
        android:hint="Tilt"
        android:inputType="number"
        android:layout_width="match_parent"
        android:layout_height="wrap_content" />

    <Button
        android:id="@+id/button"
        android:text="Move Camera"
        android:inputType="number"
        android:layout_width="match_parent"
        android:layout_height="wrap_content" />

</LinearLayout>
```

dialog_camera.xml

We are obtaining the zoom, tilt, and bearing as inputs from the user to animate the new camera view. The code for our activity is as follows:

```
package com.raj.map;

import android.app.Activity;
import android.app.Dialog;
import android.os.Bundle;
import android.view.View;
import android.widget.Button;
import android.widget.EditText;

import com.google.android.gms.maps.OnStreetViewPanoramaReadyCallback;
import com.google.android.gms.maps.StreetViewPanorama;
import com.google.android.gms.maps.StreetViewPanoramaFragment;
import com.google.android.gms.maps.model.LatLng;
import com.google.android.gms.maps.model.StreetViewPanoramaCamera;
import com.google.android.gms.maps.model.
StreetViewPanoramaOrientation;


public class MapsActivity extends Activity implements
OnStreetViewPanoramaReadyCallback {

    Dialog cameraDialog;
    EditText zoom,tilt,bearing;
    Button move_camera;

    static final LatLng AGRA = new LatLng(27.174356, 78.042183);


    @Override
    protected void onCreate(Bundle savedInstanceState) {
        super.onCreate(savedInstanceState);
        setContentView(R.layout.activity_maps);
        StreetViewPanoramaFragment streetViewPanoramaFragment =
(StreetViewPanoramaFragment) getFragmentManager().findFragmentById(R.
id.map);
        streetViewPanoramaFragment.getStreetViewPanoramaAsync(this);
        cameraDialog = new Dialog(this);
        cameraDialog.setTitle("Move Camera");
        cameraDialog.setContentView(R.layout.dialog_camera);

        zoom = (EditText)cameraDialog.findViewById(R.id.zoom);
        tilt = (EditText)cameraDialog.findViewById(R.id.tilt);
        bearing = (EditText)cameraDialog.findViewById(R.id.bearing);
        move_camera = (Button)cameraDialog.findViewById(R.id.button);
```

```
        }

    @Override
    public void onStreetViewPanoramaReady(final StreetViewPanorama
panorama) {
        panorama.setPosition(AGRA);
        panorama.setOnStreetViewPanoramaClickListener(new
StreetViewPanorama.OnStreetViewPanoramaClickListener() {
            @Override
            public void onStreetViewPanoramaClick(StreetViewPanoramaOr
ientation streetViewPanoramaOrientation) {
                cameraDialog.show();
            }
        });

        move_camera.setOnClickListener(new View.OnClickListener() {
            @Override
            public void onClick(View v) {
                String zoomText = zoom.getText().toString();
                String tiltText = tilt.getText().toString();
                String bearingText = bearing.getText().toString();

if (!TextUtils.isEmpty(zoomText) && !TextUtils.isEmpty(tiltText) &
!TextUtils.isEmpty(bearingText)) {
                                try {
                    StreetViewPanoramaCamera camera = new
StreetViewPanoramaCamera.Builder()
                            .zoom(Float.valueOf(zoomText))
                            .bearing(Float.valueOf(tiltText))
                            .tilt(Float.valueOf(bearingText))
                            .build();
                    panorama.animateTo(camera, 500);
                    cameraDialog.dismiss();
                } catch (NumberFormatException nfe) {
                        Log.d("Map", "Number Format Error");
                        cameraDialog.dismiss();
                }

            }
        }
    });
    }
}
```

MapsActivity.java

This application combines the concepts we learned in the previous sections. We use the `OnStreetViewPanoramaClickListener` interface to listen for click events. We obtain the values from the `EditText` widgets and create a `StreetViewPanoramaCamera` object with the obtained values. Then, we use the `animateTo()` method to change the camera view to the new location.

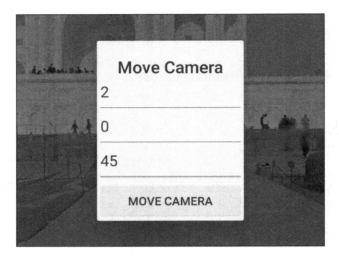

In the earlier image, I have set the zoom level to 2, the bearing angle to 0 degrees, and tilt angle to 45 degrees. When you press the **MOVE CAMERA** button, the camera view will animate to the new view.

Other functions

In this section, we are going to learn about some other functions that may be useful at times. They are:

- Orientation to point
- Point to orientation
- Getting the location

Orientation to point

This helps us convert the screen orientation into point coordinates in screen pixels. This can be done by calling the orientationToPoint() method on the StreetViewPanorama object. It takes the StreetViewPanoramaOrientation object as a parameter. Take a look at the following code in the callback method:

```
@Override
public void onStreetViewPanoramaReady(final StreetViewPanorama
panorama) {
    panorama.setPosition(AGRA);
    panorama.setOnStreetViewPanoramaClickListener(new
StreetViewPanorama.OnStreetViewPanoramaClickListener() {
        @Override
        public void onStreetViewPanoramaClick(StreetViewPanoramaOr
ientation streetViewPanoramaOrientation) {
            Point point = panorama.orientationToPoint(streetViewPa
noramaOrientation);
            Log.d("Orientation","Tilt :
"+streetViewPanoramaOrientation.tilt +" Bearing :
"+streetViewPanoramaOrientation.bearing);
            Log.d("Orientation","X : "+point.x +" Y : "+point.y);
        }
    });
}
```

In the earlier code, we converted the orientation into screen pixel coordinates. When you tap anywhere on the panorama view, the StreetViewPanoramaOrientation object will be passed to the orientationToPoint() method. It will return the X and Y coordinates as Point. The log output obtained will be similar to:

```
D/Orientation: Tilt : 9.8761215 Bearing : 22.228474
D/Orientation: X : 917 Y : 750
D/Orientation: Tilt : -4.1924515 Bearing : 343.57178
D/Orientation: X : 268 Y : 993
```

Point to orientation

Similar to the orientation to point function, we can convert the point to an orientation. To achieve this, we need to use the pointToOrientation() method on the StreetViewPanorama object. It takes screen pixels as coordinates. The example code I used is:

```
StreetViewPanoramaOrientation orientation = panorama.
pointToOrientation(new Point(400,300));
Log.d("Orientation","Tilt : "+orientation.tilt +" Bearing :
"+orientation.bearing);
```

In the earlier code, I used the coordinates as 400 and 300. The result obtained by log is:

```
D/Orientation: Tilt : 33.709534 Bearing : 351.37054
```

Getting the location

There may be a situation when you may have to obtain the LatLng coordinates of the present location when you navigate in the panorama view. On calling the getLocation() method on the StreetViewPanorama object, the function will return the StreetViewPanoramaLocation object. From this, we can retrieve the LatLng coordinates. The code I used is:

```
LatLng location = panorama.getLocation().position;
Log.d("Location","Latitude : "+location.latitude +" Longitude :
"+location.longitude);
```

It will return a log message similar to:

```
D/Location: Latitude : 27.172926 Longitude : 78.04201499999999
```

Self-test questions

Q1. Street view provides which view?

1. 360 degree view
2. 180 degree view
3. 90 degree view

Q2. What should we use to implement Street View?

1. `MapFragment`
2. `StreetViewPanoramaFragment`

Q3. To support lower API devices, we should use which function?

1. `SupportStreetViewPanoramaFragment`
2. `StreetViewPanoramaFragment`

Q4. The `setPosition()` method is used to set the location.

1. True
2. False

Q5. The `setStreetNamesEnabled()` method is used to disable/enable the street name.

1. True
2. False

Summary

In this chapter, we learned about Street View. We learned how to add `StreetViewPanoramaFragment` and also support lower API devices with `SupportStreetViewPanoramaFragment`. We learned how to disable custom user functions. Also, we worked with click events and change events. Then, we learned about using custom camera views. Finally, we finished the chapter with some other functions, such as orientation to point.

In the next chapter, we are going to learn about Google Map Intents.

Google Maps Intents

In the previous chapter, we learned how to work with Street View. In this chapter, we are going to work with Google Maps Intents. Instead of displaying maps and panoramas in our application, we are going to use the native Google Maps application to perform tasks. Let's discuss this in detail.

In this chapter, we will cover the following topics:

- Need for Google Maps Intents
- Define Intent requests
- Display maps
- Search locations
- Using navigation
- Display StreetViewPanorama

The need for Google Maps Intents

Sometimes, there are situations where you do not want to make your app complex by natively rendering the map in your application. Also, it is a tedious task to develop a turn-by-turn navigation app. In these situations, we can launch the native Google Maps application to perform tasks, since the application is preinstalled on most of the Android devices.

Defining Intent requests

Before defining Intent requests, let's learn some basics about Intents. Intents help us launch an activity of our own application or another application. Google Maps provides several Intents that can be used with our application. Four operations can be performed using Google Maps. They are as follows:

- Display a map in Google Maps of a specified location with a specified zoom level
- Search for a specified location and display it on Google Maps
- Display turn-by-turn navigation using one of the three modes: driving, walking, and bicycling
- Display the Street View imagery

To make an Intent request, we must initially define an `Intent` object. The Intent should contain three components. They are:

- Action
- URI
- Package

Let's discuss this in detail.

Action

It defines what action should be performed. Here, we use an action to view the data. It is given as: `ACTION_VIEW`.

The action is usually set in Intent as:

```
Intent intent = new Intent(Intent.ACTION_VIEW, intentUri);
```

URI

URIs are used to specify a desired action. It also provides data, which performs an action. The URI to display a map is as follows:

```
Uri intentUri = Uri.parse("geo:27.174356, 78.042183");
```

Here, the keyword `geo` defines the action to display a map at the specified coordinates.

Package

We need to set the package of Google Maps to handle the Intent. If no package is set, the system provides an option to select the app that can handle the Intent:

```
intent.setPackage("com.google.android.apps.maps");
```

Here, `intent` is the Intent object. The `com.google.android.apps.maps` term is the package name of the native Google Maps application.

Finally, Google Maps can be started by:

```
startActivity(intent);
```

Problems occur at a time when there is no app to handle the Intent. So, we need to check whether the app exists before we start the activity. It can be checked by calling the `resolveActivity()` method on the `Intent` object.

The safest implementation is:

```
if (intent.resolveActivity(getPackageManager()) != null) {
    startActivity(intent);
}
```

Display maps

In this section, we are going to learn how to display a desired location in Google Maps. Here, we need to use the keyword `geo` along with the coordinates that should be displayed in the map. Let's test this with an example.

Our main layout consists of only a single button, which helps us launch Google Maps. The code is as follows:

```
<LinearLayout xmlns:android="http://schemas.android.com/apk/res/
android"
    android:layout_width="match_parent"
    android:layout_height="match_parent"
    android:gravity="center"
    android:orientation="vertical">
    <Button
        android:id="@+id/btn"
        android:text="Display in Google map"
        android:layout_width="wrap_content"
        android:layout_height="wrap_content" />
</LinearLayout>
```

activity_maps.xml

Our activity contains the code to handle the click button. It checks whether Google Maps exists. If it exists, it will launch the application. The code is as follows:

```
package com.raj.map;

import android.app.Activity;
import android.content.Intent;
import android.net.Uri;
import android.os.Bundle;
import android.view.View;
import android.widget.Button;

import com.google.android.gms.maps.model.LatLng;


public class MapsActivity extends Activity{

    static final LatLng AGRA = new LatLng(27.174356, 78.042183);
    Button launch;

    @Override
    protected void onCreate(Bundle savedInstanceState) {
        super.onCreate(savedInstanceState);
        setContentView(R.layout.activity_maps);
        launch = (Button)findViewById(R.id.btn);
        launch.setOnClickListener(new View.OnClickListener() {
            @Override
            public void onClick(View v) {
                launchMap();
            }
        });
    }

    public void launchMap(){


    String uriString = String.format("geo:%f,%f", AGRA.latitude,
      AGRA.longitude);
        Uri intentUri = Uri.parse(uriString);
        Intent intent = new Intent(Intent.ACTION_VIEW, intentUri);
        intent.setPackage("com.google.android.apps.maps");

        if (intent.resolveActivity(getPackageManager()) != null) {
```

```
                    startActivity(intent);
                }
            }
        }
```

MapsActivity.java

Here, we launched Google Maps and displayed the location, Agra. We created a separate launchMap function, which is called to launch the application and display the location.

First, we created a URI encoded string. Then, we set the action for our Intent. We set the Google Maps package by calling the setPackage() method on the Intent object, and checked whether the package exists using the resolveActivity() method on the Intent object. Finally, the activity was launched using startActivity().

There should not be any change in the URI format. It should be similar to geo:latitude,longitude. If there is a problem with the format, the location will not be displayed.

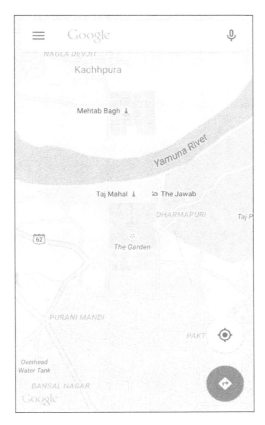

Display maps with a specified zoom level

In the previous section, we learned how to display a location in Google Maps. We are now going to learn how to display a location with the help of zoom levels. Zoom levels range from `0` and `21`. It is specified by the `z` parameter and it should be in the following format:

```
geo:latitude,longitude?z=zoom
```

In the previous code, change the URI as follows:

```
String uriString = String.format("geo:%f,%f?z=%d",
    AGRA.latitude, AGRA.longitude,12);
```

Here, in the code, we added the `z` parameter with its value as `12`, indicating the zoom level. When you execute it, you will get an output similar to following screenshot:

Searching for a location

In the previous section, we displayed a location on the map using its coordinates. Now, let's discuss how to search for and display a location using a string query. It can be done in the following ways:

- `geo:latitude,longitude?q=my+street+address`

- `geo:0,0?q=my+street+address`

- `geo:0,0?q=latitude,longitude(label)`

For zoom, we use the `z` parameter. Here, we used `q` as the parameter. In the second and third way, we used `0,0` as the latitude and longitude and passed the query. The map takes the coordinates `0,0` as the base and begins its search. There may be situations where the same address may exist in many places all over the world. To prevent this confusion, we use the latitude and longitude as a specified value instead of `0,0`. So, it looks for the address near the coordinates.

The street name should be separated by +.

The `q` parameter defines the location to be highlighted in the map. Some places in the map are identified by a label. In these situations, we can use the label to search the location.

Let's now search and display a location in the map. The complete code in the `launchMap()` method is as follows:

```
public void launchMap(){
    Uri intentUri = Uri.parse("geo:0,0?q=Agra,+Uttar+Pradesh,+Ind
ia");

    Intent intent = new Intent(Intent.ACTION_VIEW, intentUri);
    intent.setPackage("com.google.android.apps.maps");

    if (intent.resolveActivity(getPackageManager()) != null) {
        startActivity(intent);
    }
}
```

Here, we used `0,0` as the base latitude and longitude. The address is given in hierarchical order.

The city name is given as `Agra`.

The state name is given as `Uttar Pradesh`.

The country name is given as `India`.

These are separated by +. First, Google Maps limits the search to the country, then the state and the city.

The complete URI is defined as:

```
Uri intentUri =
    Uri.parse("geo:0,0?q=Agra,+Uttar+Pradesh,+India");
```

When we execute the code, we will get an output similar to the following screenshot:

Here, in the map, the location is pointed to by a red marker.

Advanced search

We searched for an address in the previous section. Similarly, we can search for places of interest such as restaurants, beach houses, and gas filling stations.

It should be passed to the same q parameter.

For example, I want to search for a beach resort near me. So, I need to pass the query as beach resort with the coordinates as 0,0.

The URI is defined as:

```
Uri intentUri = Uri.parse("geo:0,0?q=beach resort");
```

On executing the code, the output will be similar to the following screenshot:

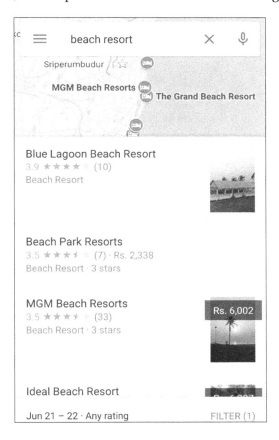

This example returns results from the nearest location. If we want to search in a specific location instead of the nearest location, we need to pass the latitude and longitude instead of 0,0.

In the following example, I will search for restaurants in New York.

The URI is defined as:

```
Uri intentUri =
  Uri.parse("geo:40.7033127,-73.979681?q=restaurant");
```

Here, I am passing the query string as restaurant with the latitude and longitude coordinates of New York. When we execute the code, Google Maps will display all the restaurants in New York.

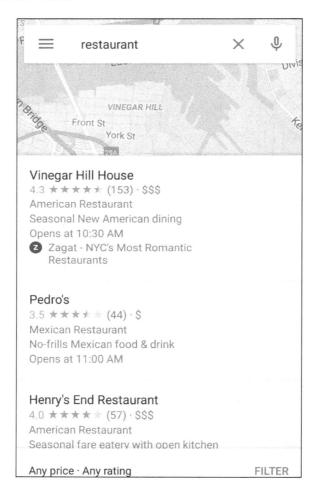

Label location

The Google Maps API provides another useful feature that helps us pass the latitude and longitude coordinates to the native Google Maps application and display them with a label. This will be helpful for locations that do not have any markers to indicate them.

This can be done by passing the latitude and longitude coordinates as a query and text, which should be displayed as a label in brackets. The URI is as follows:

```
Uri intentUri =
Uri.parse("geo:0,0?q=27.175015,78.042155(Taj Mahal + Agra)");
```

Here, I have passed the latitude and longitude coordinates of `Taj Mahal` and labeled it as **Taj Mahal**. When we execute the code, the output will be similar to the following screenshot:

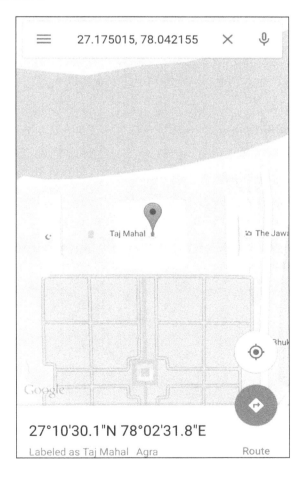

Using navigation

Till now, we have only learned about displaying locations, and searching for places of interest such as restaurants, beach resorts, and fuel filling stations using the native Google Maps application. Now, we are moving a step further. We are going to learn about navigation using the Google Maps application. It is a tedious task to design our own navigation application from scratch. So, if we want to develop and deploy an application as fast as possible, we can use the native Google Maps application. Let's learn about this in the forthcoming sections.

To search and display a location, we used the keyword `geo` in the Intent request. Similarly, now we need to use the `google.navigation` keyword.

Two parameters can be passed, they are:

- `q`
- `mode`

The street address, or the latitude and longitude coordinates, can be passed through the `q` parameter. The navigation modes can be passed through the `mode` parameter. Three values can be given to the mode parameter as follows:

- `d` indicates driving
- `w` indicates walking
- `b` indicates bicycling

The format should be as follows:

```
google.navigation:q=a+street+address
google.navigation:q=latitude,longitude
```

The `mode` parameter is optional. If we do not specify any navigation modes, it will take driving as its default value.

For example, I will use the following code to navigate to an interest:

```
Uri intentUri = Uri.parse("google.navigation:q=Besant+Nagar,+
Chennai");
```

This would fetch me a result similar to:

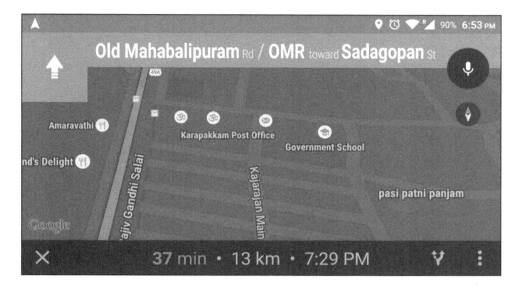

This is easier than what we thought, isn't it? As soon as you run the code, Google Maps starts navigating to the destination.

Now, let's make something more complex like a custom application.

Our custom application consists of `MapFragment` along with radio buttons, to choose the navigation mode, such as **Walking, Driving**, and **Bicycling**. The user's last known location is displayed in the map. When the user touches a location on the map, the Google Maps Intent is started for navigation using the native Google Maps application. The UI will be similar to the following screenshot:

The previous screenshot is the initial screen, which is loaded when we start the app. Let's now discuss the coding part. Make sure you have added all the required permissions.

Our main layout consists of `MapFragment` along with three radio buttons within a `Radio` group. The code is as follows:,

```
<LinearLayout xmlns:android="http://schemas.android.com/apk/res/
android"
    android:layout_width="match_parent"
    android:layout_height="match_parent"
    android:orientation="vertical">
    <fragment
        android:id="@+id/map"
        android:layout_width="match_parent"
        android:layout_height="400sp"
        android:name="com.google.android.gms.maps.MapFragment" />
    <RadioGroup
        android:layout_marginTop="50sp"
        android:layout_gravity="center"
        android:layout_width="wrap_content"
        android:layout_height="wrap_content" >

        <RadioButton
            android:id="@+id/drive"
            android:layout_width="wrap_content"
            android:layout_height="wrap_content"
            android:text="Driving"
            android:checked="true" />

        <RadioButton
            android:id="@+id/walk"
            android:layout_width="wrap_content"
            android:layout_height="wrap_content"
            android:text="Walking" />
        <RadioButton
            android:id="@+id/cycle"
            android:layout_width="wrap_content"
            android:layout_height="wrap_content"
            android:text="Bicycling" />

    </RadioGroup>
</LinearLayout>
```

`activity_maps.xml`

In our `MapsActivity` class, we are using some of the concepts we learned in the previous chapters, such as markers and location data.

Initially, we implemented the `ConnectionCallbacks` and `OnConnectionFailedListener` interfaces to use location data using the Google Play location services. Then, we initialized the Google API client.

When the location is obtained using the Google Play location services, we set the camera to the obtained location. Then, we use the `OnMapClickListener()` interface to handle the callback when the map is clicked. The custom-defined function is called by passing the coordinates and the mode, which is obtained from the radio button. The function is as follows:

```
public void launchMap(LatLng latLng,String mode){

String uriString =
    String.format("google.navigation:q=%f,%f&mode=%s",
    latLng.latitude,latLng.longitude,mode);
        Uri intentUri = Uri.parse(uriString);
        Intent intent = new Intent(Intent.ACTION_VIEW, intentUri);
        intent.setPackage("com.google.android.apps.maps");

        if (intent.resolveActivity(getPackageManager()) != null) {
            startActivity(intent);
        }
    }
```

This custom function launches the native Google Maps application for navigation using a particular mode. The complete code for `MapsActivity` is as follows:

```
package com.raj.map;

import android.app.Activity;
import android.content.Intent;
import android.location.Location;
import android.net.Uri;
import android.os.Bundle;
import android.util.Log;
import android.widget.RadioButton;

import com.google.android.gms.common.ConnectionResult;
import com.google.android.gms.common.api.GoogleApiClient;
import com.google.android.gms.location.LocationServices;
import com.google.android.gms.maps.CameraUpdateFactory;
import com.google.android.gms.maps.GoogleMap;
import com.google.android.gms.maps.MapFragment;
import com.google.android.gms.maps.model.LatLng;
```

```java
import com.google.android.gms.maps.model.MarkerOptions;


public class MapsActivity extends Activity implements
  GoogleApiClient.ConnectionCallbacks, GoogleApiClient.
OnConnectionFailedListener {
    GoogleApiClient googleApiClient;
    GoogleMap map;
    Location location;
    RadioButton drive,walk,bicycle;

    @Override
    protected void onCreate(Bundle savedInstanceState) {
        super.onCreate(savedInstanceState);
        setContentView(R.layout.activity_maps);
        MapFragment mapFragment = (MapFragment)
          getFragmentManager().findFragmentById(R.id.map);
        map = mapFragment.getMap();
        googleApiClient = new GoogleApiClient.Builder(this)
                .addConnectionCallbacks(this)
                .addOnConnectionFailedListener(this)
                .addApi(LocationServices.API)
                .build();
        googleApiClient.connect();

        drive = (RadioButton)findViewById(R.id.drive);
        walk  = (RadioButton)findViewById(R.id.walk);
        bicycle = (RadioButton)findViewById(R.id.cycle);

    }
//This function will be called when the map is clicked
    public void launchMap(LatLng latLng,String mode){

String uriString =
  String.format("google.navigation:q=%f,%f&mode=%s",
    latLng.latitude,latLng.longitude,mode);
        Uri intentUri = Uri.parse(uriString);
        Intent intent = new Intent(Intent.ACTION_VIEW, intentUri);
        intent.setPackage("com.google.android.apps.maps");

        if (intent.resolveActivity(getPackageManager()) != null) {
            startActivity(intent);
        }
    }

    @Override
```

```java
            public void onConnected(Bundle bundle) {

                location =
                 LocationServices.FusedLocationApi.getLastLocation(googleApiC
    lient);
                if(location != null) {
                    map.addMarker(new MarkerOptions().position(new
                     LatLng(location.getLatitude(), location.
    getLongitude())))).setTitle("My Location");
                    map.moveCamera(CameraUpdateFactory.newLatLngZoom(new
                     LatLng(location.getLatitude(),
                     location.getLongitude()), 12));
                }
                map.setOnMapClickListener(new
                 GoogleMap.OnMapClickListener() {
                    @Override
                    public void onMapClick(LatLng latLng) {
    //To check which mode is selected in checkbox
                        if(drive.isChecked()){
                            Log.d("Map","Drive");
                            launchMap(latLng, "d");
                        }else if(walk.isChecked()){
                            Log.d("Map","Walk");
                            launchMap(latLng, "w");
                        }else{
                            Log.d("Map", "BiCycle");
                            launchMap(latLng,"b");

                        }

                    }
                });
            }


        @Override
        public void onConnectionSuspended(int i) {

        }

        @Override
        public void onConnectionFailed(ConnectionResult
          connectionResult) {

        }
    }
```

Here, we are checking whether the radio button is checked or not by calling the `isChecked()` method on the radio button object.

For example, to launch the navigation in the driving mode, I would call the following function:

```
launchMap(latLng, "d");
```

Here, the `d` string indicates that the mode is driving.

Then, in the `launchMap()` method, we concatenate the strings to form the string in the required format. When we execute the code, we will get a screen similar to the following:

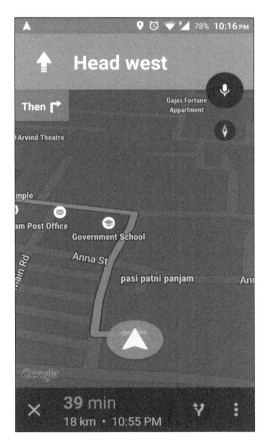

Displaying StreetViewPanorama

Finally, we have reached the last, and one of the most exciting parts of this chapter. In this section, we are going to learn how to launch Street View for our Android application.

We need to use the `google.streetview` keyword.

The format should be as follows:

```
google.streetview:cbll=latitude,longitude&cbp=0,bearing,0,zoom,tilt
google.streetview:panoid=id&cbp=0,bearing,0,zoom,tilt
```

Now, let's discuss the parameters. They are as follows:

- `cbll`: This parameter is compulsory. This parameter is used to specify the latitude and longitude as comma separated values. One thing to note is that Google Maps will display the panorama nearest to the specified location.

- `cbp`: The `cbp` parameter is an optional one. This takes five values. This is used to specify the bearing, tilt, and zoom. The first and third parameters are not supported. Bearing, zoom, and tilt should be specified in the second, fourth, and fifth positions.

- `panoid`: This parameter is compulsory. This is used to specify the panorama ID to display the Street View. Google Maps will use the panorama ID if both `cbll` and `panoid` are specified.

Now, let's try this with an example. We are going to display a street view panorama of Newark with a specified bearing and tilt. The complete code in this activity is as follows:

```java
package com.raj.map;

import android.app.Activity;
import android.content.Intent;
import android.net.Uri;
import android.os.Bundle;
import android.view.View;
import android.widget.Button;

import com.google.android.gms.maps.model.LatLng;


public class MapsActivity extends Activity{

    static final LatLng NEWARK =
      new LatLng(40.735188, -74.172414);
```

```
Button launch;

@Override
protected void onCreate(Bundle savedInstanceState) {
    super.onCreate(savedInstanceState);
    setContentView(R.layout.activity_maps);
    launch = (Button)findViewById(R.id.btn);
    launch.setOnClickListener(new View.OnClickListener() {
        @Override
        public void onClick(View v) {
            launchMap();
        }
    });
}

public void launchMap(){

    String uriString =
        String.format("google.streetview:cbll=%f,%f&cbp=%d,%d,%d,%d,
%d",
        NEWARK.latitude,NEWARK.longitude,0,60,0,0,15);
    Uri intentUri = Uri.parse(uriString);
    Intent intent = new Intent(Intent.ACTION_VIEW, intentUri);
    intent.setPackage("com.google.android.apps.maps");

    if (intent.resolveActivity(getPackageManager()) != null) {
        startActivity(intent);
    }
}
}
```

MapsActivity.java

The coordinates of Newark, for which we are going to display the panorama, is defined as:

```
static final LatLng NEWARK = new LatLng(40.735188, -74.172414);
```

The complete URI string is defined as:

```
google.streetview:cbll="+NEWARK.latitude+","+NEWARK.
longitude+"&cbp=0,60,0,0,15
```

The NEWARK.latitude term returns the latitude from the defined LatLng object. Similarly, NEWARK.longitude returns the longitude. Here, the cbp parameters are defined as 0,60,0,0,15. The bearing is 60 degrees and the tilt is 15 degrees. When we run the code, the output will be similar to the following screenshot:

Self-test questions

Q1. The `com.google.android.apps.maps` package is used to launch Google maps?

1. True
2. False

Q2. The activity can be started by?

1. `startActivity`
2. `StartActivity()`

Q3. Which keyword should be used to display the map?

1. `geo`
2. `google.streetview`
3. `google.navigation`

Q4. The driving mode can be specified using?

1. d
2. w
3. b

Q5. The `cbp` parameter is used to set the latitude and longitude?

1. True
2. False

Summary

In this chapter, we learned about Google Maps Intents. We learned how to display maps using the native Google Maps application. Then, we learned about advanced search using the Google Maps application. We proceeded to implement the navigation using different modes, such as driving and walking. We developed a custom application for navigation using the Google Maps application. Finally, we concluded the chapter by launching StreetViewPanorama from our application.

In our next and final chapter, we are going to develop a custom application with more advanced and complex features.

10
Creating a Custom Map Application

In our previous chapters, we learned all the basic concepts required to create a full-fledged map application such as `MapFragment`, markers, street view, location services, and camera views. In this chapter, we are going to create a simple custom map application with some cool stuff.

We will cover the following topics:

- What the custom application does
- What additional libraries/classes we use
- Prerequisites
- Implementation

What the custom application does

Our custom map application is a diary of our favorite locations. It helps us store the location with the address in SQLite database, which helps us fetch and display it later. We can also use the sliding navigation drawer with the hamburger menu and material design's **Floating Action Button** (**FAB**).

The map uses the Google Play location service to fetch the user's recent location and display it.

What additional libraries/classes do we use

During the Google I/O, Google unveiled a new design library to help us easily implement the material design in our Android application. We use the Android design library to implement FAB in our application.

Additionally, we use SQLite to store marker details such as the position, color, address fetched, and name that the marker denotes.

We use shared preferences as well to store some temporary data.

Prerequisites

We are going to create the project completely with Android Studio. We will start by creating a new project in Android Studio. Here, I have used the package name as `packt.mycustommap`. You can use the package name of your choice.

You will then have to register your application in the Google Developer Console with the SHA1 fingerprint and package name, and obtain the API key.

Instead of hardcoding the string, it is recommended that we define the string variables in `strings.xml` in `res/values/strings.xml`.

Make sure your activity extends to `AppCompatActivity`.

Adding dependencies

The dependencies should be added to the app's `build.gradle` file. Our app depends on the Google Play services library and the Android design support library.

Add the following dependencies to `build.gradle`:

```
compile 'com.google.android.gms:play-services:7.5.0'
compile 'com.android.support:design:22.2.0'
```

The complete dependencies look similar to the following code:

```
dependencies {
    compile fileTree(dir: 'libs', include: ['*.jar'])
    compile 'com.android.support:appcompat-v7:22.2.0'
    compile 'com.google.android.gms:play-services:7.5.0'
    compile 'com.android.support:design:22.2.0'
}
```

Using the material design icons

Google has released material design icons for use in our application. You can download them from `https://google.github.io/material-design-icons/`.

Adding permissions

We need all the permissions that we used in our previous chapters. We are also using location services; hence, we need to add permission to access **Coarse Location** and **Fine** Location. The complete permission in manifest looks similar to the following code:

```
<uses-permission
  android:name="android.permission.READ_EXTERNAL_STORAGE"/>
    <uses-permission android:name="android.permission.INTERNET" />
    <uses-permission
  android:name="android.permission.ACCESS_NETWORK_STATE" />
    <uses-permission
  android:name="android.permission.WRITE_EXTERNAL_STORAGE" />
    <uses-permission
  android:name="com.google.android.providers.gsf.permission.READ_
GSERVICES" />
    <uses-permission
  android:name="android.permission.ACCESS_FINE_LOCATION"/>
    <uses-permission
  android:name="android.permission.ACCESS_COARSE_LOCATION"/>
```

Defining the API key and Google Play services version

The API key we obtained from the Google Developer Console in the previous section must be defined in the manifest. Add the snippet to define the API key and the Google Play services version:

```
<meta-data
        android:name="com.google.android.gms.version"
        android:value="@integer/google_play_services_version"
/>private
    <meta-data
        android:name="com.google.android.maps.v2.API_KEY"
        android:value="@string/google_maps_key" />
```

Implementation

This is the most exciting part of this chapter. In a nutshell, our application has a single activity with four fragments. Also, it has a SQLite database with a single table to store marker data.

Defining the app theme

The app theme can be customized by using the `styles.xml` file in res | values | styles.xml.

The primary color is the color of the action bar. The primary dark color is the color of the status bar. The accent color is the color for FAB. The sample app looks like the following image:

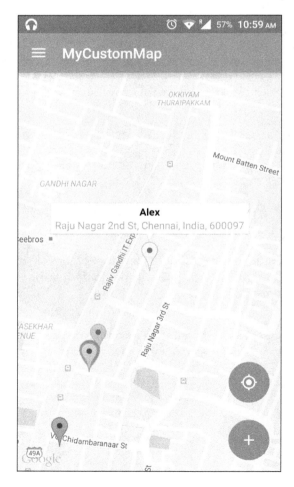

In the preceding screenshot, you can see the usage of primary, primary dark, and accent colors.

The style is defined as:

```
<style name="AppTheme" parent="Theme.AppCompat.Light.DarkActionBar">
    <item name="colorPrimary">#2196F3</item>
    <item name="colorPrimaryDark">#1976D2</item>
    <item name="colorAccent">#FF4081</item>
</style>
```

For more material design colors, you can go to http://www.materialpalette.com/.

Defining strings

It is recommended that we define all the strings and string arrays in strings.xml in res | layout | strings.xml.

The complete strings used in our project are defined as:

```
<resources>
    <string name="app_name">MyCustomMap</string>
    <string name="action_settings">Settings</string>
    <string name="drawer_open">drawer_open</string>
    <string name="drawer_close">drawer_close</string>
    <string
     name="google_maps_key">AIzaSyCoGMtqAWS_b99oAgHlJ52Nt3QqQpE4MeM</string>
    <string name="marker_hint">Marker Name</string>
    <string name="address_hint">Address</string>
    <string name="toast_add_success">Marker Added
      successfully</string>
    <string name="toast_add_error">Error Adding Marker</string>
    <string name="toast_field_empty">Fields are empty</string>
    <string name="no_marker">No Markers Found</string>
    <string name="marker_deleted">Marker Deleted</string>
    <string-array name="menu">
        <item>Home</item>
        <item>All markers</item>
        <item>Clear Data</item>
    </string-array>
    <string-array name="colors">
        <item>AZURE</item>
        <item>BLUE</item>
        <item>CYAN</item>
        <item>GREEN</item>
```

```
            <item>MAGNETA</item>
            <item>ORANGE</item>
            <item>RED</item>
            <item>ROSE</item>
            <item>VIOLET</item>
            <item>YELLOW</item>
        </string-array>
    </resources>
```

Similarly, dimensions are defined in `dimens.xml` in `res | layout | dimens.xml`.

Defining and creating a database

The first step is to define the SQLite database and table structure. Before we do this, we need to create a `Marker` class to handle all the get and set methods. This class is our table model, which has all the data to be stored in the database.

Our marker table has six columns such as `id`, `name`, `latitude`, `longitude`, `address`, and `color`. The complete `Marker` class is given by:

```
package packt.mycustommap;


public class Marker {

    private int _id;
    private String _name;
    private String _latitude;
    private String _longitude;
    private String _address;
    private String _color;

    public Marker(){

    }

    public Marker(int id,String name,String latitude,
     String longitude, String address, String color) {

        this._id = id;
        this._name = name;
        this._latitude = latitude;
        this._longitude = longitude;
        this._address = address;
        this._color = color;
```

```
    }
    public Marker(String name,String latitude,
     String longitude, String address, String color) {

        this._name = name;
        this._latitude = latitude;
        this._longitude = longitude;
        this._address = address;
        this._color = color;
    }

    public int getID(){
        return this._id;
    }

    public void setID(int id){
        this._id = id;
    }

    public String getName(){
        return this._name;
    }

    public void setName(String name){
        this._name = name;
    }

    public String getLatitude(){
        return this._latitude;
    }

    public void setLatitude(String latitude){
        this._latitude= latitude;
    }

    public String getLongitude(){
        return this._longitude;
    }
    public void setLongitude(String longitude){
        this._longitude = longitude;
    }
    public String getAddress(){
        return this._address;
    }
```

```
        public void setAddress(String address){
            this._address = address;
        }

        public String getColor(){
            return this._color;
        }

        public void setColor(String color){
            this._color = color;
        }


    }
```

Marker.java

The preceding code has a Marker constructor and the methods to get and set the table fields.

The next class is the DBHandler class, which performs all the SQLite database operations such as creating tables, adding data to tables, deleting data from the tables, and fetching data. Our DBHandler class extends to the SQLiteOpenHelper class. The two methods which are overridden are onCreate() and onUpgrade().

In the onCreate() method, we create the table. This method is called when the database is created. The onUpgrade() method deletes and recreates the table. We have six other methods. They are:

- addMarker(): This method is used to add marker data to the database
- getMarker(): This method is used to retrieve marker data from the database
- getAllMarkers(): This method is used to retrieve data of all the markers
- deleteMarker(): This is used to delete a marker
- getMarkerCount(): This is used to get the total number of markers
- deleteTable(): This is used to delete a table

The complete DBHandler class is given by:

```
package packt.mycustommap;


import android.content.ContentValues;
import android.content.Context;
import android.database.Cursor;
import android.database.sqlite.SQLiteDatabase;
```

```
import android.database.sqlite.SQLiteOpenHelper;
import java.util.ArrayList;
import java.util.List;


public class DBHandler extends SQLiteOpenHelper {


    private static final int DATABASE_VERSION = 1;
    private static final String DATABASE_NAME = "markers";
    private static final String TABLE_MARKERS = "markers_data";
    private static final String KEY_ID = "id";
    private static final String KEY_NAME = "name";
    private static final String KEY_LATITUDE = "latitude";
    private static final String KEY_LONGITUDE = "longitude";
    private static final String KEY_ADDRESS = "address";
    private static final String KEY_COLOR = "color";


    public DBHandler(Context context) {
        super(context, DATABASE_NAME, null, DATABASE_VERSION);
    }
    @Override
    public void onCreate(SQLiteDatabase db) {
        String CREATE_MARKERS_TABLE = "CREATE TABLE " +
          TABLE_MARKERS + "("
                + KEY_ID + " INTEGER PRIMARY KEY AUTOINCREMENT," +
                 KEY_NAME + " TEXT,"
                + KEY_LATITUDE + " TEXT," + KEY_LONGITUDE + " 
            TEXT," + KEY_ADDRESS + " TEXT," + KEY_COLOR + " TEXT" +
");";
        db.execSQL(CREATE_MARKERS_TABLE);


    }


    @Override
    public void onUpgrade(SQLiteDatabase db, int oldVersion,
     int newVersion) {
        db.execSQL("DROP TABLE IF EXISTS " + TABLE_MARKERS);
        onCreate(db);
    }


    public long addMarker(Marker marker) {
        SQLiteDatabase db = this.getWritableDatabase();

        ContentValues values = new ContentValues();
```

```java
            values.put(KEY_NAME, marker.getName());
            values.put(KEY_LATITUDE, marker.getLatitude());
            values.put(KEY_LONGITUDE, marker.getLongitude());
            values.put(KEY_ADDRESS, marker.getAddress());
            values.put(KEY_COLOR,marker.getColor());

            long id =  db.insert(TABLE_MARKERS, null, values);

            db.close();
            return id;
        }

    public Marker getMarker(int id) {
        SQLiteDatabase db = this.getReadableDatabase();

        Cursor cursor = db.query(TABLE_MARKERS,
          new String[] { KEY_ID,
                         KEY_NAME,
            KEY_LATITUDE,KEY_LONGITUDE,KEY_ADDRESS,KEY_COLOR },
            KEY_ID + "=?",
                new String[] { String.valueOf(id) }, null,
                    null, null, null);
        if (cursor != null)
            cursor.moveToFirst();


Marker marker = new
  Marker(cursor.getInt(cursor.getColumnIndex(KEY_ID)),
                cursor.getString(cursor.getColumnIndex(KEY_NAME)),
cursor.getString(cursor.getColumnIndex(KEY_LATITUDE)),
                cursor.getString(cursor.getColumnIndex(KEY_
LONGITUDE)),cursor.getString(cursor.getColumnIndex(KEY_ADDRESS)),
                cursor.getString(cursor.getColumnIndex(KEY_COLOR)));
        cursor.close();
return marker;
        }

    public List<Marker> getAllMarkers() {
        List<Marker> markerList = new ArrayList<Marker>();

        String selectQuery = "SELECT  * FROM " + TABLE_MARKERS;

        SQLiteDatabase db = this.getWritableDatabase();
        Cursor cursor = db.rawQuery(selectQuery, null);

        if (cursor.moveToFirst()) {
```

```
                    do {
                        Marker marker = new Marker();

                        marker.setID(cursor.getInt(cursor.getColumnIndex(KEY_
ID)));
                        marker.setName(cursor.getString(cursor.
getColumnIndex(KEY_NAME)));
                        marker.setLatitude(cursor.getString(cursor.
getColumnIndex(KEY_LATITUDE)));
                            marker.setLongitude(cursor.getString(cursor.
getColumnIndex(KEY_LONGITUDE)));
                        marker.setAddress(cursor.getString(cursor.
getColumnIndex(KEY_ADDRESS)));
                        marker.setColor(cursor.getString(cursor.
getColumnIndex(KEY_COLOR)));
                        markerList.add(marker);
                    } while (cursor.moveToNext());
                }
cursor.close();
            return markerList;
        }
    //This function is used to delete a marker data from table
    public void deleteMarker(Marker marker) {
        SQLiteDatabase db = this.getWritableDatabase();
        db.delete(TABLE_MARKERS, KEY_ID + " = ?",
                new String[] { String.valueOf(marker.getID()) });
        db.execSQL("UPDATE "+TABLE_MARKERS+" set id = (id - 1) WHERE
id > "+marker.getID());
        db.execSQL("UPDATE SQLITE_SEQUENCE SET seq ="+ (marker.getID()
- 1) +" WHERE name = '"+TABLE_MARKERS+"';");
        db.close();
    }
    //This function is used to get total number of markers present in
the database
    public int getMarkerCount() {
        String countQuery = "SELECT  * FROM " + TABLE_MARKERS;
        SQLiteDatabase db = this.getReadableDatabase();
        Cursor cursor = db.rawQuery(countQuery, null);
        int count = cursor.getCount();
        cursor.close();
        return count;
    }
    //This function is used to delete the table
    public void deleteTable(){
        SQLiteDatabase db = this.getWritableDatabase();
        db.delete(TABLE_MARKERS, null, null);
```

```
        db.execSQL("DELETE FROM SQLITE_SEQUENCE WHERE name= '"+TABLE_
MARKERS+"';");
        db.close();
    }
}
```

DBHandler.java

Creating layouts

Our project consists of one activity layout, four fragment layouts, and a list view item layout. Our main activity layout consists of FrameLayout and ListView in DrawerLayout. FrameLayout is used to dynamically add fragments and ListView is used for the sliding navigation drawer with the hamburger menu. The code is as follows:

```
<android.support.v4.widget.DrawerLayout
    android:id="@+id/drawer_layout"
    xmlns:android="http://schemas.android.com/apk/res/android"
    android:layout_width="match_parent"
    android:layout_height="match_parent">
    <RelativeLayout xmlns:android="http://schemas.android.com/apk/res/
android"
        android:layout_width="match_parent"
        android:layout_height="match_parent">
        <FrameLayout
            android:id="@+id/content_frame"
            android:layout_width="match_parent"
            android:layout_height="match_parent"/>
    </RelativeLayout>
    <ListView
        android:id="@+id/nav_drawer"
        android:layout_width="260dp"
        android:layout_height="match_parent"
        android:layout_gravity="start"
        android:background="@android:color/white"
        android:choiceMode="singleChoice"
        android:divider="@android:color/transparent"
        android:dividerHeight="0dp"
        android:drawSelectorOnTop="false">
    </ListView>
</android.support.v4.widget.DrawerLayout>
```

activity_main.xml

The next layout is the main fragment layout. It has `FrameLayout` with two FABs. `FrameLayout` is used to dynamically load `MapFragment`. The two FABs are used to detect locations using GPS and to add a marker.

The layout screenshot is as follows:

The icon drawables are used from the Google material icon pack. The code is as follows:

```xml
<?xml version="1.0" encoding="utf-8"?>
<RelativeLayout xmlns:android="http://schemas.android.com/apk/res/
android"
    android:layout_width="match_parent"
    android:layout_height="match_parent"
    xmlns:app="http://schemas.android.com/apk/res-auto">
    <FrameLayout
        android:id="@+id/content_frame_map"
        android:layout_width="match_parent"
        android:layout_height="match_parent">
        <android.support.design.widget.FloatingActionButton
            android:id="@+id/fab_add"
            android:layout_width="wrap_content"
            android:layout_height="wrap_content"
            android:layout_gravity="bottom|right"
            android:src="@drawable/ic_add_white"
            android:layout_marginRight="@dimen/fab_margin"
            android:layout_marginBottom="@dimen/fab_margin"
            app:elevation="6dp"
            app:fabSize="normal" />
        <android.support.design.widget.FloatingActionButton
            android:id="@+id/fab_locate"
            android:layout_width="wrap_content"
            android:layout_height="wrap_content"
            android:layout_gravity="bottom|right"
            android:src="@drawable/ic_gps_fixed"
            android:layout_marginRight="@dimen/fab_margin"
            android:layout_marginBottom="@dimen/fab2_bottom_margin"
            app:elevation="6dp"
            app:fabSize="normal" />
    </FrameLayout>
</RelativeLayout>
```

`main_fragment.xml`

The next layout is the add marker fragment layout. This layout is used to add the marker details to the database. It consists of `FrameLayout`, which is used to dynamically load `MapFragment`. Then, we use two `EditText` widgets within `TextInputLayout`. The `EditText` widget is used for the marker name and address. `TextInputLayout` is a part of the new Android design support library, which always shows the hint. It has a spinner to select the preferred color for the marker. Two `TextView` widgets are used to display the latitude and longitude. Two FABs are used to perform save and discard operations. Have a look at the following screenshot:

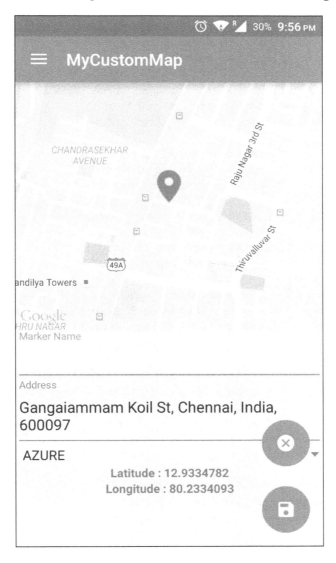

The code is as follows:

```xml
<?xml version="1.0" encoding="utf-8"?>
<RelativeLayout xmlns:android="http://schemas.android.com/apk/res/
android"
    xmlns:app="http://schemas.android.com/apk/res-auto"
    android:orientation="vertical"
    android:layout_width="match_parent"
    android:layout_height="match_parent">
    <FrameLayout
        android:id="@+id/content_frame_addmap"
        android:layout_width="match_parent"
        android:layout_height="300sp"/>
<ScrollView
    android:layout_below="@+id/content_frame_addmap"
    android:layout_width="match_parent"
    android:layout_height="match_parent">
    <RelativeLayout
        android:orientation="vertical"
        android:layout_width="match_parent"
        android:layout_height="match_parent">

    <android.support.design.widget.TextInputLayout
        android:id="@+id/txt1"
        android:layout_width="match_parent"
        android:layout_height="wrap_content">
        <EditText
            android:id="@+id/marker_name"
            android:layout_width="match_parent"
            android:layout_height="wrap_content"
            android:hint="@string/marker_hint" />

    </android.support.design.widget.TextInputLayout>
    <android.support.design.widget.TextInputLayout
        android:layout_below="@+id/txt1"
        android:id="@+id/txt2"
        android:layout_width="match_parent"
        android:layout_height="wrap_content">
    <EditText
        android:id="@+id/marker_address"
        android:layout_width="match_parent"
        android:layout_height="wrap_content"
        android:hint="@string/address_hint" />
    </android.support.design.widget.TextInputLayout>
```

```
    <Spinner
        android:layout_below="@id/txt2"
        android:id="@+id/spinner"
        android:layout_width="match_parent"
        android:layout_height="wrap_content"
        android:gravity="center"/>

<TextView
    android:layout_below="@+id/spinner"
    android:id="@+id/latText"
    android:textStyle="bold"
    android:gravity="center"
    android:layout_width="match_parent"
    android:layout_height="wrap_content" />
<TextView
    android:layout_below="@+id/latText"
    android:id="@+id/lngText"
    android:textStyle="bold"
    android:gravity="center"
    android:layout_width="match_parent"
    android:layout_height="wrap_content" />
</RelativeLayout>
</ScrollView>
    <FrameLayout
        android:id="@+id/content_frame_map"
        android:layout_width="match_parent"
        android:layout_height="match_parent">
        <android.support.design.widget.FloatingActionButton
            android:id="@+id/fab_save"
            android:layout_width="wrap_content"
            android:layout_height="wrap_content"
            android:layout_gravity="bottom|right"
            android:src="@drawable/ic_save"
            android:layout_marginRight="@dimen/fab_margin"
            android:layout_marginBottom="@dimen/fab_margin"
            app:elevation="6dp"
            app:fabSize="normal" />
        <android.support.design.widget.FloatingActionButton
            android:id="@+id/fab_discard"
            android:layout_width="wrap_content"
            android:layout_height="wrap_content"
            android:layout_gravity="bottom|right"
            android:src="@drawable/ic_cancel"
```

```
                android:layout_marginRight="@dimen/fab_margin"
                android:layout_marginBottom="@dimen/fab2_bottom_margin"
                app:elevation="6dp"
                app:fabSize="normal" />
        </FrameLayout>

    </RelativeLayout>
```

add_marker.xml

The next layout is the marker list fragment layout. It has a TextView and a ListView widget. ListView displays the list of all the markers from the database. TextView is used to display a message if no markers are found. The code is as follows:

```
<?xml version="1.0" encoding="utf-8"?>
<LinearLayout xmlns:android="http://schemas.android.com/apk/res/
android"
    android:layout_width="match_parent"
    android:layout_height="match_parent"
    android:orientation="vertical" >
    <TextView
        android:id="@+id/txt"
        android:textSize="25sp"
        android:gravity="center"
        android:layout_width="match_parent"
        android:layout_height="match_parent" />

    <ListView
        android:id="@+id/mList"
        android:layout_width="match_parent"
        android:layout_height="wrap_content"
    android:layout_marginLeft="16dp"
        android:layout_marginRight="16dp"
        android:clickable="false"
        android:dividerHeight="0dp" />

</LinearLayout>
```

marker_list.xml

The resulting screenshot is as follows:

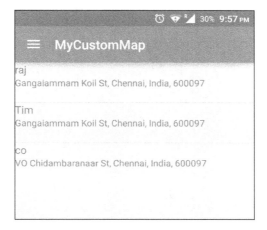

The preceding screenshot shows the list layout. The next layout is for a single list item. It consists of two `TextView` control elements, one for the marker name and the other for the address. The code is as follows:

```xml
<?xml version="1.0" encoding="utf-8"?>
<LinearLayout xmlns:android="http://schemas.android.com/apk/res/
android"
    android:layout_width="match_parent"
    android:layout_height="match_parent"
    android:gravity="center_vertical"
    android:orientation="vertical" >
    <TextView
        android:id="@+id/txtName"
        android:layout_width="match_parent"
        android:layout_height="wrap_content"
     android:layout_marginTop="8dp"
        android:maxLines="1"
        android:textSize="16sp" />
    <TextView
        android:id="@+id/txtAddress"
        android:layout_width="match_parent"
        android:textAlignment="center"
        android:layout_marginBottom="8dp"
        android:layout_height="wrap_content" />

</LinearLayout>
```

`marker_list_single.xml`

The final layout is a single fragment. It is used to display a single marker, which is loaded when we click on a list item. It consists of `FrameLayout` with two FABs for delete and cancel operations. The output will be as follows:

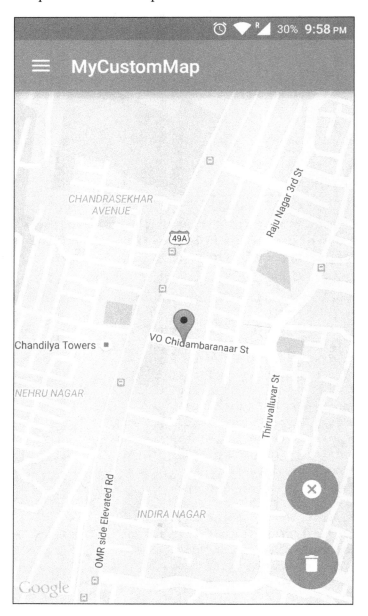

The code is as follows:

```xml
<?xml version="1.0" encoding="utf-8"?>
<RelativeLayout xmlns:android="http://schemas.android.com/apk/res/
android"
    android:layout_width="match_parent"
    android:layout_height="match_parent"
    xmlns:app="http://schemas.android.com/apk/res-auto">
    <FrameLayout
        android:id="@+id/content_frame_map_single"
        android:layout_width="match_parent"
        android:layout_height="match_parent">
        <android.support.design.widget.FloatingActionButton
            android:id="@+id/fab_delete"
            android:layout_width="wrap_content"
            android:layout_height="wrap_content"
            android:layout_gravity="bottom|right"
            android:src="@drawable/ic_delete_white"
            android:layout_marginRight="@dimen/fab_margin"
            android:layout_marginBottom="@dimen/fab_margin"
            app:elevation="6dp"
            app:fabSize="normal" />
        <android.support.design.widget.FloatingActionButton
            android:id="@+id/fab_cancel"
            android:layout_width="wrap_content"
            android:layout_height="wrap_content"
            android:layout_gravity="bottom|right"
            android:src="@drawable/ic_cancel"
            android:layout_marginRight="@dimen/fab_margin"
            android:layout_marginBottom="@dimen/fab2_bottom_margin"
            app:elevation="6dp"
            app:fabSize="normal" />
    </FrameLayout>
</RelativeLayout>
```

single_fragment.xml

Creating activities and fragments

First, let's start with MainActivity. Our MainActivity extends to AppCompatActivity. Then, we will initialize DrawerLayout and ListView for DrawerLayout. Also, we will use ActionBarDrawerToggle to open and close the Navigation drawer when the hamburger menu is pressed.

When the list item in the drawer is pressed, the corresponding fragment is loaded. Clear Data completely deletes the table. Then, we replace the FrameLayout contents with MainFragment. The onPostCreate() method is overridden and the syncState() method is called on the ActionBarDrawerToggle object to keep everything in sync. The onConfigurationChanged() method is overridden to keep in sync when the configuration changes such as orientation.

The hamburger menu is enabled by using:

```
getSupportActionBar().setDisplayHomeAsUpEnabled(true);
getSupportActionBar().setHomeButtonEnabled(true);
```

The complete code in MainActivity is as follows:

```
package packt.mycustommap;


import android.app.Fragment;
import android.app.FragmentTransaction;
import android.content.res.Configuration;

import android.support.v4.widget.DrawerLayout;
import android.support.v7.app.ActionBarDrawerToggle;
import android.support.v7.app.AppCompatActivity;
import android.os.Bundle;
import android.view.MenuItem;
import android.view.View;
import android.widget.AdapterView;
import android.widget.ArrayAdapter;
import android.widget.ListView;


public class MainActivity extends AppCompatActivity {
    private DrawerLayout drawerLayout;
    private ListView drawerList;
    private ActionBarDrawerToggle drawerToggle;
    private DBHandler db;


    @Override
    protected void onCreate(Bundle savedInstanceState) {
        super.onCreate(savedInstanceState);
        setContentView(R.layout.activity_main);
```

```
        db = new DBHandler(getApplicationContext());

    //This is used to enable the hamburger menu
        getSupportActionBar().setDisplayHomeAsUpEnabled(true);
        getSupportActionBar().setHomeButtonEnabled(true);

        drawerLayout = (DrawerLayout)findViewById(R.id.drawer_layout);
        drawerList = (ListView)findViewById(R.id.nav_drawer);

        drawerToggle = new ActionBarDrawerToggle(this, drawerLayout,
                R.string.drawer_open, R.string.drawer_close) {

            public void onDrawerOpened(View drawerView) {
                super.onDrawerOpened(drawerView);
                invalidateOptionsMenu();
            }

            public void onDrawerClosed(View view) {
                super.onDrawerClosed(view);
                invalidateOptionsMenu();
            }
        };
        drawerToggle.setDrawerIndicatorEnabled(true);
        drawerLayout.setDrawerListener(drawerToggle);

        ArrayAdapter<String> adapter = new ArrayAdapter<String>(this,
                android.R.layout.simple_list_item_1, android.R.id.
text1, getResources().getStringArray(R.array.menu));
        drawerList.setAdapter(adapter);
        drawerList.setOnItemClickListener(new AdapterView.
OnItemClickListener() {
            @Override
            public void onItemClick(AdapterView<?> parent, View view,
int position, long id) {
onDrawerListItemClick(position);

            }
        });
        Fragment main = new MainFragment();
        FragmentTransaction ft = getFragmentManager().
beginTransaction();
        ft.replace(R.id.content_frame, main);
        ft.setTransition(FragmentTransaction.TRANSIT_FRAGMENT_FADE);
        ft.addToBackStack(null);
```

```
        ft.commit();
    }
    //This is used to handle the click in the navigation drawer list
item
public void onDrawerListItemClick(int position){
        if(position == 0){
            Fragment main = new MainFragment();
            FragmentTransaction ft = getFragmentManager().
beginTransaction();
            ft.replace(R.id.content_frame, main);
            ft.setTransition(FragmentTransaction.TRANSIT_FRAGMENT_
FADE);
            ft.addToBackStack(null);
            ft.commit();
            drawerLayout.closeDrawers();
        }else if(position == 1){
            Fragment list = new MarkerList();
            FragmentTransaction ft = getFragmentManager().
beginTransaction();
            ft.replace(R.id.content_frame, list);
            ft.setTransition(FragmentTransaction.TRANSIT_FRAGMENT_
FADE);
            ft.addToBackStack(null);
            ft.commit();
            drawerLayout.closeDrawers();

        }else if(position ==2){
            db.deleteTable();
            Fragment main = new MainFragment();
            FragmentTransaction ft = getFragmentManager().
beginTransaction();
            ft.replace(R.id.content_frame, main);
            ft.setTransition(FragmentTransaction.TRANSIT_FRAGMENT_
FADE);
            ft.addToBackStack(null);
            ft.commit();
            drawerLayout.closeDrawers();

        }

    @Override
    public boolean onOptionsItemSelected(MenuItem item) {
        int id = item.getItemId();
        if (drawerToggle.onOptionsItemSelected(item) || id == R.id.
action_settings) {
```

```
                    return true;
                }
                return super.onOptionsItemSelected(item);
        }


        @Override
        protected void onPostCreate(Bundle savedInstanceState) {
            super.onPostCreate(savedInstanceState);
            drawerToggle.syncState();
        }
        @Override
        public void onConfigurationChanged(Configuration newConfig) {
            super.onConfigurationChanged(newConfig);
            drawerToggle.onConfigurationChanged(newConfig);
        }

}                        db.deleteTable();
                        Fragment main = new MainFragment();
                        FragmentTransaction ft = getFragmentManager().
beginTransaction();
                        ft.replace(R.id.content_frame, main);
                        ft.setTransition(FragmentTransaction.TRANSIT_
FRAGMENT_FADE);
                        ft.addToBackStack(null);
                        ft.commit();
                        drawerLayout.closeDrawers();


                    }
                }
            });
        Fragment main = new MainFragment();
        FragmentTransaction ft = getFragmentManager().
beginTransaction();
        ft.replace(R.id.content_frame, main);
        ft.setTransition(FragmentTransaction.TRANSIT_FRAGMENT_FADE);
        ft.addToBackStack(null);
        ft.commit();
    }



    @Override
    public boolean onOptionsItemSelected(MenuItem item) {
        int id = item.getItemId();
```

```
        if (drawerToggle.onOptionsItemSelected(item) || id == R.id.
action_settings) {
            return true;
        }
        return super.onOptionsItemSelected(item);
    }

    @Override
    protected void onPostCreate(Bundle savedInstanceState) {
        super.onPostCreate(savedInstanceState);
        drawerToggle.syncState();
    }
    @Override
    public void onConfigurationChanged(Configuration newConfig) {
        super.onConfigurationChanged(newConfig);
        drawerToggle.onConfigurationChanged(newConfig);
    }

}
```

MainActivity.java

The next is MainFragment, which dynamically loads MapFragment in FrameLayout. It has two FABs to locate and add a marker. To locate a marker, we used the Google Play location services and obtained the recent location as we saw in the previous chapters. We used shared preferences to store the temporary data we obtained, such as the latitude and longitude. When **Locate FAB** is pressed, we animate the camera to the obtained location and place a marker to indicate the current location. Here, we used a handler to delay the loading of the marker after we initialized MapFragment.

MainFragment loads all the markers from the SQLite database, displaying it in MapFragment with the name of the marker as the title and the address as the snippet with the marker color specified. Also, we use the getColor() function to convert the color string into the corresponding float values. When **Add FAB** is pressed, the Add marker fragment is displayed. The code is as follows:

```
package packt.mycustommap;

import android.app.Fragment;
import android.app.FragmentTransaction;
import android.content.SharedPreferences;
import android.location.Location;
import android.os.Bundle;
import android.os.Handler;
import android.support.design.widget.FloatingActionButton;
import android.util.Log;
```

```
import android.view.LayoutInflater;
import android.view.View;
import android.view.ViewGroup;

import com.google.android.gms.common.ConnectionResult;
import com.google.android.gms.common.api.GoogleApiClient;
import com.google.android.gms.location.LocationServices;
import com.google.android.gms.maps.CameraUpdateFactory;
import com.google.android.gms.maps.GoogleMap;
import com.google.android.gms.maps.MapFragment;
import com.google.android.gms.maps.model.BitmapDescriptorFactory;
import com.google.android.gms.maps.model.CameraPosition;
import com.google.android.gms.maps.model.LatLng;
import com.google.android.gms.maps.model.MarkerOptions;


public class MainFragment extends Fragment implements
        GoogleApiClient.ConnectionCallbacks, GoogleApiClient.
OnConnectionFailedListener{
    private FloatingActionButton locate, add;
    private Location location;
    private double latitude;
    private double longitude;
    private GoogleApiClient googleApiClient;
    private GoogleMap map;
    private com.google.android.gms.maps.model.Marker locationMarker;
    private MapFragment mapFragment;
    private SharedPreferences pref;
    private DBHandler db;

    @Override
    public View onCreateView(LayoutInflater inflater,ViewGroup
container, Bundle savedInstanceState) {
        View view = inflater.inflate(R.layout.main_fragment,
container, false);

        db = new DBHandler(getActivity());


        googleApiClient = new GoogleApiClient.Builder(getActivity())
                .addConnectionCallbacks(this)
                .addOnConnectionFailedListener(this)
                .addApi(LocationServices.API)
                .build();
```

```
            googleApiClient.connect();

            pref = getActivity().getPreferences(0);
            locate = (FloatingActionButton)view.findViewById(R.id.fab_
locate);
            add     = (FloatingActionButton)view.findViewById(R.id.fab_
add);

            add.setOnClickListener(new View.OnClickListener() {
                @Override
                public void onClick(View view) {
                    Fragment add = new AddMarker();
                    FragmentTransaction ft = getFragmentManager().
beginTransaction();
                    ft.replace(R.id.content_frame, add);
                    ft.setTransition(FragmentTransaction.TRANSIT_FRAGMENT_
OPEN);
                    ft.addToBackStack(null);
                    ft.commit();
                }
            });

            locate.setOnClickListener(new View.OnClickListener() {
                @Override
                public void onClick(View view) {
                    locate();
                }
            });

            loadMap();
            Handler handler = new Handler();
            handler.postDelayed(new Runnable() {
                @Override
                public void run() {
                    loadmarkers();
                }
            },1000);

            return view;
    }

    public void locate(){

        if (location != null) {
```

```
            latitude = location.getLatitude();
            longitude = location.getLongitude();
            map = mapFragment.getMap();
            map.getUiSettings().setMapToolbarEnabled(false);
            if(locationMarker != null)
                locationMarker.remove();
            CameraPosition cameraPosition = new CameraPosition.
Builder().
                    target(new LatLng(latitude,longitude)).
                    zoom(16).
                    build();
            map.animateCamera(CameraUpdateFactory.newCameraPosition(ca
meraPosition));
            locationMarker = map.addMarker(new MarkerOptions().
position(new LatLng(latitude, longitude))
                    .title("Marker")
                    .snippet("My Location")
                    .icon(BitmapDescriptorFactory.fromResource(R.
drawable.ic_location)));
        }

    }
    public void loadMap(){
        mapFragment = MapFragment.newInstance();
        FragmentTransaction fragmentTransaction =
                getFragmentManager().beginTransaction();
        fragmentTransaction.add(R.id.content_frame_map, mapFragment);
        fragmentTransaction.commit();
    }
    //It is used to load the markers on the map
    public void loadmarkers(){
        map = mapFragment.getMap();

        Log.d("MyMap","Count = "+db.getMarkerCount());

            if(db.getMarkerCount() > 0){
            List<Marker> markerList = db.getAllMarkers();
            for (int i = 0; i < db.getMarkerCount(); i++) {
                Marker mkr = markerList.get(i);
                map.addMarker(new MarkerOptions().position(new
LatLng(Double.valueOf(mkr.getLatitude()),Double.valueOf(mkr.
getLongitude()))))
                        .title(mkr.getName())
                        .icon(BitmapDescriptorFactory.
defaultMarker(getColor(mkr.getColor())))
```

```
                                 .snippet(mkr.getAddress()));

            }
        }

    }

    @Override
    public void onConnected(Bundle bundle) {
        location = LocationServices.FusedLocationApi.getLastLocation(
                googleApiClient);

        if(location != null) {
            SharedPreferences.Editor edit = pref.edit();
            edit.putLong("LATITUDE",Double.doubleToLongBits(location.
getLatitude()));
            edit.putLong("LONGITUDE",Double.doubleToLongBits(location.
getLongitude()));
            edit.commit();

        }

    }

    @Override
    public void onConnectionSuspended(int i) {

    }

    @Override
    public void onConnectionFailed(ConnectionResult connectionResult)
{

    }
    //Used to return float value from the color string
    public float getColor(String clr){
        if(clr.equals("AZURE")){
            return 210;
        }else if( clr.equals("BLUE")) {
            return 240;
        }else if( clr.equals("CYAN")) {
            return 180;
        }else if( clr.equals("GREEN")) {
            return 120;
```

```
        }else if( clr.equals("MAGNETA")) {
            return 300;
        }else if( clr.equals("ORANGE")) {
            return 30;
        }else if( clr.equals("RED")) {
            return 0;
        }else if( clr.equals("ROSE")) {
            return 330;
        }else if( clr.equals("VIOLET")) {
            return 270;
        }else if( clr.equals("YELLOW")) {
            return 60;
        }else {
            return 0;
        }}


    }
```

MainFragment.java

The next is the AddMarker fragment, which has two input fields for the name and the address. The address is automatically fetched using reverse geocoding. The camera is animated to the current location by the values obtained from the shared preferences. We have a spinner to select a color for the marker. The marker is draggable and, when the drag ends, the latitude, longitude, and address are updated with respect to the current marker position. We have two FABs for the save and discard operations.

When **Save FAB** is pressed, the marker details are saved to the database using the addMarker() method. When **Discard** is pressed, the MainFragment is loaded. The code is as follows:

```
package packt.mycustommap;

import android.app.Fragment;
import android.app.FragmentTransaction;
import android.content.SharedPreferences;
import android.location.Address;
import android.location.Geocoder;
import android.location.Location;
import android.os.Bundle;
import android.os.Handler;
import android.support.design.widget.FloatingActionButton;
import android.view.LayoutInflater;
import android.view.View;
import android.view.ViewGroup;
```

```
import android.widget.AdapterView;
import android.widget.ArrayAdapter;
import android.widget.EditText;
import android.widget.Spinner;
import android.widget.TextView;
import android.widget.Toast;

import com.google.android.gms.maps.CameraUpdateFactory;
import com.google.android.gms.maps.GoogleMap;
import com.google.android.gms.maps.MapFragment;
import com.google.android.gms.maps.model.*;
import com.google.android.gms.maps.model.Marker;

import java.io.IOException;
import java.util.List;
import java.util.Locale;

public class AddMarker extends Fragment {

    private EditText mk_name,mk_address;
    private MapFragment mapFragment;
    private SharedPreferences pref;
    private GoogleMap map;
    private double latitude;
    private double longitude;
    private Spinner color;
    private DBHandler db;
    private String nameText;
    private TextView lat,lng;
    private FloatingActionButton save,discard;
    private com.google.android.gms.maps.model.Marker locationMarker;
  static Handler handler;
    @Override
    public View onCreateView(LayoutInflater inflater,ViewGroup
container, Bundle savedInstanceState) {
        View view = inflater.inflate(R.layout.add_marker, container,
false);
        pref = getActivity().getPreferences(0);
        db = new DBHandler(getActivity());
handler = new Handler(Looper.getMainLooper()){


            @Override
            public void handleMessage(Message msg) {
```

```
                mk_address.setText((String)msg.obj);


            };
        };


        mk_name = (EditText)view.findViewById(R.id.marker_name);
        mk_address = (EditText)view.findViewById(R.id.marker_address);


        lat = (TextView)view.findViewById(R.id.latText);
        lng = (TextView)view.findViewById(R.id.lngText);
        color = (Spinner)view.findViewById(R.id.spinner);
        ArrayAdapter<String> adapter = new ArrayAdapter<String>(
                getActivity(), android.R.layout.simple_spinner_item,
getResources().getStringArray(R.array.colors));


        color.setAdapter(adapter);
        color.setOnItemSelectedListener(
                new AdapterView.OnItemSelectedListener() {

                    @Override
                    public void onItemSelected(AdapterView<?> arg0,
View arg1, int arg2, long arg3) {

                        int position = color.
getSelectedItemPosition();
                        SharedPreferences.Editor edit = pref.edit();
                        edit.putString("COLOR",getResources().
getStringArray(R.array.colors)[+position]);
                        edit.commit();
                        // TODO Auto-generated method stub
                    }

                    @Override
                    public void onNothingSelected(AdapterView<?> arg0)
{

                        // TODO Auto-generated method stub


                    }
                }
        );


        save = (FloatingActionButton)view.findViewById(R.id.fab_save);
        discard = (FloatingActionButton)view.findViewById(R.id.fab_
discard);
```

```
        discard.setOnClickListener(new View.OnClickListener() {
            @Override
            public void onClick(View view) {
                Fragment main = new MainFragment();
                FragmentTransaction ft = getFragmentManager().
beginTransaction();
                ft.replace(R.id.content_frame, main);
                ft.setTransition(FragmentTransaction.TRANSIT_FRAGMENT_
CLOSE);
                ft.addToBackStack(null);
                ft.commit();
            }
        });
        save.setOnClickListener(new View.OnClickListener() {
            @Override
            public void onClick(View view) {
                nameText = mk_name.getText().toString();
                if (!nameText.equals("")){
                long id = db.addMarker(new packt.mycustommap.
Marker(nameText
                        ,String.valueOf(Double.longBitsToDouble(pref.
getLong("LATITUDE_NEW",0)))
                        ,String.valueOf(Double.longBitsToDouble(pref.
getLong("LONGITUDE_NEW",0)))
                        ,mk_address.getText().toString()
                        ,pref.getString("COLOR","")));
                if(id != -1){
                    Toast.makeText(getActivity(),R.string.toast_add_
success,Toast.LENGTH_SHORT).show();
                }else{
                    Toast.makeText(getActivity(),R.string.toast_add_
error,Toast.LENGTH_SHORT).show();

                }}
                else{
                    Toast.makeText(getActivity(),R.string.toast_field_
empty,Toast.LENGTH_SHORT).show();

                }
            }
        });
        loadMap();
        Handler handler = new Handler();
        handler.postDelayed(new Runnable() {
            @Override
```

```
                public void run() {
                        initializeMap();
                }
        },1000);
        return view;
    }
    public void loadMap(){
        mapFragment = MapFragment.newInstance();
        FragmentTransaction fragmentTransaction =
                getFragmentManager().beginTransaction();
        fragmentTransaction.add(R.id.content_frame_addmap,
mapFragment);
        fragmentTransaction.commit();
    }
    public void initializeMap(){
        map = mapFragment.getMap();
        if (pref.getLong("LATITUDE",0) != 0 || pref.
getLong("LONGITUDE",0) != 0) {
                latitude = Double.longBitsToDouble(pref.
getLong("LATITUDE",0));
                longitude = Double.longBitsToDouble(pref.
getLong("LONGITUDE", 0));

                SharedPreferences.Editor edit = pref.edit();
                edit.putLong("LATITUDE_NEW",Double.
doubleToLongBits(latitude));
                edit.putLong("LONGITUDE_NEW",Double.
doubleToLongBits(longitude));
                edit.commit();

                lat.setText("Latitude : "+latitude);
                lng.setText("Longitude : "+longitude);
                map = mapFragment.getMap();
                map.getUiSettings().setMapToolbarEnabled(false);
                if(locationMarker != null)
                    locationMarker.remove();
                CameraPosition cameraPosition = new CameraPosition.
Builder().
                        target(new LatLng(latitude,longitude)).
                        zoom(16).
                        build();
                map.animateCamera(CameraUpdateFactory.newCameraPosition(ca
meraPosition));
                locationMarker = map.addMarker(new MarkerOptions().
position(new LatLng(latitude, longitude))
```

```
                .title("Marker")
                .snippet("My Location")
                .draggable(true)
                .icon(BitmapDescriptorFactory.fromResource(R.
drawable.ic_location)));
            Location loc = new Location("");
            loc.setLatitude(latitude);
            loc.setLongitude(longitude);

Thread thread = new Thread(new Runnable(){
                @Override
                public void run(){
                    getAddress(loc);
                }
            });
            thread.start();

        map.setOnMarkerDragListener(new GoogleMap.
OnMarkerDragListener() {
            @Override
            public void onMarkerDragStart(Marker marker) {

            }

            @Override
            public void onMarkerDrag(Marker marker) {

            }

            @Override
            public void onMarkerDragEnd(Marker marker) {
                Location loc = new Location("");
                lat.setText("Latitude : "+marker.getPosition().
latitude);
                lng.setText("Longitude : "+marker.getPosition().
longitude);
                loc.setLatitude(marker.getPosition().latitude);
                loc.setLongitude(marker.getPosition().longitude);
                SharedPreferences.Editor edit = pref.edit();
                edit.putLong("LATITUDE_NEW",Double.
doubleToLongBits(marker.getPosition().latitude));
                edit.putLong("LONGITUDE_NEW",Double.
doubleToLongBits(marker.getPosition().longitude));
```

```
                                    edit.commit();

Thread thread = new Thread(new Runnable(){
                        @Override
                        public void run(){
                            getAddress(loc);
                        }
                    });
                    thread.start();


            }
        });
    }
}


    public void getAddress(Location location){
        Geocoder geocoder = new Geocoder(getActivity(), Locale.
getDefault());
        List<Address> addresses = null;
        String addressText = null;
        latitude = location.getLatitude();
        longitude = location.getLongitude();
        try {
            addresses = geocoder.getFromLocation(latitude, longitude,
1);
        } catch (IOException | IllegalArgumentException e) {
            e.printStackTrace();
        }
        if (addresses != null && addresses.size() > 0) {
            Address address = addresses.get(0);
            addressText = String.format(
                    "%s, %s, %s, %s", address.getMaxAddressLineIndex()
> 0 ? address.getAddressLine(0) : "",
                    address.getLocality(),
                    address.getCountryName(),
                    address.getPostalCode());

        }
        if(addressText != null) {

                Message message = Message.obtain();
                message.obj = addressText;
                handler.sendMessage(message);
        }
```

```
    }


  }
```

AddMarker.java

The next layout is the `MarkerList` fragment. It is a simple layout used to display all the marker details, such as the name and address in `ListView`. The `getAllMarkers()` method returns all the marker details from the database. When the corresponding list item is clicked, `SingleFragment` is loaded. It displays the corresponding single marker in a map. The code is as follows:

```java
package packt.mycustommap;

import android.app.Fragment;
import android.app.FragmentTransaction;
import android.content.SharedPreferences;
import android.os.Bundle;
import android.view.LayoutInflater;
import android.view.View;
import android.view.ViewGroup;
import android.widget.AdapterView;
import android.widget.ListAdapter;
import android.widget.ListView;
import android.widget.SimpleAdapter;
import android.widget.TextView;

import java.util.ArrayList;
import java.util.HashMap;
import java.util.List;


public class MarkerList extends Fragment {

    private EditTextListView list;
    private EditTextTextView text;
    private EditTextDBHandler db;
    private EditTextList<Marker> mkrData;
    private EditTextSharedPreferences pref;
    private EditTextArrayList<HashMap<String, String>> users = new
ArrayList<HashMap<String, String>>();
    @Override
    public View onCreateView(LayoutInflater inflater, ViewGroup
container, Bundle savedInstanceState) {
```

```
        View view = inflater.inflate(R.layout.marker_list, container,
false);

        list = (ListView)view.findViewById(R.id.mList);
        text = (TextView)view.findViewById(R.id.txt);

        pref = getActivity().getPreferences(0);


        db = new DBHandler(getActivity());
        if(db.getMarkerCount() !=0 ) {
            text.setVisibility(View.GONE);
            mkrData = db.getAllMarkers();
            for (int i = 0; i < db.getMarkerCount(); i++) {
                Marker markerData = mkrData.get(i);
                String name = markerData.getName();
                String address = markerData.getAddress();
                HashMap<String, String> map = new HashMap<String,
String>();

                map.put("name",name);
                map.put("address",address);
                users.add(map);

            }
            ListAdapter adapter = new SimpleAdapter(getActivity(),
users,
                R.layout.marker_list_single,
                new String[] { "name","address" }, new int[] {
                R.id.txtName, R.id.txtAddress});
            list.setAdapter(adapter);

            list.setOnItemClickListener(new AdapterView.
OnItemClickListener() {
                @Override
                public void onItemClick(AdapterView<?> parent, View
view, int position, long id) {
                    Marker mkr = mkrData.get(position);
                    int mk_id = mkr.getID();
                    SharedPreferences.Editor edit = pref.edit();
                    edit.putInt("ID",mk_id);
                    edit.commit();
                    Fragment single = new SingleFragment();
```

```
                        FragmentTransaction ft = getFragmentManager().
beginTransaction();
                        ft.replace(R.id.content_frame, single);
                        ft.setTransition(FragmentTransaction.TRANSIT_
FRAGMENT_OPEN);
        return view;
    }
}                       ft.addToBackStack(null);
                        ft.commit();
        return view;
    }
}
                    }
                });

        return view;
    }
}       }else{
            text.setText(R.string.no_marker);
            text.setVisibility(View.VISIBLE);
        }

        return view;
    }
}
```

MarkerList.java

The final fragment is SingleFragment, which displays the single marker corresponding to the last click in the MarkerList fragment. We have two FABs to delete and discard. By pressing the **Delete FAB**, the marker detail is deleted from the database. By pressing **Discard**, the user is taken to the previous screen. The marker is deleted using the deleteMarker() method on the DBHandler object. The code is as follows:

```
package packt.mycustommap;

import android.app.Fragment;
import android.app.FragmentTransaction;
import android.content.SharedPreferences;
import android.os.Bundle;
import android.os.Handler;
import android.support.design.widget.FloatingActionButton;
import android.view.LayoutInflater;
import android.view.View;
```

```
import android.view.ViewGroup;
import android.widget.Toast;

import com.google.android.gms.maps.CameraUpdateFactory;
import com.google.android.gms.maps.GoogleMap;
import com.google.android.gms.maps.MapFragment;
import com.google.android.gms.maps.model.CameraPosition;
import com.google.android.gms.maps.model.LatLng;
import com.google.android.gms.maps.model.MarkerOptions;


public class SingleFragment extends Fragment {

    private EditTextMapFragment mapFragment;
    private EditTextSharedPreferences pref;
    private EditTextGoogleMap map;
    private EditTextDBHandler db;
    private EditTextFloatingActionButton delete,cancel;
    private EditTextView view;

    @Override
    public View onCreateView(LayoutInflater inflater, ViewGroup
container, Bundle savedInstanceState) {
        view = inflater.inflate(R.layout.single_fragment, container,
false);

        db = new DBHandler(getActivity());

        pref = getActivity().getPreferences(0);

        loadMap();
        Handler handler = new Handler();
        handler.postDelayed(new Runnable() {
            @Override
            public void run() {
                loadmarker();
            }
        },1000);

        delete = (FloatingActionButton)view.findViewById(R.id.fab_
delete);
        cancel = (FloatingActionButton)view.findViewById(R.id.fab_
cancel);
```

```
            delete.setOnClickListener(new View.OnClickListener() {
                @Override
                public void onClick(View view) {

                    deleteMarker();
                }
            });
            cancel.setOnClickListener(new View.OnClickListener() {
                    ft.replace(R.id.content_frame, list);
                    ft.setTransition(FragmentTransaction.TRANSIT_FRAGMENT_
CLOSE);
                    ft.addToBackStack(null);
                    ft.commit();
                }
            });
            return view;
        }


    public void loadMap(){
        mapFragment = MapFragment.newInstance();
        FragmentTransaction fragmentTransaction =
                getFragmentManager().beginTransaction();
        fragmentTransaction.add(R.id.content_frame_map_single,
mapFragment);
        fragmentTransaction.commit();
    }
    //This method is used to load marker on Google map
    public void loadmarker(){
        map = mapFragment.getMap();
        map.getUiSettings().setMapToolbarEnabled(false);
        Marker mkr = db.getMarker(pref.getInt("ID",0));
        map.addMarker(new MarkerOptions().position(new LatLng(Double.
valueOf(mkr.getLatitude()), Double.valueOf(mkr.getLongitude())))
                    .title(mkr.getName())
                    .snippet(mkr.getAddress()));
        CameraPosition cameraPosition = new CameraPosition.Builder().
                target(new LatLng(Double.valueOf(mkr.getLatitude()),
Double.valueOf(mkr.getLongitude())))).
                zoom(16).
                build();
        map.animateCamera(CameraUpdateFactory.newCameraPosition(camer
aPosition));

    }
```

```java
    // This method is called when the delete fab is clicked
    public void deleteMarker(){
        Marker mkr = db.getMarker(pref.getInt("ID",0));
        db.deleteMarker(mkr);
        Fragment list = new MarkerList();
        FragmentTransaction ft = getFragmentManager().
beginTransaction();
        ft.replace(R.id.content_frame, list);
        ft.setTransition(FragmentTransaction.TRANSIT_FRAGMENT_CLOSE);
        ft.addToBackStack(null);
        ft.commit();
        Toast.makeText(getActivity(),R.string.marker_deleted,Toast.
LENGTH_SHORT).show();


    }
}
```

`SingleFragment.java`

Finally, you can run the app on your Android smartphone. Make sure the location and Internet settings are enabled on your device to avoid errors. We now have a cool, simple Android app.

> This code was tested on an Android 5.0.2 device with 1080p display resolution. Make sure you have adjusted the dimensions to suit your device's display resolution.
>
> The Android design support library is new and it may contain some minor bugs, which will be fixed eventually.

Summary

In this final chapter, we have learned to create a super cool, material design-inspired map application. We have used many concepts which we learned in the previous chapters. These will give you a clear idea on how to create a map-based application. Hope you have enjoyed the learning process.

Happy coding!

Answers to Self-test Questions

This appendix contains answers to all the self-test questions that appear at the end of every chapter. Now, let's have a look at the answers to respective questions.

Chapter 1, Setting Up the Development Environment

Q1	1
Q2	False
Q3	1
Q4	True
Q5	1 and 2

Chapter 2, Configuring an API Key and Creating Our First Map Application

Q1	1
Q2	1
Q3	2
Q4	3
Q5	2
Q6	1

Chapter 3, Working with Different Map Types

Q1	2
Q2	2
Q3	2
Q4	True
Q5	True
Q6	True

Chapter 4, Adding Information to Maps

Q1	False
Q2	1
Q3	2
Q4	1
Q5	3
Q6	False
Q7	3

Chapter 5, Interacting with a Map

Q1	True
Q2	False
Q3	1
Q4	1
Q5	2
Q6	1
Q7	True

Chapter 6, Working with Custom Views

Q1	False
Q2	False
Q3	1
Q4	2
Q5	1

Chapter 7, Working with Location Data

Q1	1
Q2	1
Q3	True
Q4	True
Q5	False

Chapter 8, Knowing about the Street View

Q1	1
Q2	2
Q3	1
Q4	True
Q5	True

Chapter 9, Google Maps Intents

Q1	True
Q2	1
Q3	1
Q4	1
Q5	False

Index

Thank you for buying
Learning Android Google Maps

About Packt Publishing

Packt, pronounced 'packed', published its first book, *Mastering phpMyAdmin for Effective MySQL Management*, in April 2004, and subsequently continued to specialize in publishing highly focused books on specific technologies and solutions.

Our books and publications share the experiences of your fellow IT professionals in adapting and customizing today's systems, applications, and frameworks. Our solution-based books give you the knowledge and power to customize the software and technologies you're using to get the job done. Packt books are more specific and less general than the IT books you have seen in the past. Our unique business model allows us to bring you more focused information, giving you more of what you need to know, and less of what you don't.

Packt is a modern yet unique publishing company that focuses on producing quality, cutting-edge books for communities of developers, administrators, and newbies alike. For more information, please visit our website at www.packtpub.com.

About Packt Open Source

In 2010, Packt launched two new brands, Packt Open Source and Packt Enterprise, in order to continue its focus on specialization. This book is part of the Packt Open Source brand, home to books published on software built around open source licenses, and offering information to anybody from advanced developers to budding web designers. The Open Source brand also runs Packt's Open Source Royalty Scheme, by which Packt gives a royalty to each open source project about whose software a book is sold.

Writing for Packt

We welcome all inquiries from people who are interested in authoring. Book proposals should be sent to author@packtpub.com. If your book idea is still at an early stage and you would like to discuss it first before writing a formal book proposal, then please contact us; one of our commissioning editors will get in touch with you.

We're not just looking for published authors; if you have strong technical skills but no writing experience, our experienced editors can help you develop a writing career, or simply get some additional reward for your expertise.

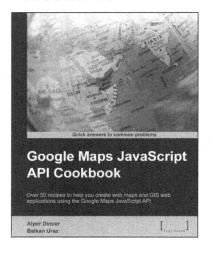

Google Maps JavaScript API Cookbook

ISBN: 978-1-84969-882-5   Paperback: 316 pages

Over 50 recipes to help you create web maps and GIS web applications using the Google Maps JavaScript API

1. Add to your website's functionality by utilizing Google Maps' power.

2. Full of code examples and screenshots for practical and efficient learning.

3. Empowers you to build your own mapping application from the ground up.

Instant Google Map Maker Starter

ISBN: 978-1-84969-528-2   Paperback: 50 pages

Learn what you can do with Google Map Maker and get started with building your first map

1. Learn something new in an Instant!
   A short, fast, focused guide delivering immediate results.

2. Understand the basics of Google map maker.

3. Add places of interest such as your hotels, cinemas, schools, and more.

4. Edit and update details for existing places.

Please check **www.PacktPub.com** for information on our titles

Google Apps: Mastering Integration and Customization

ISBN: 978-1-84969-216-8   Paperback: 268 pages

Scale your applications and projects onto the cloud with Google Apps

1. This is the English language translation of: Integrer Google Apps dans le SI, copyright Dunod, Paris, 2010.

2. The quickest way to migrate to Google Apps - enabling you to get on with tasks.

3. Overcome key challenges of Cloud Computing using Google Apps.

4. Full of examples and including a case study: 'Advanced integration with information systems'.

Google Visualization API Essentials

ISBN: 978-1-84969-436-0   Paperback: 252 pages

Make sense of your data: make it visual with the Google Visualization API

1. Wrangle all sorts of data into a visual format, without being an expert programmer.

2. Visualize new or existing spreadsheet data through charts, graphs, and maps.

3. Full of diagrams, core concept explanations, best practice tips, and links to working book examples.

Please check **www.PacktPub.com** for information on our titles

www.ingramcontent.com/pod-product-compliance
Lightning Source LLC
La Vergne TN
LVHW062304060326
832902LV00013B/2038